每天5分钟 VOA BBC CNN

创想外语研发团队 编著

中国纺织出版社

图书在版编目（CIP）数据

每天5分钟VOA BBC CNN / 创想外语研发团队编著. — 北京：中国纺织出版社，2018.1（2024.2重印）

ISBN 978-7-5180-4052-0

Ⅰ. ①每… Ⅱ. ①创… Ⅲ. ①新闻–英语–听说教学–自学参考资料 Ⅳ. ①G210

中国版本图书馆CIP数据核字（2017）第231838号

责任编辑：武洋洋　　　　责任印制：储志伟

中国纺织出版社出版发行

地　　址：北京市朝阳区百子湾东里A407号楼　邮政编码：100124

销售电话：010—67004422　传真：010—87155801

http: //www. c-textilep. com

E-mail: faxing@c-textilep. com

中国纺织出版社天猫旗舰店

官方微博 http: //weibo. com/2119887771

北京兰星球彩色印刷有限公司印刷　　各地新华书店经销

2018年1月第1版　2024年2月第4次印刷

开　　本：880 × 1230　1 / 32　印张：10.5

字　　数：340千字　定价：72.00元

听力是学习语言的必备基础技能，英语听力水平当然就是学好英语的第一阶梯了。很多人说，英语听力太难了，老外说话根本听不明白，英语影视剧只能看字幕，英语广播节目更听不懂了。这些烦恼，其实是平时很少听英语，或者听力素材不够全面，或者没有专门进行听力训练等等。学好英语，就要从提高英语听力开始！

“千里之行，始于足下。”听英语应该耳到、嘴到、心到，听的过程就是将语言信息进行识别、整理和分析的过程，是全身心投入的过程。听说不分家，只听不说，效果打折扣；听说结合，能说出来才是真正地听懂了！

提高英语听力，应该选择合适的听力素材。英语新闻是听说训练的绝佳素材，也是提高英语听力的有效途径，听懂了会说了，马上就能用，可将最新热点新闻与身边的朋友分享！新闻报道语言通俗鲜活，内容反映最新生活动态和世界热点，还有时髦的新词和新涵义。我们只需每天花5分钟来听听英语新闻，一定会成为超级英语听力达人！

为帮助广大英语学习者，尤其是为了大学英语四六级、雅思、托福的考生提高英语听力水平，本书精心挑选VOA、BBC和CNN中的热点新闻，包括“经济聚焦”“能源与环境”“农业看点”“卫生健康”“体育娱乐”“教育热点”“科技前沿”共7章，每章分别有VOA、BBC和CNN新闻报道共10篇。

本书主要特色：

1. 英音美音全有

本书精选VOA、BBC、CNN新闻报道，大量的英音和美音新闻听力素材，读者可以英音和美音交错学习，辩听和模仿原汁原味的英音和美音。

2. 内容新颖广泛

本书内容包含VOA、BBC、CNN报道的近期各大热点英语新闻，包括经济、科技、能源、环境、农业、体育、卫生、教育、娱乐等关于经济和生活方面的世界热点。内容贴近生活，时尚新颖，拿起就喜欢学，喜欢听。

3. 方便读者学习

每篇新闻有“新闻导读”，介绍热点新闻的相关背景知识，利于引导听力读者切入新闻材料，理解新闻内容。有“新闻热词”，摘取新闻中的重点核心词，为听新闻材料预热。有“新闻播报”，包含新闻正文内容和参考中文译文，参考中文译文附于新闻英语正文之下，方便理解听力材料内容。每篇新闻还有“精彩解析”，对疑难句、重点词组进行解析，并举例运用。新闻学习材料，内容循序渐进，方便读者学习。

本书有的新闻后面附有“新闻听力加油站”，贴心为学习者提供听力听音的技巧，帮助学习者形成科学正确的听力习惯。

目 录
Contents

读书笔记

经济聚焦

打击全球非法经济

Fighting the Global Illegal Economy (VOA News)

新闻导读

知识产权经济是由传统经济向知识经济演化进程中客观存在的一种以知识产权资源作为主导生产要素，政府、法人与公民依靠现代知识产权制度、政策、法律和世贸规则，在创造（创作）、管理、保护和运营知识产权资源，并对资本、人才以及其他有形资源进行市场配置、集约经营、管理创新和财富创造的过程中逐步形成的、具有自身运行规律、独特运营技巧和良好发展前景的经济形态。知识经济时代，就是以知识产权来“经济”的时代，就是知识产权经济时代。整个世界都面临着知识产权的挑战，没有人或者企业可以避免知识产权经济问题。

新闻热词

shadow economy 影子经济

globalization [ˌgləʊbəlaɪ'zeɪʃn] n. 全球化，全球性

siphon off 吮吸

spectrum ['spektrəm] n. 系列；范围

narcotic [nɑː'kɒtɪk] n. 毒品；麻醉品

counterfeit ['kaʊntəfɪt] adj. 仿造的，假冒的

artifact ['ɑːtɪfækt] n. 手工制品，手工艺品

participant [pɑː'tɪsɪpənt] n. 参加者，参与者

tariff ['tærɪf] n. 关税

suspicion [sə'spɪʃn] n. 怀疑；疑心

deterioration [dɪˌtɪəriə'reɪʃn] n. 恶化；变坏；衰退

intellectual property 知识产权

enact [ɪ'nækt] v. 颁布；通过；制定（法规）

hyperbole [haɪ'pɜːbəli] n. 夸张；夸张法

新闻播报

The term illicit economy refers to all illegal economic activity. Sometimes referred to as the **shadow economy**, black market or informal economy, it represents the dark side of **globalization**. It undermines economic potential, **siphons off** legitimate profits, and hampers future economic growth and investment.

The illicit economy is one of the most daunting challenges we face today. It is growing by leaps and bounds, accounting for 8 to 15 percent of the global Gross Domestic Product, said Senior Director for National Security and Diplomacy Anti-Crime Programs, David Luna.

"The global illicit economy is experiencing a boom across a wide **spectrum** of activities: **narcotics**, kidnapping-for-ransom, arms trafficking, human smuggling and trafficking, the trade in stolen and **counterfeit** goods, smuggling of antiquities and cultural **artifacts**, bribery, and money laundering."

参考译文

非法经济指的是非法的经济活动。非法经济又名影子经济、黑市、非正规经济，代表着全球化的阴暗面。非法经济会破坏经济潜力、吞食合法利益、阻碍未来经济增长与投资。

非法经济是我们目前每天都要面临的最让人却步的挑战之一。

它发展速度迅猛，占全球GDP的8%-15%，国家安全与外交反犯罪项目组的高级总监大卫·卢娜说。

“全球非法经济正以多种经济活动形式飞速发展，包括：麻醉毒品、绑架以敲诈勒索、武器走私、人口走私贩卖、偷盗及假冒货物贸易、走私古物和文化产品、行贿、洗钱。”

The illicit economy robs legitimate markets by undercutting legitimate businesses. Black market **participants** do not pay sales or corporate taxes or import **tariffs**. They do not necessarily guarantee the quality or authenticity of the goods they offer, and thus could be cheating their customers. Authorities that cannot stop them may be viewed with **suspicion**, leading to distrust of institutions and a **deterioration** in the quality of life for millions of people.

One way to fight the global illicit economy is to crack down on intellectual property infringement.

参考译文

非法经济通过削减合法商贸交易的方式夺走了合法市场。黑市的交易者不必支付营业税、公司税或者进口关税。他们不必保证所提供的货物是否货真价实，因此就可能欺骗消费者。有关部门若是不加以制止，就会让大众心中存疑，继而导致各个组织机构的信任危机，以及无数百姓生活质量的恶化。

打击全球非法经济的方法之一是制裁知识产权侵权行为。

“Protection of **intellectual property** is at the very heart of economic growth and innovation. When innovators and creators know their creations are safe from theft, they are more inclined to bring new products and ideas to society that enrich and improve our lives.”

“Weak protection, on the other hand, makes it difficult for private companies to reap the benefits of their investments in R&D and thus reduces their incentive to make those investments," said Director Luna.

参考译文

"保护知识产权是经济发展与创新的核心。只有当创新者、创造者知道自己的创造不会被窃取时，他们才更愿意为社会带来新产品和新理念，丰富和提升人们的生活。"

"另一方面，如果知识产权保护薄弱，私营企业就很难通过投资研发来获取利润，继而降低了他们进行投资的热情，"卢娜说。

Thus we must **enact** and implement strong and effective laws to combat criminal activities. At the same time, governments, businesses and citizens need to cooperate across national boundaries to defend our shared interests. Above all, we must all work together, said Director Luna.

"It is not **hyperbole** to say the convergence of illicit networks is an existential threat to human progress. We must stand together to meet and defeat this threat."

参考译文

因此我们必须制定并实施有力有效的法律，打击犯罪活动。同时，政府、商业组织、市民需要跨境合作以维护我们共同的利益。最重要的是，我们必须通力合作，卢娜说。

"将非法网络的集合视为对人类进步的现有威胁，这并非危言耸听。我们必须合作以应对并打垮这个威胁。"

精彩解析

1. Authorities that cannot stop them may be viewed with suspicion, leading to distrust of institutions…

有关部门若是不加以制止，就会让大众心中存疑，继而导致各个组织机构的信任危机……

lead to 导致，引起

例句 Politicians say it could lead to a dissolution of parliament.

政客们说这可能会导致议会解散。

2. One way to fight the global illicit economy is to crack down on intellectual property infringement.
打击全球非法经济的方法之一是制裁知识产权侵权行为。

crack down 制裁；打击

例句 New measures will also be introduced to crack down on forced marriages.

新措施也将推出，严厉打击强迫性婚姻。

新闻听力加油站

扩大词汇量

1. 普通词汇。尽管新闻报道所使用的词汇量很大，但是语言的基本词汇是稳定的。如BBC新闻广播中的新闻报道常用词汇约2 000个，这些词汇的重复率在报道中是很高的，如Foreign Aid，Terrorist，Nuclear Energy，Nationa Election等政治性词汇，WTO，finance，share-list等经济类词汇，Space Station，robot，Mars，Clinical等科技类词汇，Super Bowl，Olympics，World Cup等体育类词汇。而新闻英语中的特有用语就更具稳定性。若能掌握这些词汇，再加上一些听力技巧，基本听懂新闻报道就不是件难事了。

2. 专有词汇。新闻报道是有关世界范围的最新消息，因在报道中常涉及许多人名、地名、国名、公司名称等，如Bush，Afghan，Iran，IBM等。除此之外，新闻报道中还常常出现一些河流、山脉及名胜古迹等专有名词，如Alps，Amazon，Pyramid等，熟悉这些专有名词可使听者更快更准确地了解所听的新闻。

美联储加息可能性很大

The Federal Reserve Probably Raises Interest Rates (VOA News)

新闻导读

美国联邦储备系统（The Federal Reserve System或Federal Reserve），简称美联储，负责履行美国的中央银行的职责。这个系统是根据《联邦储备法》（Federal Reserve Act）于1914年11月16日成立的。联邦储备系统由位于华盛顿特区的联邦储备委员会和12家分布全国主要城市的地区性的联邦储备银行组成。珍妮特·耶伦为现任美联储最高长官。作为美国的中央银行，美联储从美国国会获得权力，行使制定货币政策和对美国金融机构进行监管等职责。美联储通过公开市场操作来影响联邦基金利率。公开市场操作是指美联储通过买卖债券向市场投放或者收回货币的行为。公开市场委员会设定联邦基金利率目标后，美联储通过公开市场操作改变市场上货币的发行量，实现预先设定的目标利率。例如，目前市场上的联邦基金利率是2.5%，而公开市场委员会决定把利率提高到2.75%。为实现这个目标，美联储在公开市场上卖出债券，收回货币。这时金融机构持有的货币减少，超额储备金降低，银行间储备金的贷款利率上升。

新闻热词

stock [stɒk] n. 股票，证券

turmoil ['tɜːmɔɪl] n. 动荡，恐慌

slowdown ['sləʊdaʊn] n. 放慢，放缓

muddy ['mʌdi] v. 使更为复杂，使难以理解
flash [flæʃ] v. 使闪光，使闪耀
mandate ['mændeɪt] v. 授权，委任
deflation [ˌdiː'fleɪʃn] n. 通货紧缩
deter [dɪ'tɜː(r)] v. 阻止，制止
purchase ['pɜːtʃəs] v. 购买；采购
reduction [rɪ'dʌkʃn] n. 减少；降低
tangible ['tændʒəbl] adj. 真实的，实际的
inflation [ɪn'fleɪʃn] n. 通货膨胀
policy ['pɒləsi] n. 政策，方针
inevitable [ɪn'evɪtəbl] adj. 不可避免的；必然发生的
eloquently ['eləkwəntli] adv. 善辩地，有说服力地
clarity ['klærəti] n. 清楚，明晰
announcement [ə'naʊnsmənt] n. 通告，宣告

新闻播报

Until the recent **stock turmoil** triggered by the **slowdown** in China, many expected a September rate hike. But uncertainty over global economic growth **muddied** the waters. Even job numbers showing U.S. unemployment at a seven-year low have not eased concerns, says Bankrate.com's Mark Hamrick on Skype.

"This August jobs report neither **flashes** a green light for the Federal Reserve to raise interest rates, nor does it flash a red light. Meaning, that it is still in this caution zone."

参考译文

由于中国经济放缓导致全球股市震动，业内人士预测9月将上调

利率。然而，却让全球经济增长的不稳定性搅了局。Bankrate公司专家马克·哈姆里克在Skype上称，尽管美国失业人口达到了7年以来的最低值，但这并没有缓解人们对它的担心程度。

“8月份的就业报告既没有让联邦储蓄为增加利率而亮绿灯，也没有亮红灯。这就说明它仍然在警戒线以内。”

The caution reflects the Fed's dual **mandate**, full employment and stable prices. Hiking rates too soon could spark **deflation** and its ripple effects says Joseph Minarik, head of research at the Committee for Economic Development.

"If the Federal Reserve raises interest rates too quickly and too much and **deters** demand, particularly for major **purchases** in the economy, the result can be a cascading **reduction** – starting with consumer demand, going on to employment."

参考译文

这样的担心反映了联邦储蓄的“双重使命”，稳定价格，实现充分就业。经济发展委员会研究部主任约瑟夫·米纳雷克称，增加利率将导致通货膨胀等一系列连锁反应。

“如果联邦储蓄增加利率过快或过多，将抑制消费需求，特别是减少主要采购量，其结果将会是消费需求的锐减，其次是就业人口。”

The International Monetary Fund urges the Fed to wait until at least next year. IMF William Murray: We continue to believe that the Federal Reserve can afford to hold interest rates low until there are more **tangible** signs of wage or price **inflation**.

But delay also carries risks. Among them, few **policy** options when the U.S. economy hits another downturn says Joe Brusuelas, a financial consulting firm McGladrey.

"The Fed needs, before this business cycle ends, to get the Federal Funds rate somewhere at or above 200 basis points (2 percent), so when the **inevitable** recession comes, they can have firepower."

参考译文

国际货币基金组织敦促联邦储蓄要至少等到明年才可以上调利率。国际货币基金组织发言人威廉·穆雷称：我们依旧相信在工资膨胀或价格膨胀出现迹象之前，联邦储蓄能够保持低利率。

但是，这样做也存在风险。McGladrey财务咨询公司首席经济学家Joe Brusuelas称，如果美国经济再遇低迷，那么相应的政策选择将少之又少。

"在此次商业周期结束之前，联邦储蓄需要将联邦基金保持在200基点或以上的范围（2%），所以，当不可避免的经济衰退到来时，它们将提供支持。"

But the Fed is keeping all options open. That's a worry for a market that likes certainty, says Maria Fiorini Ramirez at consulting firm MFR.

"We've all been on pins and needles in terms of when they're going to do it," she said. "So either they should say that because of weaker growth and all the other reasons that they **eloquently** discuss, say that 'we're not going to do anything' or just do it and say: 'this is it for now.'"

Anyone seeking **clarity** will have to wait. No **announcement** is expected until after members of the Federal Open Market Committee meet September 16 and 17.

参考译文

MFR咨询公司的Maria Fiorini Ramirez称，但是联邦储蓄依旧拥有如此多的选择。那么，这对于喜欢稳定的经济市场来说前景担忧。

她说："关于他们何时采取行动，我们总会坐立不安。所以，他们要么会因为经济疲软和所有其他所讨论的原因，说'我们不打算采取措施。'要么会立即行动后说'现在只能这样。'"

所有人都在等待事情明了化。9月16日至17日，联邦公开市场委员会委员将召开会议，在这之前或将不会发表任何声明。

精彩解析

1. But uncertainty over global economic growth muddied the waters.
然而，却让全球经济增长的不稳定性搅了局。

muddy the waters 把水搅浑，把事情弄糟

例句 You are not going to muddy the waters this time.

你这次不要搅这趟混水吧。

2. The result can be a cascading reduction – starting with consumer demand…
其结果将会是消费需求的锐减……

consumer demand 消费者需求

例句 Consumer demand is booming last half year.

上半年消费需求旺盛。

3. We've all been on pins and needles in terms of when they're going to do it.
关于他们何时采取行动，我们总会坐立不安。

on pins and needles 坐立不安，如坐针毡

例句 On hearing the news, she was on pins and needles.

听到这个消息，她坐立不安。

3 伊朗旅游业迎来高速发展

The Tourist Industry in Iran Has Gained Fast Development (VOA News)

新闻导读

1980年，美国对伊俄核合作不满，多次指责伊朗以“和平利用核能”为掩护秘密发展核武器，并一直对其采取遏制政策。“9·11”事件之后，美国将伊朗视为支持恐怖主义的国家和“邪恶轴心”国家之一。2006年12月，安理会决定就核问题对伊朗进行制裁，决议要求伊朗立即暂停铀浓缩和后处理活动，立即暂停与重水有关的项目。2007年3月，联合国安理会通过1747号决议，进一步对伊朗实施制裁。2008年3月，联合国安理会通过1803号决议，扩大对伊朗的制裁范围。2013年10月16日，在日内瓦举行的伊朗与伊核问题六国谈判有了新亮点，伊朗提出了解决伊核问题的新方案，包括时间表，以换取西方取消经济制裁。2015年7月14日，伊朗和伊核问题六国（美国、英国、法国、俄罗斯、中国和德国）达成全面协议，如果一切顺利，西方国家及联合国对伊朗的经济制裁最早可在年底开始解除。这意味着，伊朗的石油行业、旅游业、航空业、汽车制造业、医药行业都将迎来快速增长。

新闻热词

unexplored [ˌʌnɪk'splɔːd] adj. 未经勘探的，未开发的

architecture ['ɑːkɪtektʃə(r)] n. 建筑式样，建筑风格

landscape ['lændskeɪp] n. 风景；风景画

isolation [ˌaɪsə'leɪʃn] n. 隔离，隔离状态

tourist ['tʊərɪst] n. 旅行者，观光客

venture ['ventʃə(r)] v. 冒险去（某处）

embassy ['embəsi] n. 大使馆；大使馆全体成员

restriction [rɪ'strɪkʃn] n. 限制，规定

insurance [ɪn'ʃʊərəns] n. 保险；保险业

traveler ['trævlə] n. 旅行者

sights [saɪts] n. 风景，名胜

generate ['dʒenəreɪt] v. 形成，造成

economy [ɪ'kɔnəmi] n. 节约；经济

hurdle ['hɜːdl] n. 障碍，困难

新闻播报

Tour companies describe Iran as one of the **unexplored** jewels of the Middle East, with stunning **architecture**, breathtaking **landscapes** and warm people. But the country's **isolation** since the 1979 Islamic Revolution has seen visitor numbers from the West fall. Latest figures show just 90,000 arrivals from North America and the European Union in 2013.

"The difficulties we've had in Iran have definitely hurt the **tourist** industry in the sense that people are afraid to go. But those people that **ventured** and overcame these considerations and visited Iran were never sorry."

参考译文

精彩绝伦的古建筑，令人惊叹的自然景色，热情好客的伊朗

人，旅游公司认为伊朗是一块未被挖掘的中东瑰宝。1979年，伊朗发生了伊斯兰革命，至此之后一直保持隔绝状态，前往伊朗旅游的西方游客逐渐减少。最新数据表明在2013年，前往伊朗旅游的北美和欧盟游客仅为9万人。

“伊朗目前所面临的困难确实损害了伊朗旅游业的发展，人们不敢来这里旅游。但是那些排除万难来到伊朗的游客绝对不虚此行。”

Iran's **embassy** reopened in London this week. The July deal struck by Tehran and six world powers over the country's nuclear program is already helping ease travel **restrictions**. This British travel agency has seen a spike in demand.

"Two things have happened since the nuclear deal. First of all, the Foreign Office have changed their advice against travel to Iran, and that's made it much simpler for people to get **insurance** and that sort of thing, so the numbers have gone up again. We've had to put on three extra departures this year alone to cope with demand for the autumn season to Iran."

参考译文

本周，伊朗驻伦敦使馆重新开放。今年7月，德黑兰和六国就伊朗核问题所达成的协议更是缓解了对旅游的限制。这家英国旅行社的赴伊游客与日俱增。

“核协议达成之后发生了两件事。第一件，外交部改变了劝阻游客赴伊旅游的建议，这让游客办理保险等的事情变得简单，赴伊游客数量又一次增加。为了解决赴伊旅游的秋季高峰期，我们单在今年就不得不额外增加3个旅行团。

British **traveler** Buggsie Heath-Brown is about to join one of this tours.

"We decided to get on one of the first trips that we could to get out there; see the **sights**, meet the people before the big rush of the rest of the world."

Iran says it wants to attract 20 million visitors a year by 2025, **generating** up to $30 billion in revenues.

参考译文

英国游客Buggsie Heath-Brown即将要参加这批旅行团中的一个。

"我们决定参加首批旅行团中的一个；在全球游客到来之前欣赏那里的风景。"

伊朗希望在2025年之前每年能够吸引2 000万游客赴伊旅游。年收入将达到300亿美金。

"Now that this outside face of Iran is beginning to change, I think that tourism offers a great opportunity for the Iranian **economy**."

Tour operators say obtaining a visa is still a major **hurdle** for many visitors, while international sanctions on Iran's banking system mean that most transactions have to be in cash.

参考译文

"伊朗将以新的面貌示人，我想旅游业为伊朗经济提供了巨大机遇。"

旅行社称对于许多游客来说，申请护照仍然是最大的阻拦，国际对伊朗银行系统的制裁意味着绝大多数交易都必须使用现金。

精彩解析

1. People are afraid to go.

人们不敢来这里。

be afraid to 害怕，不敢

例句 He is afraid to touch the snake.

他不敢碰那条蛇。

2. Two things have happened since the nuclear deal.
核协议达成之后发生了两件事。

nuclear deal 核协议

例句 Iran plans to implement a recent nuclear deal with six world powers.

伊朗计划与六大国达成新的核协议。

3. We've had to put on three extra departures this year alone to copc with demand for the autumn season to Iran.
为了解决赴伊旅游的秋季高峰期，我们单在今年就不得不额外增加3个旅行团。

cope with 对付，应对，处理

例句 I must cope with the difficulties!

我必须应对这些难题！

读书笔记

汇丰银行大幅削减运营成本

HSBC Will Sharply Cut Operating Costs (BBC News)

新闻导读

香港上海汇丰银行有限公司（The Hong Kong and Shanghai Banking Corporation Limited，英文缩写HSBC）为汇丰控股有限公司的全资附属公司，属于汇丰集团的创始成员，也是香港最大的注册银行以及香港三大发钞银行之一。香港上海汇丰银行于1865年3月在香港开业，同年于上海及伦敦开设分行，又在旧金山设立代理行。香港上海汇丰银行及各附属公司总部位于中环皇后大道中1号香港汇丰总行大厦，主要在亚太地区设立约700多间分行及办事处。2009年3月2日汇丰控股结束旗下美国汇丰融资以HFC及Beneficial为品牌消费贷款业务，并会集中全力缩减有抵押及无抵押房地产组合，分别涉及未偿还结欠额为460亿美元及160亿美元。同时亦会继续缩减汽车融资及其他无抵押个人贷款业务，合共1 004亿美元资产组合，共剩下与信用卡相关之消费贷款业务组合466亿美元。绝大部分分行在履行对客户的承诺后，亦将关闭，并裁减6 100人，每年节省7亿美元成本。

新闻热词

bank [bæŋk] n. 银行

Turkey ['tɜːki] n. 土耳其（国家）

shrink [ʃrɪŋk] v. 使收缩，使减少

significantly [sɪg'nɪfɪkəntli] adv. 显著地，明显地
reveal [rɪ'viːl] v. 显示，表明
recognize ['rekəgnaɪz] v. 认出，识别
growth [grəʊθ] n. 发展，增长
focus ['fəʊkəs] n. 重点，焦点
asset ['æset] n. 资产，财产
headquarter [ˌhed'kwɔːtə] n. 总部，总公司

新闻播报

BBC News with Charles Carroll.
查尔斯·卡罗尔为你播报BBC新闻。

One of the world's biggest **banks**, HSBC, has announced the first details of a major cost-cutting exercise. It's to sell its businesses in Brazil and **Turkey**, reduce its asset base and **shrink** its investment bank. Kamal Ahmed reports.

参考译文

全世界最大银行之一——汇丰银行公布削减成本重大举措的首批细节，该公司将出售在巴西和土耳其的业务，减少资产基础，并收缩其银行投资。卡麦勒·艾哈迈德报道。

"Europe's largest bank has announced that it wants to be **significantly** smaller. HSBC has **revealed** that its UK operations will be hit hard as it battles to find over 3.2 billion pounds of cost-savings. Stuart Gulliver, the bank's chief executive, said that it was time to **recognize** the world had changed, and the **growth** in Asia had to be the new **focus**. The bank is selling businesses in Turkey and Brazil, and will look to reduce the value of its risky **assets** by 290 billion pounds. HSBC also said that it will make a decision on whether it will retain its **headquarters** in London by the end of the year."

参考译文

"欧洲最大银行宣布缩减规模，汇丰银行透露希望削减32亿英镑的成本，其在英国的业务将受最大影响。银行总裁斯图尔特·格利佛表示，是时候承认世界已经不一样了，在亚洲的发展将是新重点。这家银行正在出售在土耳其和巴西的业务，并希望减少2 900亿英镑的风险资产。汇丰银行还表示将在年底之前决定是否保留其在伦敦的总部。"

精彩解析

1. It's to sell its businesses in Brazil and Turkey, reduce its asset base and shrink its investment bank.

该公司将出售在巴西和土耳其的业务，减少资产基础，并收缩其银行投资。

asset base 资产基础，资产基准

资产基础是一种国际上企业价值评估时，需要评估的项目和方法。不仅需要对原资产负债表中的资产与负债的项目重估其评估基准日的价值，并且还需要在原负债表中增加和剔除若干的资产科目和负债科目。例如，商誉。根据历史成本要求，除作为企业购入的无形资产按会计方法入账之外，其他的无形资产都没有计入会计的资产负债表之内。

例句 This bank continues to invest in strengthening its asset base.

该银行继续投资加强其资产基础。

2. HSBC also said that it will make a decision on whether it will retain its **headquarters** in London by the end of the year.

汇丰银行还表示将在年底之前决定是否保留其在伦敦的总部。

make a decision 做出决定，下决心

例句 The central bank will make a decision on the loan plan as soon as possible.

央行将会尽快就贷款计划做出决定。

读书笔记

5 希腊债务协议可能很快达成

A Deal About Greek Debt May Be Close at Hand (BBC News)

新闻导读

希腊债务危机，源于2009年12月希腊政府公布政府财政赤字，而后全球三大信用评级相继调低希腊主权信用评级，从而揭开希腊债务危机的序幕。希腊债务危机的直接原因即是政府的财政赤字，除希腊外欧洲大部分国家都存在较高的财政赤字，因此，希腊债务危机也引爆了欧洲债务危机。此次危机是继迪拜债务危机之后全球又一大债务危机。2012年5月，希腊人纷纷到银行去提领存款，银行出现挤兑现象。2009年10月初，希腊政府突然宣布，2009年政府财政赤字和公共债务占国内生产总值的比例预计将分别达到12.7%和113%，远超欧盟《稳定与增长公约》规定的3%和60%的上限。鉴于希腊政府财政状况显著恶化，全球三大信用评级机构惠誉、标准普尔和穆迪相继调低希腊主权信用评级，希腊债务危机正式拉开序幕。希腊债务危机的根本原因是，该国经济竞争力相对不强，经济发展水平在欧元区国家中相对较低，经济主要靠旅游业支撑。金融危机爆发后，世界各国出游人数大幅减少，对希腊造成很大冲击。此外，希腊出口少进口多，在欧元区内长期存在贸易逆差，导致资金外流，从而举债度日。

新闻热词

surge [sɜːdʒ] v. 飞涨，激增

prevent [prɪ'vent] v. 阻碍，阻止

debt [det] n. 债务，欠款

austerity [ɒ'sterəti] n. 紧缩，紧缩政策

creditor ['kredɪtə(r)] n. 债权人，债主

proposal [prə'pəʊzl] n. 提议，提案

repayment [rɪ'peɪmənt] n. 偿还，偿付

bailout ['beɪlaʊt] n. 紧急援助，救援

skepticism ['skeptɪsɪzəm] n. 怀疑态度，怀疑论

withdrawn [wɪð'drɔːn] v. 取回，收回

新闻播报

Hello, I'm Nick Kelly with the BBC news.

Stock markets have **surged** in the Far East amid signs that a deal to **prevent** Greece defaulting on its **debt** may be close at hand.

参考译文

尼克·凯里为你播报BBC新闻。

远东股市大涨，诸多迹象表明可能很快达成有关阻止希腊违约的协议。

The Greek government has outlined further **austerity** measures to appease its **creditors**. The German Chancellor Angela Merkel speaking after an emergency summit in Brussels said this constituted progress but work was needed to steady the **proposals**. Chris Moris is in Brussels.

参考译文

希腊政府已提出进一步的紧缩措施来安抚其借贷者。德国总理安吉拉·默克尔在布鲁塞尔紧急峰会后讲话称已经取得进步，但还

需要将这些提议确定下来。克里斯·莫里斯在布鲁塞尔报道。

"Greece has to make a big debt **repayment** to the IMF in a week's time, on the same day that its current EU **bailout** expires. So time is short. And as he left the summit, the Greek Prime Minister Alexi Tsipras said the ball is now in the court of the European leaders. But after bruising five months negotiations, there's still plenty of **skepticism** about Greece around the Euro Zone. Earlier, finance ministers prompted by Germany's Wolfgang Schebler argued about whether capital control should be introduced as significant amounts of money continue to be **withdrawn** from Greek banks."

参考译文

"希腊必须在一周内向国际货币基金组织偿还大笔贷款，就在同一天其欧盟援助计划也到期。所以时间很紧迫，希腊总理阿列克谢·蒂西普拉斯在离开峰会时称现在要由欧洲领导人来做决定了。但在经过五个月的协商后，人们仍对希腊在欧元区的地位表示怀疑。早些时候，在德国人沃尔夫冈的提示下，财长们开始辩论是否实施资本控制，因为仍有相当大笔的资金被从希腊银行提取。"

精彩解析

1. But after bruising five months negotiations, there's still plenty of skepticism about Greece around the Euro Zone.
   但在经过五个月的协商后，人们仍对希腊在欧元区的地位表示怀疑。

   plenty of 很多，许多

   例句 She had plenty of imagination.

   她有丰富的想象力。

2. Earlier, finance ministers prompted by Germany's Wolfgang

Schebler argued about whether capital control should be introduced…

早些时候，在德国人沃尔夫冈的提示下，财长们开始辩论是否实施资本控制……

argue about 争论，辩论

例句 I won't argue about the matter.

我不会争论这件事。

读书笔记

全球石油价格下降——供大于求

Global Oil Prices Fall—Oil Supply Outstrips Demand (CNN News)

新闻导读

石油是一种黏稠的、深褐色液体。地壳上层部分地区有石油储存。主要成分是各种烷烃、环烷烃、芳香烃的混合物。石油主要被用来作为燃油和汽油，也是许多化学工业产品如溶液、化肥、杀虫剂和塑料等的原料。石油价格与全球宏观经济状态息息相关，因此油价是一个关键性价格。原油价格受多种因素影响，主要因素包括：原油需求与原油价格成正比例关系；原油供给与原油价格成反比例关系；美元指数与原油价格成反比例关系；地缘冲突与原油价格成正比例关系。中国出现经济增长放缓，使2000年以来国际油价飙升得以放缓。

新闻热词

barrel ['bærəl] n. 桶，一桶的量

determine [dɪ'tɜːmɪn] v. 是……的决定因素

industry ['ɪndəstri] n. 工业，产业

economic [ˌiːkə'nɒmɪk] adj. 经济的，经济上的

surplus ['sɜːpləs] n. 过剩，过剩量

beneath [bɪ'niːθ] prep. 在……之下；在……下面

horizontal [ˌhɒrɪ'zɒntl] adj. 水平的，卧式的

unleash [ʌn'liːʃ] v. 释放；放纵……而出

outstrip [ˌaʊt'strɪp] v. 超过，胜过

consequence ['kɒnsɪkwəns] n. 结果，后果，影响

profit ['prɒfɪt] n. 收益，利润

新闻播报

Crude oil is measure in barrels. Last summer, its global price was $100 per barrel. Yesterday, it was trading at less than half that, at about $46.50 a **barrel**.

参考译文

原油按照桶测量。去年夏天，每桶原油的价钱为100美元。昨天，原油的交易价格还不到去年夏天的一半，每一桶的价钱约为46.5美元。

Why does that matter?

Well, the price of crude affects everything from gas prices to car prices, to stock prices. And it **determines** the number of jobs in the large global oil **industry**. The current glut of oil, the surplus of it, gives us a clear lesson in the **economic** principle of supply and demand.

参考译文

为什么原油的价钱很重要呢？

原油的价格会影响石油、汽车以及股票等一切事物的价格。也决定了全球石油市场的工作岗位数量。当今石油过剩，供大于求，给我们上了一堂供求关系的经济学原理课。

When it comes to oil, it used to be all about the Middle East. Today, the Persian Gulf still has plenty of crude, but the boom is global.

We produced a **surplus** of 2 million to 3 million barrels per day. Oil buried deep **beneath** the earth surface in shale rock can now be accessed with new technologies like fracking and **horizontal** drilling.

参考译文

当涉及石油，过去想到的就是中东。现在，波斯湾仍有大量的石油，但是繁荣却是全球现象。

现在每天我们生产过剩200万到300万桶原油。石油深埋于地表的页层下面，可以采用水力压裂和水平钻探等最新的技术来开采。

In 2014, U.S. oil productions saw its biggest jump in more than 100 years, and it's not the only country to **unleash** a flood of crude. Production in Canada and Brazil has also hit record levels.

At the same time, there are more alternatives to oil, like natural gas and renewables. When oil supply **outstrips** demand, prices fall.

And cheap oil has **consequences**. It's great for consumers, costing less to fuel our cars and heat homes. But it can be tough for companies in the oil patch. It hurts **profits** and leads to job cuts. And the really sharp dip can unsettle global markets.

参考译文

2014年，美国实现100年以来原油增长最大增幅，但是美国并不是唯一一个石油大量增长的国家。加拿大和巴西石油产量也破历史新高。

同时，现在替代石油的可选择性能源也多了，例如，天然气和其他可再生能源。当石油供大于求时，价钱就下降了。

石油价钱下降会造成影响。对于消费者而言，供暖以及燃油费的成本降低了。但是对于油田公司而言，会损害公司收益并导致公司裁员。而且石油价格急剧下降会扰乱全球市场。

精彩解析

1. The current glut of oil, the surplus of it, gives us a clear lesson in the economic principle of supply and demand.

   当今石油过剩，供大于求，给我们上了一堂供求关系的经济学原理课。

   give sb. a lesson 给某人上课，授课

   例句 She gave the two young men lessons in French.

   她给两位年轻人上法语课。

2. When it comes to oil, it used to be all about the Middle East.

   当涉及石油，过去想到的就是中东。

   used to 过去常常

   例句 I used to swim in the river when I was a child.

   我小时候常常去河里游泳。

3. It hurts profits and leads to job cuts.

   它会损害公司收益并导致公司裁员。

   lead to 导致，引起

   例句 In given conditions, a bad thing can lead to good results.

   在一定条件下，一件坏事可以引发好的结果。

读书笔记

7 油价降低造成OPEC影响力减弱

Lower Gasoline Price Results In OPEC's Influence Declined (CNN News)

新闻导读

石油输出国组织，即OPEC——Organization of Petroleum Exporting Countries，中文音译为欧佩克。1960年9月，由伊朗、伊拉克、科威特、沙特阿拉伯和委内瑞拉的代表在巴格达开会，决定联合起来共同对付西方石油公司，维护石油收入，14日，五国宣告成立石油输出国组织（Organization of Petroleum Exporting Countries——OPEC），简称“欧佩克”。1962年11月6日欧佩克在联合国秘书处备案，成为正式的国际组织。现有12个成员国是：沙特阿拉伯、伊拉克、伊朗、科威特、阿拉伯联合酋长国、卡塔尔、利比亚、尼日利亚、阿尔及利亚、安哥拉、厄瓜多尔和委内瑞拉。欧佩克总部设在奥地利首都维也纳。现在，欧佩克旨在通过消除有害的、不必要的价格波动，确保国际石油市场上石油价格的稳定，保证各成员国在任何情况下都能获得稳定的石油收入，并为石油消费国提供足够、经济、长期的石油供应。

新闻热词

hybrid ['haɪbrɪd] adj. 混合的，混合动力的

vehicle ['viːəkl] n. 车辆，交通工具

minority [maɪ'nɒrəti] n. 少数

mileage ['maɪlɪdʒ] n. 英里数，里程

average ['ævərɪdʒ] adj. 平均的

influence ['ɪnfluəns] n. 影响，影响力

historically [hɪ'stɒrɪkli] adv. 在历史上，从历史上

clout [klaʊt] n. 影响力

coordinate [kəʊ'ɔːdɪneɪt] v. 协调，调和

stabilize ['steɪbəlaɪz] v. 使稳定，使安定

decision [dɪ'sɪʒn] n. 决定，决议

plunge [plʌndʒ] v. 骤降，猛跌

political [pə'lɪtɪkl] adj. 政治的，政治上的

新闻播报

An increasing number of Americans are trading in their **hybrid** or electric cars for purely gas-powered **vehicles**, including SUVs.

According to Edmunds.com, new hybrid sales are down from last year and a **minority**, 45 percent of hybrid owners, are trading in for another hybrid, many opting instead for gasoline-powered cars.

参考译文

越来越多的美国人正将混合动力或纯电动汽车换成包括SUV在内以汽油为燃料的车辆。

据Edmunds.com网站公布的消息称，新型混合动力车的销量去年开始走下坡路，而且少数人，45%的混合动力车是车主之间进行交易，许多人反而选择汽油汽车。

Why? Well, carmakers have improved the gas **mileage** of their vehicles and gas-powered cars generally cost less than hybrids. Probably the biggest reason, though, gas prices. AAA says the national

average for a gallon is 2.47. A year ago, it was 3.66. So people are less worried about the cost of filling up.

The biggest **influence** on gas prices is the cost of crude oil and OPEC **historically** has been a major factor in determining that.

参考译文

为什么？汽车制造商们已改善自家车辆的油耗而且汽油为燃料的汽车一般成本低于混合动力车。可能的最大原因是天然气的价格。AAA表示全国平均水平范围内每加仑汽油是2.47美元。一年之前的价格是3.66美元。所以人们不太担心加油的成本。

天然气价格的最主要影响因素是原油的成本，而OPEC在历史上一直在这方面起到决定性因素。

Whenever you hear about oil, the word OPEC isn't far behind. OPEC stands for the Organization of Petroleum Exporting Countries.

It's a group of 12 nations that have a lot of **clout** in the energy market because they produce about one third of the world's total oil and export it around the globe. That's about 30 million barrels of oil every single day. It was formed in 1960. The goal—to **coordinate** oil production to ensure that members are pumping enough supply to meet demand.

参考译文

每当你听到石油，总会或多或少提及OPEC。OPEC指的是石油输出国组织。

这个组织的12个国家在能源市场有很大的影响力，因为这些国家生产全球约三分之一的石油并且出口到世界各地。每天约3 000万桶的石油。这个组织成立于1960年。其目标为协调石油产量，确保成员国有足够供应满足需求。

If all 12 countries play by the rules, it can help to regulate and **stabilize** global oil prices. But there are also plenty of major oil producing nations that are not part of the OPEC club, including the United States, Canada, Mexico, Russia. And they dttenon't ad OPEC meetings and as such, they're not bound by the cartel's **decisions**.

And as these nations have increased their production over the past two years, OPEC's influence in the market has **plunged**. There's now an excess of oil supply, which has pushed down prices significantly. The price drop has caused **political** problems in some OPEC countries that rely on oil sales heavily to fund their governments.

参考译文

如果所有的12个国家照章办事，它可以帮助调节及稳定全球石油价格。但也有包括美国、加拿大、墨西哥、俄罗斯在内的大量石油生产大国并非隶属于这个组织。它们不参加OPEC会议，因此这些国家不受其约束。

随着这些国家在过去2年内增加了自身的生产，OPEC在市场的影响力正在减弱。现在石油供应过多，进而明显压低价格。价格下跌引发严重依赖石油销售来资助自身政府的一些OPEC国家的政治问题。

精彩解析

1. An increasing number of Americans are trading in their **hybrid** or electric cars for purely gas-powered vehicles, including SUVs.
越来越多的美国人正将混合动力或纯电动汽车换成包括SUV在内以汽油为燃料的车辆。

a number of 许多，一些

例句 A large number of people were present.

很多人出席了。

2. OPEC stands for the Organization of Petroleum Exporting Countries.

OPEC指的是石油输出国组织。

stand for 代表，表示

例句 What does EU stand for?

EU代表什么？

3. But there are also plenty of major oil producing nations that are not part of the OPEC club…

但也有大量石油生产大国并非隶属于这个组织……

plenty of 很多，大量的

例句 There is plenty of coal in this area.

这个地区有丰富的煤。

读书笔记

8 大众尾气检测造假

Volkswagen Has Cheated on the Emission Tests (CNN News)

新闻导读

大众汽车（Volkswagen）是一家总部位于德国沃尔夫斯堡的汽车制造公司，也是世界四大汽车生产商之一的大众集团的核心企业。大众汽车，意为大众使用的汽车，汽车的标志历史曾发生过多次变化。今天的标志中的VW为全称中头一个字母。该标志看似由三个用中指和食指作出的“V”组成，表示大众公司及其产品必胜–必胜–必胜。大众汽车集团旗下有大众、斯柯达（SKODA）、宾利（Bentley）、布加迪（Bugatti）、保时捷（Porsche）、斯堪尼亚（SCANIA）、MAN、奥迪（Audi）、西亚特（Seat）、兰博基尼（Lamborghini）、杜卡迪（DUCATI）等多个品牌。2015年9月中旬，大众汽车曝出尾气排放检测丑闻，涉嫌在柴油车辆上安装造假软件，用于识别车辆是在行驶还是进行检测，然后对发动机排放进行控制以帮助检测达标。全球大约有1100万车辆受到影响，在美国市场涉及约50万辆。

新闻热词

diesel ['diːzl] *n.* 柴油机，柴油机机车

temporary ['temprəri] *adj.* 临时的，暂时的

scandal ['skændl] *n.* 丑闻

emission [i'mɪʃn] *n.* 排放，辐排放物

register ['redʒɪstə(r)] n. 登记，注册

category ['kætəgəri] n. 种类，类别

urgent ['ɜːdʒənt] adj. 紧迫的，紧急的

imperative [ɪm'perətɪv] adj. 极重要的，必要的

compliance [kəm'plaɪəns] n. 遵守，服从

prosecutor ['prɒsɪkjuːtə(r)] n. 检察官，公诉人

intangible [ɪn'tændʒəbl] adj. 无形的，难以确定的

furious ['fjʊəriəs] adj. 狂怒的，暴怒的

refit [ˌriː'fɪt] v. 改装

新闻播报

The sale of some Volkswagen **diesel** models has been banned in Switzerland. The **temporary** move comes amid a deepening **scandal** over VW's rigging of diesel car **emissions** tests and could affect 180,000 cars not yet sold or **registered** in Switzerland. The ban does not apply to vehicles already on the road or cars with Euro6 emission **category** engines.

参考译文

瑞士已经禁止部分大众柴油车型的销售。此举是由于日益加深的大众柴油汽车尾气排放测试丑闻，预计可能会影响180 000辆瑞士尚未出售或注册的汽车。此项禁令不适用于已经上路的车辆或欧盟6排放类型发动机汽车。

New Volkswagen CEO Matthias Mueller said his most **urgent** task is to win back trust.

"Acting carefully is more important than acting quickly," he says.

"It's **imperative** that this kind of thing can never happen again at Volkswagen which is why the group is going to enforce even stricter standards of **compliance** and governance. That is my commitment," he says.

参考译文

新大众首席执行官马蒂亚斯·缪勒说，他最迫切的任务就是要赢回信任。

他说："小心行事比快速行事更为重要""有必要保证大众不会再发生这类事情，这就是为什么大众要执行更为严格的遵循和治理标准。这是我的承诺。"他说道。

Meanwhile regulators and **prosecutors** around the world are investigating the issue while investors and customers are launching lawsuits.

Well, it's incredibly damaging, the sheer scale of it and the deliberate nature means it will really have a very significant impact on VW's brand. The damage done already could amount to 10 billion dollars wiped off its **intangible** value.

参考译文

与此同时，世界各地的监管机构和检察官正在调查这一问题，投资者和客户正发起诉讼。

好吧，破坏之大难以想象，从规模到本质上，大众品牌将受到严重的影响，此次损害无形价值可能达到一百亿美元。

Volkswagen said 11 million vehicles worldwide were fitted with cheating software.

Customers and motor dealers are **furious** because they say Volkswagen has yet to specify which vehicles models and years of manufacture are affected, and whether cars are going to be recalled for **refits**.

参考译文

大众称全世界有1100万辆汽车装配了欺骗性的软件。

客户和汽车经销商对此都极为愤怒，因为他们说大众还尚未指出是哪种车型、哪年生产的汽车受到影响，以及汽车是否会被召回改装。

精彩解析

1. The ban does not apply to vehicles already on the road or cars with Euro6 emission category engines.
   此项禁令不适用已经上路的车辆或欧盟6排放类型发动机汽车。
   apply to 适合，适用于
   例句 School regulations apply to every student.
   校规适用于每个学生。

2. It will really have a very significant impact on VW's brand.
   大众品牌将受到严重的影响。
   have an impact on sth. 对……有影响，对……起作用
   例句 They can also have an impact on tourism.
   它们也会对旅游业造成影响。

3. The damage done already could amount to 10 billion dollars wiped off its intangible value.
   此次损害无形价值可能达到一百亿美元。
   wipe off 擦去，去除
   例句 I can never wipe off the memory that I met my current stepmom for the first time.
   我无法抹去第一次遇到我继母的记忆。

新闻听力加油站

怎样处理新闻中的专有名词

在收听VOA新闻广播中，听众会遇到大量的专有名词（包括地名、人名、建筑物名、机构和条约名等），给理解增加了难度。其中地名常表示事件的发生地、消息来源或代表某国政府；人名是事件的当事者或发言人；机构、条约和建筑物名常用来代表一定的组织机构和政府。这些专用名词对听众理解新闻起着重要作用。那么初学者在收听过程中应该怎样处理众多的专有名词呢？我们认为，总的原则是：就大不就小，分清主次，辨明从属。现分述如下：

地名主要指大洲、大洋、海域、河流、岛屿、国家及其首都名，还有历史名城，国际会议城，各国下属的州、省、邦名等。这些地名在新闻广播中使用的频率较高，可以说每一个节目中，甚至每一条新闻中都会涉及几个。

人名主要指各国的主要领导人（包括国王、国家元首、政府首脑、外交部长、国防部长和各部门的新闻发言人等），各大国际组织的头号人物以及一些重要的新闻人物（包括在野党首要领导、反对派领导人等）。人名和地名一样，出现频率极高。但是人名一般都比地名要长，而且有的非英语国家的人名特别难记，有的则和汉语译名的读音“风马牛不相及”，如日本人的名字，初学者想记住他们是要花大气力的。

能源与环境

为尼日利亚提供能源机会

Energy Opportunities for Nigeria (VOA News)

新闻导读

尼日利亚缺乏稳定的电力供应，制造企业、贸易企业及普通家庭年均花费3.5万亿奈拉（约合219亿美元）购买柴油和汽油进行发电。尼日利亚现已成为世界最大的发电机进口国之一，每年进口额达179亿奈拉（约合1.1亿美元）。尽管尼日利亚发电量已由2010年的3000兆瓦提高至2012年的4 500兆瓦，但尼电力消费与供应之间的缺口依然巨大。目前，尼日利亚全国共有5 172 979名电力用户，其中尚有280万未安装电表，比高达54.15%。尼国家电力改革委员（NERC）要求尼日利亚各配电公司18个月内为所有用户安装电表，为实现这一目标，还需购买价值1 700亿奈拉（约合10.6亿美元）的电表。

新闻热词

feasibility [ˌfiːzə'bɪləti] n. 可行性；可能性

photovoltaic [fəʊtəʊvɒl'teɪɪk] adj. 光电池的

microgrid ['maɪkrəgrɪd] n. 微网格

generation [ˌdʒenə'reɪʃn] n.（能源的）产生

sustainability [səˌstenə'bɪlɪti] n. 可持续性，能维持性

module ['mɒdjuːl] n. 模块；组件

advance [əd'vɑːns] v. 发展，进步

connection [kə'nekʃn] n. 连接部分，接头

priority [praɪ'ɒrəti] n. 优先，优先权

pilot ['paɪlət] n. 试验性的方案；试点性的项目

infrastructure ['ɪnfrəstrʌktʃə(r)] n. 基础设施；基础建设

新闻播报

The U.S. Trade and Development Agency recently awarded a grant to the Nigerian company, Community Social Enterprises Limited, or CESEL, for a **feasibility** study supporting the roll-out of 25 solar **photovoltaic** microgrids across Nigeria. Together, the **microgrids** will produce more than 5 megawatts.

This project will help Nigeria to capitalize on its tremendous solar energy potential by scaling up the deployment of off-grid **generation** and minigrid systems, ultimately increasing access to electricity. The study will focus on providing solar energy for rural and peri-urban communities that generally lack reliable access to electricity. The microgrid systems will operate on a "pay-as-you-go" structure using mobile payments, with production and consumption monitored on a real-time basis. This structure will ensure payment and **sustainability**, as well as provide consistent, reliable power at a lower price than diesel generators.

参考译文

近日，美国贸易发展局（The U.S. Trade and Development Agency）向尼日利亚能源创业公司（CESEL）拨款，助力其就支持尼日利亚建造25座太阳能光伏微电网一事进行可行性研究。这些微电网的总发电量将达到500多万瓦。

该项目将助力尼日利亚通过扩大离网发电和微型发电系统的部

署来充分利用巨大的太阳能潜力，最终增加电能供应。该研究将侧重于为农村地区和城郊社区提供太阳能，因为这些地方基本上都存在电能供应乏力的问题。微型发电系统将采取“用多少付多少”的移动付款模式，这种模式下的发电量和用电量都是实时监控的。这种模式能确保及时付款、用户始终有电可用，也能以比柴油发电机更低的价格提供持续可靠的电能。

CESEL selected the U.S. firm, Renewvia Energy Corporation (Atlanta, GA), to conduct the feasibility study. The project presents opportunities for U.S. businesses to make sales in solar PV **modules**, batteries, electrical equipment, control systems and meters across Nigeria.

We are proud to connect CESEL with a leading U.S. company on this important project to expand energy access in Nigeria, said Lida Fitts, USTDA's Regional Director for Sub-Saharan Africa.

参考译文

尼日利亚能源创业公司选择美国公司Renewvia 能源公司（亚特兰大代理商）着手进行这项可行性研究。该项目为很多美国企业提供了销售太阳能光伏组件、电池、电气设备、控制系统和仪表的机会。

我们很骄傲能为尼日利亚能源创业公司与领先的美国企业牵线搭桥，让双方就这个重要项目进行合作以改善尼日利亚的电能供应情况，美国贸易发展局撒哈拉以南非洲地区总监丽达表示道。

We're delighted to be selected as technical services partner for this project with CESEL, said Trey Jarrard, CEO of Renewvia. We look forward to continuing development of solar microgrids in Sub-Saharan Africa, and we're excited to play such an important role in helping to **advance** Nigeria's support for off-grid power.

The grant was signed by the U.S. Consul General of in Lagos John Bray and Dr. Patrick Tolani of CESEL. This project advances the goals of Power Africa to increase electricity **connections** and power generation.

参考译文

Renewvia 公司首席执行官特雷表示，我们很高兴能被选为尼日利亚能源创业公司在这个项目上的技术服务合作伙伴。我们期待能在撒哈拉以南非洲地区继续发展太阳能微电网。我们也很高兴能在助力尼日利亚发展太阳能微电网方面发挥重要作用。

这笔拨款是由美国驻拉各斯总领事约翰和尼日利亚能源创业公司的帕特里克博士共同签署的。该项目也促进了非洲电力项目目标的实现，增加了电力连接和发电量。

The U.S. Trade and Development Agency helps companies create U.S. jobs through the export of U.S. goods and services for **priority** development projects in emerging economies. USTDA links U.S. businesses to export opportunities by funding project planning activities, **pilot** projects, and reverse trade missions while creating sustainable **infrastructure** and economic growth in partner countries. The United States is proud to work with its partner Nigeria and the private sector to help meet the energy needs of the people of Nigeria.

参考译文

美国贸易发展局帮助很多美国公司创造了就业机会，方式是将美国的商品和服务出口到新兴经济体的优先发展项目。美国贸易发展局为美国企业带来了很多出口机会，方式是在伙伴国家资助项目规划活动、试点项目和反向贸易任务，同时构建可持续的基础设施，实现经济发展。美国很骄傲能与尼日利亚及其私营企业成为合作伙伴，帮助尼日利亚满足其人民的能源需求。

精彩解析

1. This project will help Nigeria to capitalize on its tremendous solar energy potential by scaling up the deployment of off-grid generation and minigrid systems...

   该项目将助力尼日利亚通过扩大离网发电和微型发电系统的部署来充分利用巨大的太阳能潜力……

   capitalize on 充分利用某事物

   例句 Everyone should capitalize on his opportunity.

   每个人都应当利用机会。

2. We're delighted to be selected as technical services partner for this project with CESEL...

   我们很高兴能被选为尼日利亚能源创业公司在这个项目上的技术服务合作伙伴……

   be delighted to 很高兴做某事

   例句 He said he would be delighted to help her over all her difficulties.

   他说他很乐意帮她克服一切困难。

3. ...and we're excited to play such an important role in helping to advance Nigeria's support for off-grid power.

   ……我们也很高兴能在助力尼日利亚发展太阳能微电网方面发挥重要作用。

   play a role in 在……方面起作用

   例句 The UN would play a major role in monitoring a ceasefire.

   联合国在监督停火方面会发挥重要作用。

北极理事会——遥远北方的管家

Arctic Council—Stewards of the Far North (VOA News)

新闻导读

北极理事会第十届部长级会议于5月11日在美国阿拉斯加州费尔班克斯结束，与会成员国外长签署了北极地区加强国际科研合作的协议。会议发表了《费尔班克斯宣言》，回顾了北极理事会过去两年推进北冰洋安全、保障和管理以及改善经济和生活条件方面的进展，并为今后两年提出了工作重点：利用芬兰知名的教育体系和高新技术来影响北极社区，加强北极地区天气监测，并为北极理事会的环保倡议而继续努力。北极理事会成立于1996年，其宗旨是保护北极地区环境，促进地区经济、社会和福利持续发展。成员国为美国、俄罗斯、加拿大、瑞典、挪威、芬兰、丹麦和冰岛8个国家，中国是北极理事会的正式观察员国。

新闻热词

region ['riːdʒən] n. 地区，地域

average ['ævərɪdʒ] n. 平均水平

formerly ['fɔːməli] adv. 原来，原先；以前

ecosystem ['iːkəʊsɪstəm] n. 生态系统

approach [ə'prəʊtʃ] n. 方法；途径

forum ['fɔːrəm] n. 论坛；讨论会

indigenous [ɪn'dɪdʒənəs] adj. 当地的;本土的

biennial [baɪ'eniəl] adj. （事件）两年一次的

vessel ['vesl] n. 轮船；大船

implement ['ɪmplɪment] v. 实施，执行

signatory ['sɪgnətri] n. 签字人，签约国

privilege ['prɪvəlɪdʒ] v. 给与……特权，特免

新闻播报

The Arctic **region** is warming faster than any other region on earth, more than twice the rate of the global **average** according to recent reports. This means, among other things, that areas of the Arctic Ocean that were **formerly** inaccessible to humans are opening up for increased human traffic.

But the warming of the Arctic raises the risks for fragile land and marine **ecosystems**, which must be managed through a balanced **approach**, lest they become damaged beyond recovery.

参考译文

北极圈变暖的速度属全球第一，最近的报道显示，其变暖速度是全球平均速度的两倍。这意味着，目前北冰洋地区人类可进入的区域正在逐渐扩大。

但北极圈的变暖给脆弱的土地和海洋生态系统带来了风险，这两者需要平衡的途径来维系，否则就会遭到不可修复性的破坏。

This is where the Arctic Council comes in. A high-level **forum** of the eight nations with territory in the region and representatives of **indigenous** peoples who live in the region, the **biennial** Arctic Council Ministerial Meeting gives Arctic nations and peoples a forum in which to address these concerns, balancing the protection of the Arctic's fragile environment with responsible, sustainable development.

参考译文

这就是北极理事会成立的目的。北极理事会部长级会议是一个高层论坛，集聚北极地区的8个国家和当地民众代表，它两年一度的召开给了北极圈地区国家和人民一个解决上述关切问题的机会，在保护北极脆弱生态环境与实现负责任的可持续发展之间找到了平衡点。

On May 10th and 11th, in Fairbanks, Alaska, the Council held its 10th Ministerial Meeting, which marked the conclusion of the two-year U.S. chairmanship of this body. Under U.S. leadership, the Council completed an assessment of the telecommunications infrastructure in the Arctic; launched a new Arctic Ship Traffic Database to keep track of **vessels** passing through the Arctic; and **implemented** two agreements signed by Council members during the last meeting, one on improving search-and-rescue in the Arctic region, and the second on preparing and responding to potential oil pollution incidents in the Arctic.

参考译文

5月10日—11日，在阿拉斯加的费尔班克斯举行了第十届北极理事会部长级会议，这次会议上宣布结束美国两年来对北极理事会的领导。在美国的领导下，该理事会完成了对北极圈电信基础设施的评估工作；设立了新的北极圈航行数据库，以追踪在北极圈内航行舰艇的情况；实施了两份在这次会议中北极理事会成员国签订的协议，一份是提升北极圈搜救能力的，一份是应对并为可能的油污染事件做准备的。

Secretary of State Rex Tillerson and the other foreign ministers also signed two documents at the Fairbanks Ministerial: a binding agreement that will promote scientific cooperation throughout the Arctic, and the Fairbanks Declaration, a non-binding statement that affirms the **signatories**' commitment to maintain peace, stability, and constructive cooperation in the Arctic; promotes the economic development of indigenous peoples there; and recognizes that climate change is a serious threat to the Arctic, and calls for timely action to address this threat.

参考译文

美国国务卿蒂勒森以及其他一些外长还在费尔班克斯的部长级会议上签订了两份文件：一份具有约束力，将会促进北极圈地区的科学合作；另一份名为《费尔班克斯宣言》，不具有约束力，这份宣言确认了签约国要致力于维护北极圈地区的和平、稳定和建设性合作，促进了北极圈地区的经济发展，承认气候变化是对北极圈的严重威胁，并呼吁及时采取行动，解决这一威胁。

The United States had been **privileged** to lead the Arctic Council at a time when the Arctic region has been facing unprecedented change and challenges, said Secretary Tillerson, who hosted the meeting as Chair of the Arctic Council.

The Arctic Council has proven to be an indispensable forum in which we can pursue cooperation. I want to affirm that the United States will continue to be an active member in this Council. The opportunity to chair the Council has only strengthened our commitment to continuing its work in the future.

参考译文

美国有此殊荣，在北极圈地区面临前所未有的变故和挑战之际领导北极理事会，蒂勒森在以北极理事会主席身份主持会议期间如是说道。

北极理事会已经成为我们追求合作不可或缺的论坛。我想申明，美国将继续积极参与北极理事会的事务。主持北极理事会的机会让我们坚定了未来继续推进这项工作的决心。

精彩解析

1. … more than twice the rate of the global average according to recent report.

……最近的报道显示，其变暖速度是全球平均速度的两倍。

according to 根据，依据

例句 He is an honest businessman, according to what everyone says.

根据大家所说，他是位诚实的商人。

2. … launched a new Arctic Ship Traffic Database to keep track of **vessels** passing through the Arctic.

……设立了新的北极圈航行数据库，以追踪在北极圈内航行舰艇的情况。

keep track of 记录；追踪

例句 The computer can keep track of the patient's progress and sound an alarm in the event of danger.

计算机能跟踪病人的病情变化，并在万一发生危险时发出警报。

3. …and calls for timely action to address this threat.

……并呼吁及时采取行动，解决这一威胁。

call for 要求；呼吁

例句 The Finance Minister has renewed his call for lower interest rates.

财政部长再次呼吁降低利率。

3 气候变化让恶劣天气越来越糟

Weather Extremes Made Worse By Climate Change (VOA News)

新闻导读

根据《联合国气候变化框架公约》，气候变化是指经过相当一段时间的观察，在自然气候变化之外由人类活动直接或间接地改变全球大气组成所导致的气候改变。《联合国气候变化框架公约》（UNFCCC）第一款将因人类活动而改变大气组成的“气候变化”与归因于自然原因的“气候变率”区分开来。气候变化（climate change）主要表现为三个方面：全球气候变暖（Global Warming）、酸雨（Acid Deposition）、臭氧层破坏（Ozone Depletion），其中全球气候变暖是人类目前最迫切的问题，关乎到人类的未来！

暴雪、暴雨、洪水、干旱、冰雹、雷电、台风……极端气候在近几年异常频繁地光顾地球，这些都与全球气候变化大背景有关。2007年发布的政府间气候变化专门委员会（IPCC）第四次评估报告表明，“自20世纪70年代以来，干旱的发生范围更广、持续时间更长、程度更严重，特别是热带、亚热带地区。”“过去50年里，极端高温、低温发生了大范围的变化。昼夜低温、霜冻变得不如以前频繁，而昼夜高温、热浪则愈加常见。”极端天气气候事件发生的频率和强度都有所增强，对人类生命财产安全带来极大的危害。

新闻热词

undermine [ˌʌndəˈmaɪn] *v.* 削弱，损害

extreme [ɪkˈstriːm] *n.* 极端

potentially [pə'tenʃəli] adv. 潜在地；可能地

drought [draʊt] n. 干旱，旱季

productivity [ˌprɒdʌk'tɪvəti] n. 生产力，生产率

malnutrition [ˌmælnjuː'trɪʃn] n. 营养不良

cholera ['kɒlərə] n. 霍乱

sanitation [ˌsænɪ'teɪʃn] n. 公共卫生，环境卫生

severity [sɪ'verəti] n. 严重，严格

dramatic [drə'mætɪk] adj. 戏剧的，戏剧性的

approximately [ə'prɒksɪmətli] adv. 近似地，大约

pollution [pə'luːʃn] n. 污染

decline [dɪ'klaɪn] n. 下降

reliance [rɪ'laɪəns] n. 依靠，依赖

diabetes [ˌdaɪə'biːtiːz] n. 糖尿病

advocate ['ædvəkət] n. 倡导者；支持者

新闻播报

The impact of climate change is so great that it could **undermine** the last 50 years of gains in global health, according to the Lancet Commission report.

Weather **extremes** made worse by climate change are **potentially** catastrophic and unacceptable, says Commission's project leader Nicolas Watts, who spoke to VOA via Skype.

"In terms of **drought**, we often see corresponding decreases in agricultural **productivity**, which then in turn has a profound impact on **malnutrition**, particularly for children, and floods we often see a rise in the rates of infectious diseases, **cholera** and diarrheal diseases that happen as a result of a breakdown in **sanitation**."

参考译文

柳叶刀委员会的报告指出，气候变化的影响如此巨大，它能削弱过去50年来的全球卫生成绩。

气候变化令恶劣天气越发严重，这可能是灾难性的，是不可接受的，委员会项目负责人尼古拉斯·沃特通过Skype接受了美国之音的采访。

"就干旱来说，它通常会导致农业产量的相应减少，然后会对营养不良产生深刻影响，尤其是对儿童。而洪灾通常会导致传染疾病、霍乱、腹泻患病率的增加，这是因为洪灾导致公共卫生的崩溃。"

Increasingly, it's just hotter, which can be deadly. An extreme heatwave in 2003 left 70,000 people dead across Europe. "And those sorts of events are expected to increase in intensity and **severity** as time goes on."

The World Health Organization warns that unless **dramatic** action is taken to reduce global warming emissions by 2030, **approximately** 250,000 people will die each year from the effects of climate change. Outdoor air **pollution** is linked to some three million deaths worldwide, 1.2 million in China alone.

参考译文

而且气温在越来越热，这可能是致命的。2003年的极热天气导致整个欧洲有7万人死亡，"以后所有这些气候事件可能会越来越严重。"

世卫组织警告称，除非在2030年之前采取有效行动来导致全球变暖的排放，否则每年将有大约25万人死于气候变化的影响。室外空气污染导致全世界大约300万人死亡，单单中国就有120万。

Watts says a shift from coal-fired power plants to renewable energy can greatly reduce that danger. "We see immediate **declines** in hospital admissions and in health care costs, which reduces the burden of already struggling health budgets. But there are also benefits to be found outside of the energy sector, you can decrease the amount the **reliance** on cars and motor vehicles, and try to encourage active transport like cycling and walking, you reduce the carbon emissions from that sector, but you also decrease the rates of **diabetes** and obesity," he said.

参考译文

沃特称燃煤发电厂转向可再生能源可以大大减少这种危险。他说："我们看到入院率和医疗成本很快就下降了，这就减轻了已经很艰难的医疗预算。但能源部门之外也能受益，可以减少对汽车和机动车的依赖，鼓励骑自行车和步行就可以减少运输业的碳排放，还能减少糖尿病和肥胖率。"

Among its recommendations, the Commission supports a phase-out of coal power plants, expansion of renewable energy, investment in health systems and a commitment to a strong global climate treaty. Watts says public health is at the core of a new global agreement. "Most of what you want to do to respond to climate change is good for public health, and it is actually a much brighter future." Watts says health care professionals can be **advocates** in the battle against climate change, he says what is good for the planet is good for patient care.

参考译文

该委员会提出了一些建议，其中包括逐步淘汰火电厂、扩大可再生能源、投资医疗系统，以及致力于更强有力的全球气候协议。沃特称公共健康是新的全球协议的核心。"就气候变化而采取的行动对公共健康有益，会促成更美好的未来。”沃特说，卫生专家们可以成为对付气候变化行动中的倡导者，他说，任何有利于地球的行动都对医疗有益。

精彩解析

1. In terms of drought, we often see corresponding decreases in agricultural productivity…

就干旱来说，它通常会导致农业产量的相应减少……

in terms of 就……而言，从……方面来说

例句 In terms of finance, this company has great advantage.

就财力方面来说，这个公司有很大的优势。

2. …and floods we often see a rise in the rates of infectious diseases, cholera and diarrheal diseases that happen as a result of a breakdown in sanitation.

……而洪灾通常会导致传染疾病、霍乱、腹泻患病率的增加，这是因为洪灾导致公共卫生的崩溃。

as a result of 由于……的结果；起因

例句 He was late as a result of the snow.

由于大雪他迟到了。

3. And those sorts of events are expected to increase in intensity and severity as time goes on.

以后所有这些气候事件可能会越来越严重。

as time goes on 随着时间的推移

例句 Renewable energy will become progressively more important as time goes on.

随着时间的推移，可再生能源将变得愈发重要。

4. Most of what you want to do to respond to climate change is good for public health…

就气候变化而采取的行动对公共健康有益……

respond to 对……有某种反应

例句 She responded to the news by bursting into tears.

她听到那个消息后眼泪夺眶而出。

读书笔记

4 班加罗尔——汽车尾气变墨水

Vehicle Exhaust Is Turned into Ink in Bangalore (BBC News)

新闻导读

Graviky 实验室的印度发明家 Anirudh Sharma 联手新加坡虎牌啤酒，进行了一个“空气墨水”（air-ink）的项目。这个项目利用各种废气制成了150升的“空气墨水”，此外它还陆续来到了中国内陆、香港、印度、新加坡等地，缓解了这些地方的空气污染问题。Graviky 实验室是麻省理工大学的下设的一个研究机构。Anirudh Sharma是其创始人之一。Anirudh Sharma带领团队，花了几年时间筹划和研发了一个名为 Kaalink 的神奇设备，它能够收集汽车尾气和污染废气，并将其转化为墨水。Kaalink 的实质是一个过滤技术装置，它内部的过滤转化装置会留下多余的碳元素和有毒物质，在把清洁无害的气体排出的同时，将污染的原碳、废气和烟灰进行纯化处理，转化为相对安全的碳元素。经过不断地试验、完善与升级，这些碳元素就被转化为了安全可用的墨水，一款变废为宝的“空气墨水”（air-ink）就这样诞生了！

新闻热词

soot [sʊt] *n.* 煤烟，烟灰

retrofit ['retrəʊfɪt] *n.* 装配（新部件）；翻新，改型

irrespective [ˌɪrɪ'spektɪv] *adj.* 不考虑的，不顾的；无关的

substantially [səb'stænʃəli] *adv.* 基本上；大体上

restriction [rɪ'strɪkʃn] n. 限定，约束，限制因素

diesel ['diːzl] n. 柴油

installation [ˌɪnstə'leɪʃn] n. 安装；装置

lorry ['lɒri] n. 卡车；货车

新闻播报

Well, here in Bangalore, we've come across a small project to capture the **soot** and turn it into art.

So what we have to build is we have a **retrofit** device that attaches to the exhaust pipe and other chimneys. This device can be attached to practically any exhaust pipe **irrespective** of what is the age or what type of engine you are running. And it captures practically whatever particular matter comes out of it. Once you capture particular matter, it is **substantially** carbon which is like the basis of everything that exists in the world. At present we are recycling into inks which we believe is something that is used by practically everyone on the planet.

参考译文

这里是班加罗尔，我们遇到了一个小型项目：提取烟尘并将它变为艺术。

我们现在建造的是一种翻新的装置，它可以安装在汽车排气管或烟囱上。事实上，不管你操作的发动机有多老或者是什么型号的，这个装置都可以提取排气管中的物质。事实上，它可以提取从排气管里排出的任何物质。等我们提取排气管里的物质后，发现里面的主要成分是碳，而碳是世界上任何物质的基本构成元素。我们现在做的是把烟尘回收为油墨，因为我们认为墨实际上是这个星球上人人都会用到的物质。

Their so-called Air Ink does have a few **restrictions**. It will only ever come in black and at the moment it is not good enough quality to be used in printers.

Graviky is giving it to artists who are finding their own uses for it. Painting and screen painting for example, for use on clothes and bags.

参考译文

他们口中所谓的“空气墨水”确实还是有些使用限制的。这种物质只有黑色，并且目前，这种油墨还达不到能在印刷机里使用的质量。

Graviky实验室把这些墨交给了艺术家们，艺术家们找到了它们的用途。例如，这种墨可以用于衣服和手提包的印刷上。

If the idea catches on, users would expect to remove their exhaust pipe device called a “kaalink” , literally black ink as often as every 15 days depending on how old and dirty their **diesel** engines were.

So that’s about three or four minutes of revving. Once we read the scale often, for example a city-wide **installation**, we plan to install what we call “carbon banks” on multiple locations for it to be dropped either by the people or by our own staff.

参考译文

如果这个想法能流行起来，需要每15天移除一次使用者的汽车排气管，从中提取一种叫“kaalink”的物质，字面上解释就是“黑墨”，提取时间的频率取决于使用者车辆的柴油发动机老化程度和清洁程度。

提取完之后，大概需要3到4分钟重新启动发动机。我们在研究数据时，比如，研究要在全城安装这种设施，我们的计划是在很多地方投放这种我们叫“碳银行”的装置，然后让人们自己把烟尘放进去或者由我们的工作人员收集后放进去。

Even in the shorter term, the thought is to place these "carbon banks" in business headquarters and lorry depots where large numbers of vehicles are centralized anyway. And while the ink may only have limited uses at present, Nikhil insists that it is still better to put the carbon to good use than just collect it and dump it.

参考译文

即使是短期计划，Graviky实验室也是希望把"碳银行"投放到商业中心或货车集运站，毕竟这些地方本身就是大量车辆的聚集地。虽然这种油墨现在用途有限，项目负责人尼基尔仍然坚持认为，"碳尽其才"总比只是收集烟尘然后倒掉要好。

精彩解析

1. Well, here in Bangalore, we've come across a small project to capture the soot and turn it into art.

这里是班加罗尔，我们遇到了一个小型项目：提取烟尘并将它们变为艺术。

come across 偶然发现；偶然遇见

例句 I came across this old photograph when looking for a book yesterday.

我昨天找书的时候，偶然发现了这张老照片。

2. If the idea catches on, users would expect to remove their exhaust pipe device called a"kaalink"…

如果这个想法能流行起来，使用者从排气管中提取一种叫"kaalink"的物质……

catch on 时兴；流行

例句 It isn't surprising his ideas didn't catch on.

他的想法没有被广泛接受，这并不意外。

3. Even in the shorter term, the thought is to place these"carbon banks"in business headquarters and lorry depots where large numbers of vehicles are centralized anyway.

即使是短期计划，Graviky实验室也是希望把“碳银行”投放到商业中心或货车集运站，毕竟这些地方本身就是大量车辆的聚集地。

large numbers of 大量的，数目很多的

例句 Police are prepared for large numbers of demonstrators.

警方已经为应对大量示威者做好了准备。

新闻听力加油站

怎样听记VOA中的数字

在收听VOA英语广播的过程中，听众时常会碰到许多数字，这是我国英语学习者的一大难关，四位数以上的数字更是如此。原因是英汉两种语言的计数单位不完全一样。它们的最大区别是：汉语中有“万”和“亿”这两个计数单位，英语没有；而英语的million（百万）和billion（十亿）这两个计数单位，汉语里却是在它们的前面加上十、百、千而构成的复合计数单位，于是形成了英汉数字的不同表示法。

怎样才能克服这一困难，做到准确无误地听记英语新闻中出现的数字呢？根据我们的收听实践，发现采取以下步骤，比较容易听记：

1. 根据美国英语中每逢四位数就要变更计数单位的规则，记数时采用国际习惯每隔三位数用一逗号分开，即1 000以上的数：先从后向前数，每三位数加一“，”，第一个“，”号前为thousand，第二个“，”号前为million，第三个“，”号前为billion（在英国英语国家中为thousand million），然后一节一节表示。

2. 以trillion，billion，million和thousand为中心，收听时集中注意力听清楚是多少个trillion，多少个billion，多少个million和多少个thousand，及时记下并在它们的后面分别用“，”分开，没有具体数字的就打上“0”。当然trillion的前面还有一些更大的计数词，其规律都是一样的。

一种破坏性步行鱼的蔓延

The Spread of a Destructive Walking Fish (BBC News)

新闻导读

攀鲈属于鲈形目攀鲈亚目攀鲈科攀鲈属的小型亚洲淡水鱼。原产于中国南方、马来西亚、印度等国家。分布于亚洲，产于中国东南部至印度，为亚洲特有属。攀鲈属全球仅有2个种，中国仅龟壳攀鲈一种，分布于香港、福建、广东、广西、台湾、澳门、海南岛及云南省各大小江河下游及邻近湿地、稻田，属中国原生鱼类，以顽强的生命力和能在陆地上爬行而闻名于世。

龟壳攀鲈是攀鲈科的小型鱼类，属多年生，群或独居、昼行、杂食性偏肉食性的原生淡水鱼类，成鱼及幼鱼均属近水表之自由游泳动物，主要摄小型水生动物包括蚯蚓、昆虫、小鱼以及浮萍和一些鲜嫩水草等。栖息于静止、水流缓慢、淤泥多的水体。当生活的环境被污染，水质变质发臭，其它鱼类都无法生存相继死亡时，这种小鱼依然顽强的活着，但它并不喜欢生活在受污染的水里，每当大雨过后，水位上涨后，鱼儿们就会集体爬上岸，去寻找良好的新环境生活。它们常依靠摆动鳃盖、胸鳍、翻身等办法爬越堤岸、坡地，移居新的水域，或者潜伏于淤泥中。龟壳攀鲈的鳃上器非常发达，能呼吸空气，故离水较长时间而不死，当水体缺氧、离水时或在稍湿润的土壤中可以生活较长时间。

新闻热词

indigenous [ɪn'dɪdʒənəs] adj. 本土的，土生土长的

destructive [dɪ'strʌktɪv] adj. 破坏性的；毁灭性的

endemic [en'demɪk] adj. 某地特有的

ecosystem ['iːkəʊsɪstəm] n. 生态系统

spine [spaɪn] n. 脊柱，脊椎

predator ['predətə(r)] n. 捕食性动物

academic [ˌækə'demɪk] n. 学者

pristine ['prɪstiːn] adj. 原始状态的，纯朴的

environmental [ɪnˌvaɪrən'mentl] adj. 生态环境保护的，环保的

新闻播报

Indigenous rangers in northern Australia are leading the fight to stop the spread of a **destructive** walking fish. The climbing perch, which is **endemic** to parts of southeast Asia has been found on two of Australia's most northerly islands. It is feared that it might be disrupting local **ecosystem**. From Sydney, Phil Mercer.

参考译文

澳大利亚北部的土著管理员们在带头遏制一种破坏性步行鱼的蔓延。攀鲈是东南亚特有的鱼种，目前出现在澳大利亚两个最北部岛屿，人们担心这种鱼类可能会破坏当地的生态系统。菲尔·默瑟在悉尼报道。

With sharp **spines** over its gills, the climbing perch can drag itself over dry lands as it moves from one waterhole to another. It's the spines that can choke **predators**, including sea birds, turtles and other fish. **Academics** are working with indigenous rangers to try to stop this aggressive invader infiltrating **pristine** wetlands in northern Australia. The walking fish has a specialized lung that enables it to live out of the water for up to 6 days. Should it reach the Australian mainland, experts say it could wreak a huge **environmental** damage. Phil Mercer. BBC world news.

参考译文

攀鲈的腮部有锋利的脊柱，能拖着自己在干旱的地面上转移，行走于不同的水坑之间。它的脊柱能卡住包括海鸟、乌龟和其他鱼类在内的捕食者。学者们正与当地管理员合作，努力遏制这种掠食性入侵者渗入澳大利亚北部原始湿地。这种步行鱼有着特殊的肺部，能让它离开水可以生活长达6天。专家称一旦这种鱼类抵达澳大利亚大陆，就会给环境带来巨大的破坏。菲尔·默瑟报道。BBC世界新闻。

精彩解析

1. Indigenous rangers in northern Australia are leading the fight to stop the spread of a destructive walking fish.

澳大利亚北部的土著管理员们在带头遏制一种破坏性步行鱼的蔓延。

the spread of ……的传播，蔓延

例句 One of the biggest tasks will be to control the spread of malaria.

最大的任务之一就是控制疟疾的蔓延。

2. Academics are working with indigenous rangers to try to stop this aggressive invader infiltrating pristine wetlands in northern Australia.

学者们正与当地管理员合作，努力遏制这种掠食性入侵者渗入澳大利亚北部原始湿地。

stop sth./sb. doing sth. 阻止某物/某人做某事

例句 She stopped the boy climbing the tree.

她阻止那个男孩爬树。

新闻听力加油站

注意处理精听与泛听的关系

所谓精听是指将音响效果较好的新闻录下来，多听几遍，在较好地理解整条新闻的基础上，将新闻记下来（口头复述或笔头听写）。初学者在收听英语广播时，大多是泛泛地听，其结构是，不少词、词组、句型或同类新闻事件反复听过多少次，但最终还是不知其所以然，没有学到本可学到的知识。长此以往，不但收效不大，不利于严谨学风的培养，而且还会因长期没有多大的进展而丧失信心。精听则可以克服这方面的不足，这也是精听的目的。

所谓泛听，是指听众每天都听一定量的节目，坚持不断，听时以了解大意为主。其目的是获取信息，了解时事，增强语感以提高听力水平。增强语感是泛听所要达到的目的。泛听时要注意的问题是“坚持不断，大量广泛”这八个字。

精听和泛听是互为补充的。精听在初学阶段显得更为重要，泛听是必不可少的学习手段之一，坚持大量泛听，对提高自己的听力能力，具有举足轻重的作用；而且随着听力水平的不断提高，泛听会显得越来越重要，同时也是学习者的最终目的。

读书笔记

冰岛钻火山，开发新能源

Scientists in Iceland Are Drilling Deep into a Volcano for New Energy Source (BBC News)

新闻导读

冰岛目前是世界上唯一一个以100%可再生能源运行的国家，但显然这对他们来说还不够。冰岛已经钻开位于雷克雅涅斯的一座火山进行地热发电。钻探的深度大概为3英里（5公里），这样的深度可以获得火山内部巨大的热量。地下5公里的温度和压力相当极端，其温度将达400℃至1 000℃。在这样的深度，压力也非常大，超过大气水平的200倍。这项工程背后的能源公司合伙人预测，水可能会以“超临界蒸汽”形式存在，既不是液体，也不是气体，并且拥有比以往更多的热能。如果一口钻井能够成功钻探到这样的蒸汽，那么将会获得5 000万瓦特的能量，而一口典型的地热能钻井可获得的能量为500万瓦特。这意味着单口井能够向5万户家庭提供能源，而非5 000户家庭。

新闻热词

intriguing [ɪn'triːɡɪŋ] adj. 有趣的；吸引人的

volcano [vɒl'keɪnəʊ] n. 火山

borehole ['bɔːhəʊl] n. 钻孔，井眼

geologist [dʒi'ɒlədʒɪst] n. 地质学家

schedule ['ʃedjuː] v. 安排，计划

blast [blɑːst] v. 喷射（水流、气流等）
geothermal [ˌdʒiːəʊˈθɜːml] adj. 地热的，地温的
renewable [rɪˈnjuːəbl] adj.（资源）可再生的，可更新的
molten [ˈməʊltən] adj. 熔化的；熔融的
immense [ɪˈmens] adj. 广大的；巨大的
conventional [kənˈvenʃənl] adj. 传统的；平常的

新闻播报

Scientists in Iceland are looking into a rather **intriguing** potential energy source by drilling deep into a **volcano**. They've reached nearly five kilometres down and are close to creating the hottest **borehole** ever drilled. They believe they may be able to harvest energy from it, as our science correspondent Rebecca Morelle reports.

参考译文

冰岛科学家通过深钻火山研究一项相当新奇的势能。他们到达地下近5千米，几乎创造了有史以来最热的钻孔。他们相信或许能从中收获能源。本台科学记者丽贝卡·莫莱尔报道。

In the south of Iceland, **geologists** are heading into the unknown. Inside a giant rig, a drill has been operating for 24 hours a day since August. And it's descending into the heart of a volcano. I've climbed up the rig to come and take a closer look at the drill. It's quite thin actually, probably about 20 centimetres wide. And it just keeps on going and going and going. This is a huge piece of equipment.

参考译文

冰岛南部，地理学家在向未知事物挺进。在一个巨大的钻塔中，钻具从8月份开始便每天工作24个小时。它往下朝着火山中心钻。我

爬上了钻台，来近距离观察一下这个钻具。实际上它相当薄，宽度可能在20厘米左右，一直不停地钻。这是一台巨大的设备。

This is capable of drilling down to six kilometres. This time we are **scheduling** for five kilometres.

So far they've reached nearly 4 500 metres down into a volcanic system. Tell me what you are finding as you are going down.

It's getting hotter. And that's what we want. And we don't expect to drilling much more.

参考译文

它有能力钻到6 000米，我们这次安排的是5 000米。

目前，他们到达火山系统下将近4 500米。讲一下你们在往下工作的过程中有什么发现。

温度越来越高了，这也是我们想要的结果，而且我们不想再钻下去了。

It makes this the hottest borehole in the world and the plan is to tap into its energy. Nearby, steam is **blasting** from the ground blending into the grey sky. Iceland is one of the most volcanically active places in the world. Harnessing this through **geothermal** technology is already well-established here.

In this area, we typically drill to two or three kilometres depth to harness the steam to run the power plant and produce clean **renewable** electricity. We want to see if the resource goes deeper than that.

参考译文

这是世界上温度最高的钻孔了，计划挖掘其中的能量。在附近，蒸汽从地表迸发出来，混入灰色的天空。冰岛是世界上火山最活跃的地区之一，通过地热技术利用能源的方式已经在这个地方确定了下来。

在这个区域，我们一般的钻孔深度为2 000~3 000米，利用蒸汽经营电站，制造可再生清洁电力。我们希望弄清楚资源是不是会超过这个深度。

And this is why five kilometres down **molten** rock mixes with water, but with the extreme heat and **immense** pressure, the water becomes what's known as super critical steam. It's neither a liquid nor a gas. But it holds up far more energy than either. And it's thought that this could be converted into ten times more electricity than any **conventional** geothermal worlds.

We hold that this will open new ways and new doors for the geothermal industry globally to step into an era of more production with a less environmental impact and a lower cost.

参考译文

这就是为什么5千米深处熔岩和水混合在一起，但在极热和高压条件下，水变成超临界蒸汽，既非液体也非气体，但比两者积蓄的能量都多。而且人们认为，与传统地热领域相比，这可能会转化为10倍以上的电力。

我们相信，这会为地热行业打开新的道路和大门，从而步入低环境影响、低成本、高产量的时代。

精彩解析

1. Scientists in Iceland are looking into a rather intriguing potential energy source by drilling deep into a volcano.
   冰岛科学家通过深钻火山研究一项相当新奇的势能。

   look into 考察；调查；研究

   例句 The government will look into how to reduce unemployment.

政府将研究如何降低失业率。

2. This is capable of drilling down to six kilometres.

它有能力钻到6 000米。

be capable of 能够

例句 The larger firm was capable of providing a better range of services.

较大的公司能够提供一系列更好的服务。

3. But it holds up far more energy than either.

但比两者积蓄的能量都多。

hold up 维持；保持

例句 Children's wear is one area that is holding up well in the recession.

童装是在经济衰退中仍然保持良好发展的一个领域。

7 加州需要建造海水淡化工厂

California Needs to Build Desalination Plant (CNN News)

新闻导读

从海水中取得淡水的过程称为海水淡化。现在所用的海水淡化方法有海水冻结法、电渗析法、蒸馏法、反渗透法以及可实现盈利的碳酸铵离子交换法。目前应用反渗透膜的反渗透法以其设备简单、易于维护和设备模块化的优点迅速占领市场，逐步取代蒸馏法成为应用最广泛的方法。海水淡化主要是为了提供饮用水和农业用水，有时食用盐也会作为副产品被生产出来。海水淡化在中东地区很流行，在某些岛屿和船只上也被使用。到2003年止，世界上已建成和已签约建设的海水和苦咸水淡化厂，其生产能力达到日产淡水3 600万吨。海水淡化已遍及全世界125个国家和地区，淡化水大约养活世界5%的人口。海水淡化，事实上已经成为世界许多国家解决缺水问题，普遍采用的一种战略选择，其有效性和可靠性已经得到越来越广泛的认同。

新闻热词

absolutely ['æbsəluːtli] adv. 绝对地，完全地

drought [draʊt] n. 干旱，旱季

controversial [ˌkɒntrə'vɜːʃl] adj. 有争议的，引起争议的

desalination [ˌdiːˌsælɪ'neɪʃn] n. 脱盐，淡化，海水淡化

gallon ['gælən] n. 加仑

osmosis [ɒz'məʊsɪs] n. 渗透

highlight ['haɪlaɪt] v. 强调，突出

essentially [ɪ'senʃəli] adv. 本质上，根本上

overtime ['əʊvətaɪm] adv. 超时地，过久地

reactivate [ri'æktɪveɪt] v. 使恢复工作，重启

severe [sɪ'vɪə(r)] adj. 严峻的，严重的

floppy disk [ˌflɒpi 'dɪsk] n. 软盘

community [kə'mjuːnəti] n. 社区

dwarf [dwɔːf] v. 使相形见绌

facility [fə'sɪləti] n. 设备，设施

新闻播报

"We will run out of water. We **absolutely** will."

California is in the midst of the worst **drought** on record, and yet the need for freshwater is only increasing. In order to meet that demand, cities across the state are turning to rather **controversial** and expensive technology called **desalination**, where they turn ocean water into freshwater.

参考译文

"我们将会用尽水资源。我们绝对会的。"

加州正处于历史上最严重的干旱，而对淡水的需求只是有增无减。为了满足这种需求，各个城市转向颇受争议且造价高昂的海水淡化技术，这种技术能够把海水转化为淡水。

Fifteen desalination plants are currently in the works in California, the largest being the 1 billion Carlsbad plant slated to open this November. When operational, it will produce 50 million **gallons** of fresh water a day through a process called reverse **osmosis**, which filters out 99.9 percent of the salt.

"We certainly didn't plan on completing the plant during record drought conditions here in California, but it does **highlight** the importance of what we're doing, which is to provide a new supply of water, **essentially** drought-proof water." But this drought-proof water source comes at a price.

参考译文

目前加州有约15座海水淡化工厂，而耗资10亿元建成最大的一座卡尔斯巴德工厂将于今年11月开始运营。当开始运作时，每天将通过名为反渗透的过程，过滤掉99.9%的盐生产5 000万加仑的新鲜水。

"我们当然没有计划在加州遭遇历史性干旱期间完成我们工厂的建设。但这确实凸显出我们所做事情的重要性，即提供一种新的供应水的方法，基本上是耐旱水。"但这耐旱水资源是需要付出代价的。

The desalination process is incredibly energy-intensive and the water produced from the plant will cost about twice as much as traditional tap water. A gap the San Diego Water Authority expects will close **overtime**.

Up the coast, Santa Barbara is planning to invest 40 million to **reactivate** a plant that was built in the '90s, during the state's last **severe** drought. The plant ran for just four months before heavy rains ended the dry spell.

参考译文

海水淡化过程是令人难以置信的能源密集型，而且工厂的这种水资源的生产成本约是传统自来水的2倍。圣地亚哥的水务局预计将会因为过时而关闭。

在海岸上，圣芭芭拉分校计划投资4 000万重修最近一次严重干旱时期即20世纪90年代落成的工厂。在暴雨终结干旱前这座工厂仅仅运营了4个月。

You got **floppy disk** here. Keyboards with actual keys. Over 30 million investment, only use for four months and then sits here for 23 years.

"Desalination is expensive. But I—if you start to look at the economic impacts of a **community** running out of water, it will **dwarf** any costs of bringing desalination to this community."

The city says it will take about 12 to 14 months to update the now very outdated **facility**.

参考译文

"你这里有软盘。键盘与实际的钥匙。超过3 000万的投资，只运营4个月，然后在这里等待了23年。"

"海水淡化造价高昂。但我——如果你开始看一个社区因为水资源缺失而受到的经济影响，海水淡化引入这个社区所需的任何成本与之相比都微不足道。"

这个城市表示需要大约12到14个月更新现在非常过时的设施。

精彩解析

1. We will run out of water.

   我们将会用尽水资源。

   run out of 用完，耗尽

   例句 My car is running out of gas.

   我的车快没油了。

2. In order to meet that demand, cities across the state are turning to rather controversial and expensive technology called desalination…

加中文

in order to 为了……

例句 He got up very early in order to catch up his bus.

为了赶公交车，他起得非常早。

3. Up the coast, Santa Barbara is planning to invest 40 million to reactivate a plant that was built in the '90s, during the state's last severe drought.

在海岸上，圣芭芭拉分校计划投资4 000万重修最近一次严重干旱时期即20世纪90年代落成的工厂。

plan to 打算，计划

例句 Where do you plan to spend your holiday?

你们打算去哪里度假？

读书笔记

电动汽车电池能满足我们未来的驾驶动力吗?

Electric Vehicle Batteries Be Enough to Power Our Driving Future? (CNN News)

新闻导读

电动汽车电池分两大类，蓄电池和燃料电池。蓄电池适用于纯电动汽车，包括铅酸蓄电池、镍基电池、钠硫电池、二次锂电池、空气电池。燃料电池专用于燃料电池电动汽车，包括碱性燃料电池（AFC）、磷酸燃料电池（PAFC）、熔融碳酸盐燃料电池（MCFC）、固体氧化物燃料电池（SOFC）、质子交换膜燃料电池（PEMFC）、直接甲醇燃料电池（DMFC）。随着电动汽车的种类不同而略有差异。在仅装备蓄电池的纯电动汽车中，蓄电池的作用是汽车驱动系统的惟一动力源。而在装备传统发动机（或燃料电池）与蓄电池的混合动力汽车中，蓄电池既可扮演汽车驱动系统主要动力源的角色，也可充当辅助动力源的角色。可见在低速和启动时，蓄电池扮演的是汽车驱动系统主要动力源的角色;在全负荷加速时，充当的是辅助动力源的角色;在正常行驶或减速、制动时充当的是储存能量的角色。

新闻热词

battery ['bætri] n. 电池

lithium ['lɪθiəm] n. 锂

recharge [ˌriː'tʃɑːdʒ] v. 给（电池）充电

average ['ævərɪdʒ] adj. 平常的，平均的

sticker ['stɪkə(r)] adj. 汽车价目标签的
efficient [ɪ'fɪʃnt] adj. 有效率的
expensive [ɪk'spensɪv] adj. 昂贵的，高价的
mass [mæs] v. 使聚集，使集中
transformative [ˌtræns'fɔːmətɪv] adj. 革新的，变化的
evolve [i'vɒlv] v. 使发展，使进化

新闻播报

Lightning in a bottle. That's the **battery**. Corked and on demand. But for all the talk that batter powered cars are our future, why aren't we driving them? Think about it. What are the batteries you use every day? The rechargeable **lithium** ion ones, right? The ones in your phone or computer.

People are obsessed with how long these last. But car batteries, who's pushing for them to last longer? The battery-powered car with the longest range in the U.S. is the 80,000 Tesla S. That lasts about 265 miles before needing to **recharge**. The second longest, the 30,000 Nissan Leaf, last about 84 miles. The **average** range of a gas-powered Toyota Camry, 476 miles at a **sticker** price under 25,000.

参考译文

瓶中闪电。这就是电池。封装好后等待按需随选。所有说法都预示不远的未来会是电动汽车，但为什么我们还不能驾驶呢？想想看。你每天使用的是什么电池？可充电的锂子电池，对吗？在你的手机或电脑中的。

人们沉迷于这些电池能够持续多长时间。但对于汽车用电池而言，谁能争取让它们续航时间更长？美国电动汽车行驶里程最长的是价格在80 000美元的特斯拉。需要充电之前它持续行驶大约265英

里。排在第二位的是30 000美元的尼桑Leaf，里程是84英里。而烧油的丰田凯美瑞的平均里程是25 000美元以下的车型达到了476英里。

For all the talk of being **efficient** and ecofriendly, gas-power still wins on what matters most for people: price. That's because car batteries are **expensive**. And while Elon Musk claims his plan the Gigafactory will **mass** produce lithium ion car batteries, and lower their costs by 30 percent, will that be enough to power our driving future?

Maybe in the short term, but some researchers believe that in order to be truly **transformative**, batteries need to **evolve** into something completely different.

参考译文

虽然大家都在谈论的是高效、环保，但燃油车在价格方面仍然赢得了绝大多数人的赞同。这是因为汽车的电池造价昂贵。虽然艾伦·马斯克宣称他的电池工厂Gigafactory计划能大规模生产锂离子的汽车电池，而且降低成本30%，但这足以能满足我们未来的驾驶动力吗？

也许在短期内可以满足，但一些研究人员相信，为了真正的变革，电池需要演变成某种完全不同的东西。

精彩解析

1. Think about it.

想想看。

think about 考虑，捉摸

例句 We must think about the cost.

我们应该考虑成本。

2. Batteries need to evolve into something completely different.

电池需要演变成某种完全不同的东西。

evolve into 逐渐发展成

例句 The simple plan evolved into a complicated scheme.

这个简单的计划逐渐发展成了一项复杂的规划。

怎样理解新闻中的代词

代词在英语广播中使用的频率很低，这是广播文体的一大特点，是由广播的传播特点所决定的。据我们统计，代词的使用仅占总词数的1%。代词数量减少，但人名、地名却大大增多，具体名词也增多了，这样，能使语言表达更为精确，减少产生混乱、引起误解的可能性。但根据需要或使语言简洁起见，新闻广播中有时还会出现一定数量的代词。代词的理解在阅读中常常是中国学生的一个难点，在收听英语新闻时，这一问题就显得更为突出了。所以我们应更加留神代词的用法，在收听时做到以下几点：

1. 根据上下文来理解代词。

2. 通过对照收听Special English和Standard English同一内容的新闻来明确代词。

3. 利用历史背景知识来理解代词。世界上的许多事情，比如几大战争热点，都有其历史根源，两国之间的缓解与恶化也都有其时代背景。所以如果听众不断丰富自己的国际知识，也将有助于对新闻中的代词进行理解。

4. 坚持收听英语新闻对有关事件的系列报道。通过了解某一具体事件的发生、发展和结束这一全过程来判断代词。新闻广播中代词的使用有时并不是以一天的某一事件为出发点，而是从有关事件的一系列报道来措辞的。因此坚持收听也是解决代词理解问题的有效方法之一。

美国多地遭遇极端天气袭击

Several States in America are Suffering From Severe Weather (CNN News)

新闻导读

美国有许多世界上最变化无常的极端天气，包括飓风、龙卷风、旱灾、洪涝灾害、山火、暴风雪、热浪和寒流。来自科罗拉多州博尔德的气象学家兼作家罗伯特·亨森说：“很难在地球上找到另外一块像美国这样大小，有着如此种类繁多的极端天气的地方。”其中，美国被称为“龙卷风之乡”，每年都会有近1 000到2 000个次卷风灾害，而且强度大，这主要是和美国的地理位置、气候条件以及大气环流特征有关。美国东临大西洋，西靠太平洋，南面还有墨西哥湾，大量的水汽从东、西、南面流向美国大陆。水汽多就容易导致雷雨云，当雷雨云积聚到一定强度后，龙卷风就产生了。而美国主要处在中纬度，春夏季常受副热带高压控制。在副热带高压的控制下，大西洋、太平洋和墨西哥湾的暖湿空气源源不断地向美国大陆输送，雷雨云也就越积越多。

美国龙卷风最多的地区是中西部，其中一半都发生在春季。国家风暴预测中心说，美国中部地区11月发生如此严重的龙卷风很罕见，龙卷风高发期一般是每年的4至6月。从6月份开始，大量暖湿空气北移至堪萨斯州、内布拉斯加州和衣阿华州，7月份移到加拿大，此后，美国的龙卷风数量就减少，但仍会有龙卷风出现。统计数据显示，美国每年约有70人在龙卷风中丧生。

新闻热词

severe [sɪ'vɪə(r)] *adj.* 严峻的，恶劣的

midsection ['mɪdˌsekʃən] *n.* 中部，中间部分

population [ˌpɒpju'leɪʃn] *n.* 人口，全体居民

superintendent [ˌsuːpərɪn'tendənt] *n.* 监督人，管理人

flash [flæʃ] *n.* 突然的一阵

airlift ['eəlɪft] *v.* 空运

shingle ['ʃɪŋgl] *n.* 木瓦板

refrigerator [rɪ'frɪdʒəreɪtə(r)] *n.* 冰箱

county ['kaʊnti] *n.* 县

新闻播报

Welcome to CNN STUDENT NEWS—current events for middle and high school classrooms, no commercials.

This Tuesday, May 12th, Americans from parts of South Dakota and Iowa, stretching down to Arkansas and Texas, are recovering from **severe** weather. Over the weekend, fierce storms ripped through the country's **midsection**.

参考译文

欢迎收看不含商业广告为中学及高中课堂量身打造的CNN学生时事新闻。

5月12日的这个周二，从南达科他州、爱荷华州到阿肯色州及德克萨斯州的美国人们正从极端天气中缓和过来。上周末猛烈的暴风雨肆虐了美国中部地区。

At least five people were killed, dozens were injured, and several were still missing yesterday afternoon. More than 70 tornadoes were reported.

One of the areas hardest hit was the northeast Texas town of Van, **population**: 2,300 plus. A fire marshal there says roughly 30 percent of Van was damaged. The town's schools were closed after getting this kind of damage on Sunday.

The district **superintendent** said they felt blessed this did not happen during a school day. A high school in Iowa also lost most of its roof.

Apparent tornadoes weren't the only problem. The storms brought sudden **flash** flooding the areas of northern Texas. Helicopters were called in to **airlift** people when flood waters covered the roads nearby.

参考译文

至少5人死亡，数十人受伤，还有几人自昨天下午以来一直下落不明。据报道有70多起龙卷风。

其中受灾最为严重的一个地方是得克萨斯州东北部的凡镇，这是一个有着2 300多人口的小镇。当地一位消防局长表示该镇大约30%受到损害。这个镇的学校在周日龙卷风肆虐后被迫关闭。

地区负责人表示他们感到庆幸的是龙卷风并没有发生在上学期间。爱荷华州的一所学校的大部分屋顶也被掀翻。

显然龙卷风并不是唯一的问题。暴风雨夹带的突然洪水淹没了得克萨斯北部地区。道路被淹没后，直升机被派过来空运群众。

So, now, the EF scale, Enhanced Fujita Scale, starts at 0 and goes only to 5. Anything above 200 miles per hour is considered an EF-5 tornado.

If you have a 0, you're going to lose **shingle**s. A 1, you may lose a couple of boards on the roof. A 2, you lose all the windows, and maybe even a wall. A 3, EF-3, you will lose a couple of walls on the outside, but there were still be a part of the home standing.

An EF-4, most of the home is gone but you'll still see the **refrigerator**, you'll still a closet and you'll still the bathroom. An EF-5, you cannot find the house. It's completely gone. We don't know how big that Fujita scale will be, how big that tornado will be literally until after we look at the damage.

参考译文

现在，EF级，增强的藤田级数，从0级开始，只到5级。只要超过每小时200英里的速度都会被认为是藤田级数5级的龙卷风。

如果是0级，你将只会失去房屋的板瓦而已。如果是1级，你可能失去屋顶上的几块砖瓦，如果是2级，你会失去所有的窗户，甚至一堵墙。如果是3级，你将会失去外面的一两堵墙，但家的一部分仍然会坚挺不倒。

如果是4级，大多数的家会消失不见，但你仍然会看到冰箱，你仍然会看到壁橱，你仍然会看到浴室。而第5级，你就不会看到房子了。它已经完全消失了。直到我们看到确实损害后才能断定藤田级有几级，龙卷风有多强烈。

The greatest threat of a tornado is being hit by something that the tornado is moving. If you're outside or if you're not protected inside, if you're hit by 140 mile per hour 2x4, you're going to be killed. So, you need to be inside and the lowest, somewhere in the middle of the home, away from windows.

When you hear the word "warning" , and you hear your **county**, that's when you need to take cover. When you hear the word "watch" , that means something might happen today. Let's have a plan. When you hear the word "warning" , it's too late to make a plan. You need to already have a plan. Warning is a long word. It's a bad word.

参考译文

龙卷风最大的威胁是被它所移动的物体击中。如果你在室外或者如果你没有掩体，如果你遭受的是时速140英里2X4的龙卷风，你会有性命之忧。所以，你需要在室内而且处于最低位置，在房子中间地方，远离窗户。

当你听到你的县发布“警告”，你就需要寻找掩体。当你听到“小心”一词就意味着今天可能会发生一些事情。我们得有个计划。当你听到“警告”，制定一个计划就太晚了。你需要已经制定好的计划。警告是一个很长的单词，而且是个糟糕的单词。

精彩解析

1. At least five people were killed, dozens were injured…

至少5人死亡，数十人受伤……

at least 至少

例句 At least 60 people were killed in this gas explosion.

此次煤气爆炸中，至少60人死亡。

2. Helicopters were called in to airlift people when flood waters covered the roads nearby.

道路被淹没后，直升机被派过来空运群众。

call in 请来，找来

例句 The police have been called in to help make it clear.

已请来了警察帮忙把这件事弄清楚。

3. When you hear the word“warning”, and you hear your county, that’s when you need to take cover.

当你听到你的县发布“警告”，你就需要寻找掩体。

take cover 藏身，躲避，找掩体藏好

例句 You can’t take cover under a tree when it’s storming.

在暴风雨中你不能在树下躲避。

10 美洲地区的天灾

Natural Disasters in America (CNN News)

新闻导读

美洲（America）分为北美洲（North America）和南美洲（South America），位于太平洋东岸、大西洋西岸。美洲位于西半球，南纬60°~北纬80°，西经30°~西经160°，面积达4 206.8万平方公里，占地球地表面积的8.3%、陆地面积的28.4%，美洲地区拥有大约9.5亿居民，占到了人类总数的13.5%。美洲是唯一一个整体在西半球的大洲。北美洲和南美洲，以巴拿马运河为界，总称亚美利加洲，简称美洲，美洲又被称为“新大陆”。

北美洲地跨热带、温带、寒带，气候复杂多样。大陆中部广大地区位于北温带，由于西部山地阻挡，来自大平洋的湿润西风不能深入内地，大部分地区的降水来自东南方的大西洋，空气湿润，降水量从东南向西北逐渐减少，东南部大部分地区年平均降水量在1 000毫米以上，平原的西北部和落基山脉以西在500毫米以下，太平洋沿岸迎西风的地区降水量剧增，有的地方年平均降水量约在2 000毫米以上。南美洲介于北纬13°和南纬57°之间，大部分地区属热带雨林和热带草原气候。南美洲有丰富的森林资源。亚马孙平原和赤道附近的安第斯山低坡地带有世界最广阔的热带雨林，盛产各种珍贵的热带林木。南美洲水资源也极为丰富。

新闻热词

predict [prɪ'dɪkt] v. 预示，预告

storm [stɔːm] n. 暴风雨，暴风雪

emergency [i'mɜːdʒənsi] n. 紧急情况，突发事件

snowfall ['snəʊfɔːl] n. 降雪

memory ['meməri] n. 记忆，回忆

dangerously ['deɪndʒərəsli] adv. 危险地，可能引起危险地

amount [ə'maʊnt] n. 量，数量

reservoir ['rezəvwɑː(r)] n. 水库，蓄水池

capacity [kə'pæsəti] n. 容积，容量

ration ['ræʃn] v. 限量供应，配给供应

crisis ['kraɪsɪs] n. 危机

incredible [ɪn'kredəbl] adj. 不可思议的，难以置信的

新闻播报

Hi, everyone. I'm Carl Azuz for CNN STUDENT NEWS. We are your commercial-free source of current events for middle and high school classrooms.

General Beauregard Lee is a famous groundhog here in the South. On Groundhog Day, he **predicted** an early spring. Failed. After four winter **storms** in two weeks and states of **emergency** in Tennessee and Alabama, Southerners are saying never put your trust in the groundhog.

参考译文

大家好。欢迎收看CNN学生新闻，我是卡尔·阿祖兹。这里是为中学及高中学生们准备的免商业广告的时事新闻。

布瑞嘉·李将军是美国南部一只非常有名的土拨鼠。在土拨鼠日，这种小动物以为春天已提早到了所以钻出洞来。但结果大相径

庭。两周以来经历了4场暴风雪，田纳西州和阿巴拉巴州都已宣布进入紧急状态。南方居民表示永远不要相信土拨鼠的习惯。

The **snowfall**, a couple inches here, a few more there, might not be much compared to what folks in the Northeast have been through.

But in states that are generally not used to it, it's enough to shut down schools, delay or cancel hundreds of flights and leave grocery stores completely out of milk and bread.

There were winter storm warnings in 11 states yesterday, some of them taking no chances with the **memory** still fresh of ice storms that shut down traffic in Atlanta and the Carolinas last year.

参考译文

这场暴风雪达数英尺厚，但可能还是无法同东北部居民所经历的相提并论。

但对于不习惯暴风雪的各州来说，已足以让学校被迫关闭，航班延迟或取消，超市面包牛奶被一抢而空。

昨天11个州发布了暴风雪预警，其中亚特兰大和卡罗莱州地区的市民还没从去年的冰风暴造成交通瘫痪的阴影中走出来就开始面对暴风雪。

A very different natural disaster is drying out part of South America. Sao Paolo is the largest city in Brazil. About 20 million people live in and around Sao Paolo and they're running **dangerously** low on water.

The city has seen its lowest **amount** of rainfall since 1930. The **reservoir** that provides its main water source is down to 6 percent of its total **capacity**.

参考译文

而在南美洲一场截然不同的自然灾害正将部分地区的水源榨干。在巴西最大的城市圣保罗地区大约有2 000万人居住，现在正在闹水荒。

自1930年该城市经历过最低降雨量。其主要用水来源的水库储水量下降到总容量的6%。

Officials are now warning people they may have to **ration** water. What could be worse news is that some experts expect this **crisis** to last for years.

It's a pretty **incredible** story when it comes to the country that has the largest fresh water supply in the world, 12 percent of the world's fresh water supply comes right out of here, Brazil.

参考译文

官员们正在警告当地市民将要限量供水。更糟糕的是专家们估计这种状况可能会持续数年之久。

这非常令人难以置信，这个国家拥有世界上最大的淡水供应，占据全球淡水供应12%的就是这里——巴西。

精彩解析

1. The snowfall, a couple inches here, a few more there, might not be much compared to what folks in the Northeast have been through.
   这场暴风雪达数英尺厚，但可能还是无法同东北部居民所经历的相提并论。

   compare to 与……相比

   例句 Compared to her book, my book is much more interesting.

   与她的书相比，我的书要有趣的多。

2. It's enough to shut down schools, delay or cancel hundreds of

flights and leave grocery stores completely out of milk and bread.
这已足以让学校被迫关闭，航班延迟或取消，超市面包牛奶被一抢而空。

shut down 关闭，歇业，停业

例句 Smaller contractors had been forced to shut down.

规模较小的承包商已被迫歇业。

3. What could be worse news is that some experts expect this crisis to last for years.
更糟糕的是专家们估计这种状况可能会持续数年之久。

expert to 预期，预料

例句 The talks are expected to continue until tomorrow.

预计会谈将持续到明天。

读书笔记

农业看点

1 东非旱灾频发，急需人道主义援助

Drought in East Africa, Humanitarian Assistance Is Needed (VOA News)

新闻导读

联合国粮农组织2月14日发布的最新的《粮食价格监测和分析公报》显示，东非的旱灾导致粮食大量减产，谷物和其他主食的价格也飙升至异常水平，给当地家庭造成沉重的负担。大部分地区降雨不足也给牲畜养殖和牧民的生活带来极大的压力。由于牧场和水的短缺以及强行宰杀造成的牲畜身体状况恶化，导致肉类食品价格下滑，进而使牧民收入减少，甚至无法承担购买基本食品的开销。比如，在索马里，山羊的价格比一年前下降了60%，而在肯尼亚的牧区，山羊的价格在过去12个月中下降了30%。由于东非的旱灾，玉米、高粱和其他谷物的价格不断飙升，即将超过该地区各国的历史记录，比如在索马里首都摩加迪沙，1月份玉米价格上涨了23%。在索马里中部和南部的主要城镇，1月份的粗粮价格比去年同期翻了一番。这些国家和地区急需国际人道主义援助。

新闻热词

recurrent [rɪ'kʌrənt] *adj.* 重现的；再次发生的

escalate ['eskəleɪt] *v.* （使）扩大；（使）恶化；（使）升级

undernutrition [ʌndənju'trɪʃn] *n.* 营养不良

exacerbate [ɪg'zæsəbeɪt] *v.* 使恶化；使加剧

estimate ['estɪmeɪt] *v.* 评价，判断

starvation [stɑːˈveɪʃn] n. 极度饥饿；饿死

pastoral [ˈpɑːstərəl] adj. 畜牧的；放牧的

herder [ˈhɜːdə] n. 牧者，牧人

relief [rɪˈliːf] n. 救济；救援物资

inadequate [ɪnˈædɪkwət] adj. 不充分的;不足的

sustain [səˈsteɪn] v. 使持续；保持

intervention [ˌɪntəˈvenʃn] n. 干涉；干预

新闻播报

Over the past two decades, much of East Africa has suffered through **recurrent** droughts resulting in failed crops, dying cattle and **escalating** food prices. The result is hunger, **undernutrition** and suffering for millions of people.

This year, the rains have been scant, more so than usual. This is **exacerbating** drought in the Horn of Africa, particularly in Somalia, Ethiopia and Kenya, where around 15 million people are suffering from food insecurity as a result.

参考译文

过去20年来，东非的很多地区饱受旱灾频发之苦，导致庄稼颗粒无收，牲畜奄奄一息，物价急剧飙升。其后果就是上百万人处于食不果腹和营养不良的水深火热之中。

今年的雨量与以往相比少之又少。这就使得非洲之角的旱灾愈发恶化，索马里、埃塞俄比亚和肯尼亚尤是如此，这几个国家有近1 500万人由于旱灾的降临而遭受粮食紧缺。

The Famine Early Warning Systems Network, or FEWS NET, which is funded by the U.S. Agency for International Development, as well as the Food Security and Nutrition Analysis Unit for Somalia, are sounding the alarm in Somalia. They **estimate** that half of Somalia's population of 12.3 million people is facing hunger or **starvation**. The southern agricultural and **pastoral** areas and northeastern pastoral areas have been hardest hit.

参考译文

饥荒早期预警网络（FEWS NET，Famine Early Warning Systems Network）是由美国国际开发署以及索马里粮食安全和营养分析组织共同出资建设的，该组织目前正在索马里发出警报。据该组织估计，索马里1 230万人口中有半数人食不果腹。索马里南部的农场、牧区以及东北部的牧区受创最为严重。

Over the past few years, food insecurity has been dropping in Ethiopia. The number of people requiring humanitarian assistance there has declined by half since late 2015. But as last year's October-to-December rains failed and drought conditions developed in the country's southern and south eastern regions, farmers and **herders** who had been unable to recover from the previous drought, are once again in need of assistance. According to the Government of Ethiopia and its **relief** partners, some 5.6 million people will need relief food assistance between January and December 2017.

参考译文

过去几年来，埃塞俄比亚的粮食不安全系数不断降低。需要人道主义援助的人数自2015年末以来已经减少了将近一半。但由于去年10月至12月期间雨量的缺乏、南部和东南部旱灾的侵扰，尚未从前一次旱灾中缓过劲儿来的农民以及牧民再一次处于需要援助的境地。据埃塞俄比亚政府及其援助伙伴表示，2017年1月至12月期间有近560万人需要粮食援助。

Kenya is also suffering from **inadequate** rainfall during both the March-to-May 2016 long rain season and the October-to-December short rain season. In some parts of northern Kenya, 70 percent of water sources are already dry, and people are already suffering hunger. FEWS NET projected in January that without **sustained** relief assistance, crisis-level acute food insecurity could occur in some drought-affected areas of Kenya in the coming months.

参考译文

肯尼亚在2016年3月至5月的长雨季和10月至12月的短雨季期间也遭受了雨量不足的困扰。在肯尼亚北部的部分地区，70%的水源已经干涸，当地人温饱成为问题。饥荒早期预警网络于1月做出预测——如果没有持续的救济援助，则在未来的数月中，肯尼亚的一些旱灾爆发地区将发生严重的粮食紧缺。

So far this year, the United States government has committed more than 282 million dollars for critical relief **interventions** in the Horn of Africa. We call on our global partners to join us in this effort.

参考译文

今年到目前为止，美国政府已为非洲之角捐献了2.82亿美元的关键性救助资金。我们呼吁全球的伙伴加入我们，一起努力。

精彩解析

1. Over the past two decades, much of East Africa has suffered through recurrent droughts resulting in failed crops, dying cattle and escalating food prices.

过去20年来，东非的很多地区饱受旱灾频发之苦，导致庄稼颗粒无收，牲畜奄奄一息，物价急剧飙升。

result in 引起，导致

例句 High temperatures also result in high evaporation from the plants.

高温也导致了植物水分的大量蒸发。

2. …farmers and herders who had been unable to recover from the previous drought, are once again in need of assistance.

……尚未从前一次旱灾中缓过劲儿来的农民以及牧民再一次处于需要援助的境地。

recover from 恢复

例句 That country hasn't yet recovered from the effects of the war.

战争结束以来，那个国家尚未恢复元气。

in need of 需要

例句 Energy policy is badly in need of radical re-examination.

能源政策亟需进行彻底的重新审视。

3. We call on our global partners to join us in this effort.

我们呼吁全球的伙伴加入我们，一起努力。

call on 要求；呼吁

例句 We'd better do something to call on people to protect wild animals.

我们最好采取一些行动呼吁人们保护野生动物。

促进南亚和东南亚农业发展

Boosting Agriculture in South and Southeast Asia (VOA News)

新闻导读

美国国际开发署（USAID），是美国联邦政府的一个组织，属于美国的援外机构，成立于1961年，总部在华盛顿，2006年雇员达到1 759人。其主要承担着美国大部分对外非军事性的援助工作，目的在承办开发贷款，推动技术援助方案，分配军援及处理480公法（Public Law 480）案下所进行的农业剩余物资。作为一个独立的联邦机构，国际开发总署（USAID）按照美国国务院制定的外交政策，力图"为那些为美好生活而奋斗、灾后重建以及为生活于民主自由之国家的人们提供帮助"。它提供帮助的地区包括非洲、拉丁美洲、亚洲等地区。

新闻热词

smallholder ['smɔːlhəʊldə(r)] n. 小农，小佃农

resilience [rɪ'zɪliəns] n. 弹力；快速恢复的能力

potentially [pə'tenʃəli] adv. 潜在地；可能地

innovation [ˌɪnə'veɪʃn] n. 改革，创新

diffusion [dɪ'fjuːʒn] n. 扩散；传播

disseminate [dɪ'semɪneɪt] v. 扩散；传播

productivity [ˌprɒdʌk'tɪvəti] n. 生产力；生产能力

algorithm ['ælgərɪðəm] n. 算法，运算法则

efficiency [ɪ'fɪʃnsi] n. 功能，功效

contamination [kən,tæmɪ'neɪʃn] n. 弄脏

prosperity [prɒ'sperəti] n. 繁荣；兴旺

新闻播报

Millions of **smallholder** farmers in South and Southeast Asia are attempting to diversify beyond staple crops to increase their incomes, nutrition, and **resilience** in response to climate change and shifting market demand. Although they are **potentially** significant producers of fresh vegetables and farmed fish, most smallholders lack access to technologies that would help them produce the quantities and quality needed to earn income sustainably. To address this, the U.S. Agency for International Development, or USAID, rolled out its new Feed the Future Asia Regional Innovative Farmers Project at the Agriculture Innovation Summit in Dhaka, Bangladesh January 24th.

参考译文

南亚和东南亚的很多小农正试图在主要作物的基础上让作物种类多样化，以增加收入、提高营养、增强应对气候变化和多变市场需求的恢复力。虽然他们是大量新鲜蔬菜和养殖鱼类的潜在生产者，但大多数小农都接触不到助力生产出大量的优质产品以赚取稳定的收入的技术。为了解决这一问题，美国国际开发署（USAID）在1月24日于孟加拉国首都达卡市举行的农业创新峰会上推出了一个亚洲区域创新农民的新项目，名为“保障未来粮食供给”。

Implemented by Winrock International, the regional project will increase food security, reduce poverty, and improve environmental sustainability by facilitating agricultural **innovation** and technology

diffusion in several countries in Asia including Bangladesh.

To **disseminate** agricultural knowledge and expertise among the Asian countries, this new project will create challenge competitions to discover the most promising technologies, support partnerships and ultimately bring successful tools and practices to farmers in all stages of the supply chain – from productivity to marketing. The Honorable Additional Secretary of Bangladesh's Ministry of Agriculture Musharaf Hossain and USAID Office of Economic Growth Director Matt Curtis spoke at the event.

参考译文

该区域性项目由温洛克国际实施，将通过在孟加拉国在内的多个亚洲国家中促进农业创新和技术推广来提升粮食安全、减少贫困、增强环境的可持续性。

为了达到在亚洲各国传播农业知识和专业知识的目的，这个新项目将创造挑战竞技赛，发掘出最有希望的技术、支持合伙经营并最终为从生产到推广的供应链中各个环节的农民带来有效的工具和实践。孟加拉国农业部名誉秘书穆沙拉夫·侯赛因（Musharaf Hossain）和美国国际开发署经济增长办公室主任马特·柯蒂斯（Matt Curtis）在活动上发言。

USAID also announced the winners of the Tech4Farmers Challenge, the very first challenge competition held under the Asia Regional Innovative Farmers Project that sought ways to improve the agricultural **productivity** and income of small hold farmers in Bangladesh, Cambodia, Myanmar and Nepal.

参考译文

美国国际开发署还公布了Tech4Farmers挑战赛的获胜者，这次挑战赛也是亚洲区域创新农民项目举办的第一次挑战赛，该项目的目的是寻找提升农业产量，提高孟加拉国、柬埔寨、缅甸、尼泊尔的小农收入。

The winners were the e-Fishery's Smart Fish Feeder, an Indonesia-based technology that combines automatic feeding with sensors and **algorithms** that sense fish's appetite and adjust the amount of feed to improve **efficiency**, and the Innovative Spirulina Production, a system created by EnerGaia in Thailand that maximizes algae production with minimal resources, reducing potential for **contamination** in its bioreactor design and allows spirulina production nearly anywhere. Unlike many challenges, the Tech4Farmers Innovation Challenge did not offer a cash prize, but provided winners the information, business services and access to networks to help expand innovative solutions into new markets in low-income countries.

参考译文

获奖者分别是印度科技公司e-Fishery和泰国的EnerGaia公司：前者将自动喂食与传感器、算法结合起来，可以感知鱼类的胃口，并据此调节喂食量，提升效率；后者发明了螺旋藻创新生产系统，该系统可利用矿物资源将藻类产量最大化，降低生物反应器污染的可能性，让螺旋藻生产随处可行。Tech4Farmers创新挑战赛不同于其他赛事，它并不提供现金奖励，而是为获胜者提供信息、商业服务、网络接入，帮助获胜者在低收入国家扩大增加新市场的创新方案。

The U.S. Government, through USAID, has provided more than $6 billion in development assistance to Bangladesh since 1971. The U.S. is proud to work with Bangladesh promote **prosperity** for the people of the U.S., Bangladesh, and the Asia region.

参考译文

自1971年以来，美国政府已通过美国国际开发署提供了60多亿美元的发展援助资金。美国很自豪能与孟加拉国一道促进美国、孟加拉国和亚洲地区的繁荣。

精彩解析

1. Millions of smallholder farmers in South and Southeast Asia are attempting to diversify beyond staple crops to increase their incomes…

   南亚和东南亚的很多小农正试图在主要作物的基础上让作物种类多样化，以增加收入……

   staple crop 主要作物

   例句 Rice is a staple crop in much of Asia.

   水稻是亚洲的主要农作物。

2. … and ultimately bring successful tools and practices to farmers in all stages of the supply chain…

   ……并最终为从生产到推广的供应链中各个环节的农民带来有效的工具和实践……

   supply chain 供应链

   例句 It has been a clever innovator with its supply chain.

   在供应链方面它也是独具匠心。

3 跨境疾病导致非洲动物死亡

Trans-border Diseases Kill the Continent's Animals in Africa (VOA News)

新闻导读

动物疾病是指动物机体受到内在或外界致病因素和不利影响的作用而产生的一系列损伤与抗损伤的复杂过程，表现为局部、器官、系统或全身的形态变化和（或）功能障碍。在健康情况下，动物与其环境之间保持一种动态平衡，机体的结构和功能处于正常状态，疾病则使这种平衡受到破坏。在这一过程中，若损伤大于机体的防御能力，则疾病恶化，甚至导致死亡；反之则疾病痊愈，机体康复，间或遗留某些不良后果。动物疾病主要分为传染病、寄生虫病、普通病、群发病、散发病。动物疾病还可分为本土疾病和外来疾病。在国际交往频繁，旅游和贸易十分发达的情况下，外来疾病常通过各种交通工具中的蚊、蝇、蚤、虱、臭虫、蟑螂、老鼠和伴随动物、进口的家畜和野兽、冷冻精液和胚胎，以及畜产品和其他货物传入本国。严防外来的动物疾病，已成为国境和口岸检疫的重要任务。

新闻热词

disease [dɪ'ziːz] n. 疾病

tick [tɪk] n. 蜱

vaccination [ˌvæksɪ'neɪʃn] n. 种痘，接种疫苗

contagious [kən'teɪdʒəs] adj. 有传染性的，传染病的

protein ['prəʊtiːn] n. 蛋白质

infection [ɪn'fekʃn] n. 传染病，感染

surveillance [sɜː'veɪləns] n. 监护，监督

collaboration [kəˌlæbə'reɪʃn] n. 合作，协作

livelihood ['laɪvlihʊd] n. 营生，生计

famine ['fæmɪn] n. 饥荒，饥饿

新闻播报

The United Nations Food and Agriculture Organization is urging farmers to be on guard against transboundary animal **diseases**. Officials warn that **ticks**, lice and other pests can spread quickly from one country to the next.

Experts from across Africa say trans-border diseases kill between 10 and 20 percent of the continent's animals every year. The experts gathered in Cameroon last month to discuss the problem. They suggested large **vaccination** and pest eradication programs to stop the spread of the diseases.

参考译文

联合国粮农组织督促农民警惕跨境动物疾病。官员警告说，蜱、虱等害虫可以迅速从一个国家传播到另一个国家。

非洲各地的专家表示，跨境疾病每年导致非洲大陆10%到20%的动物死亡。专家们上个月聚集在喀麦隆讨论这个问题。他们建议采用大规模接种和有害生物根除计划来阻止疾病的传播。

Dr. Taiga is Cameroon's livestock minister. He does not use a first name. He says pests like nose bot flies and wool maggots are harming animals in some communities in his country.

Dr. Taiga says all animals in an area must be killed if one animal is affected because the diseases are **contagious**. They spread quickly from animal to animal. He says that is why the Food and Agriculture Organization (FAO) and the World Organization for Animal Health are working together to destroy the diseases. He says that when central African countries succeed in killing the pests, their human populations will enjoy better quality **protein**.

参考译文

塔伊加（Taiga）博士是喀麦隆畜牧部部长。他没有姓氏。他说，像马鼻蝇和肉蝇蛆等害虫正在危害喀麦隆一些社区的动物。

塔伊加博士表示，如果有动物感染，该地区所有动物都必须被杀死，因为这些疾病是传染性的，它们能从一种动物迅速传播到另一种动物。他说，这就是为什么粮农组织和世界动物卫生组织正在共同努力消灭这些疾病。他说，当中非国家成功消灭害虫，这里的人们就能享受到更优质的蛋白质。

Sebastien Mongomo is an animal pest expert from Equatorial Guinea. He told the conference that diseases caused by pests have killed at least 10 percent of the sheep and goats in his country this year.

Dr. Mongomo says the borders between Cameroon, Gabon and Equatorial Guinea are largely unguarded. He notes it is difficult to control the movement of animals.

参考译文

塞巴斯蒂安·蒙戈莫（Sebastien Mongomo）是赤道几内亚的动物病虫害专家。他在会上表示，虫害导致的疾病今年已经导致赤道几内亚至少10%的绵羊和山羊死亡。

蒙戈莫博士表示，喀麦隆、加蓬和赤道几内亚之间的边境几乎无人看守。他指出，这很难控制动物的流动。

Pests can spread diseases and also cause health problems known as secondary **infections**. Some infections cause the animals to become very tired. They may not eat. Then they die.

Dr. Felix Njemi is an animal health officer at the FAO. He says the large number of animal deaths is worsening the food crisis in Africa, especially in countries south of the Sahara.

参考译文

害虫可以传播疾病，还能导致继发性感染这类健康问题。有些感染会让动物变得非常疲惫，它们可能不进食然后死亡。

菲利克斯（Felix Njemi）博士是粮农组织的一位动物卫生官员。他说，大量动物死亡正在加速非洲，特别是撒哈拉以南非洲地区的粮食危机。

"The strategy is the large vaccination at the country level. Undertake **surveillance** to detect any case of the disease and strengthen **collaboration** between member nations and even between international institutions. Imagine somebody who has 10 animals and loses eight. The disease can have impact in food security."

Many poor people in African countries depend on goats and sheep for their **livelihoods**. The FAO says people become vulnerable to **famine** when pests attack and kill their animals. I'm Jonathan Evans.

参考译文

"应对战略则是在国家层面开展大规模疫苗接种，开展监测以发现疾病，并加强成员国甚至是国际机构之间的合作。想像一下有人有10头动物，然后死了8头。这种疾病会影响粮食安全。"

非洲国家的很多穷人以山羊和绵羊为生。粮农组织表示，当害虫袭击并杀死他们的动物时，人们就很容易受到饥荒伤害。我是乔纳森·埃文斯。

精彩解析

1. He says that when central African countries succeed in killing the pests, their human populations will enjoy better quality protein.

他说，当中非国家成功消灭害虫，这里的人们就能享受到更优质的蛋白质。

succeed in doing sth. 成功做某事

例句 There is no doubt that we will succeed in designing the project.

毫无疑问，我们会把这项工程成功设计出来。

2. Many poor people in African countries depend on goats and sheep for their livelihoods.

非洲国家的很多穷人以山羊和绵羊为生。

depend on 依靠，依赖

例句 All living things depend on the sun for their growth.

万物靠太阳生长。

读书笔记

法国农民使用无人机检查作物

French Farmers Are Using Drones to Examine Their Crops (VOA News)

新闻导读

法国是欧盟最大的农业生产国，也是世界主要农副产品出口国。粮食产量占全欧洲粮食产量的三分之一，农产品出口仅次于美国居世界第二位。随着法国人口城市化，农村人口不断减少，法共有耕地面积5 491.9万公顷，其中61%为农业用地、27%为林业用地、12%为非农业用地。农业用地的96%为家庭所有。农业的传统地区结构为：中北部地区是谷物、油料、蔬菜、甜菜的主产区，西部和山区为饲料作物主产区，地中海沿岸和西南部地区为多年生作物（葡萄、水果）的主产区。机械化是法国提高农业生产率的主要手段，现已基本实现了农业机械化。

新闻热词

aircraft ['eəkrɑːft] n. 航空器

farmer ['fɑːmə(r)] n. 农场主，农民

examine [ɪg'zæmɪn] v. 检查，调查

fertilizer ['fɜːtəlaɪzə(r)] n. 肥料，化肥

navigation [ˌnævɪ'geɪʃn] n. 航行

individual [ˌɪndɪ'vɪdjuəl] adj. 个人的

monitor ['mɒnitə] v. 监控，监视

technology [tek'nɒlədʒi] n. 科技，工艺

program ['prəʊgræm] n. 程序

nitrogen ['naɪtrədʒən] n. 氮，氮气

新闻播报

It used to be mostly the military that used small, unpiloted **aircraft**, called "drones." The little planes were very costly. But as they have dropped in price more people have begun to use them. Rescue workers and **farmers** are among the new users.

A company in France is using drones to help farmers **examine** their crops and limit the amount of **fertilizer** they use.

参考译文

过去通常是军方在使用小型无人机，这种小飞机非常昂贵。但随着价格的下降，越来越多人开始使用无人机。援救人员和农民也是新使用者。

法国一家公司在使用无人机来帮助农民检查作物并限制化肥的使用量。

The fast rate of development of computer technology, image sensing devices, satellite **navigation** and smartphones has led to lower-priced drones. Researchers and developers have learned how to build smaller and less-costly drones sought by **individuals**, companies and governments.

Moviemakers are using drones to film from the sky. Historians use them when they explore ancient buildings. Rescue workers use them to look for people. And now farmers are using them to **monitor** their crops.

参考译文

电脑技术、图像感应设备、卫星导航和智能手机的快速发展使得无人机价格越来越低，研究者和开发者开始研究制造个人、公司和政府想要的低成本无人机。

电影制作人开始使用无人机在天空拍摄，历史学家使用无人机来探索古代建筑。援救人员使用无人机来寻人，现在农民也开始使用无人机来观测作物。

Romain Faroux is a French businessman who starts companies. His father was a farmer. He believed drones could help farmers. He helped create a company that developed a small drone that could be controlled by people on the ground. They called it "Agridrone." It uses a special "optical sensor" to examine crops.

He says the technology used is similar to that used by smartphones—except it has wings. He says the industrialization of electronic parts for smartphones and tablets lets them get the **technology**—including GPS—at a very low price.

参考译文

罗曼·法鲁克是一位开公司的法国商人，他的父亲曾是农民。他认为无人机能帮助农民，他帮助创立了一家公司，开发地面人员能控制的无人机，他们称它为“农业无人机”，这种无人机使用特殊的光学感应器来检测作物。

他说这种无人机除了有机翼外，所使用的技术与智能手机的技术很类似。他说智能手机和平板电脑电子元件的产业化使得他们以很低的价格获得包括GPS在内的技术。

A computer **program** directs the drone to fly over the crops. The sensor on the drone records four different-colored "bands" of sunlight that are reflected off the crops.

Jean-Baptiste Bruggeman is a farmer. He says the drone flies over his crops at different times of the season. He says this provides a lot of information about his crops.

He says the drone pictures show him the exact amount of fertilizer the crops need. He says it also shows exactly where the fertilizer is needed. Some areas of a field may need more than others.

As a result, Mr. Bruggeman says there is reduced **nitrogen** from the fertilizer after the harvest. This helps nature.

参考译文

计算机程序指导无人机飞行在作物上空，无人机上的感应器能记录作物反射的四种不同颜色的太阳光光带。

让·巴蒂斯特·布鲁格曼是一位农民，他说无人机在季节的不同时间飞行在作物上空，他说这就能提供关于作物的很多信息。

他说无人机图片能让他了解作物所需化肥的确切份量，他说还能精确显示哪里需要化肥，一块土地上的一些区域可能需要更多的化肥。

布鲁格曼说，因此的结果就是庄稼收割后，来自化肥的氮的含量减少，这就对自然有益。

Romain Faroux says farmers use information gathered by the Agridrone to place fertilizer only in areas where it was needed. This saves money and reduces pollution. Before they used the drones, farmers would put the same amount of fertilizer everywhere.

Drones also save time because farmers can examine up to three hectares in about a minute. I'm Marsha James.

参考译文

罗曼·法鲁克说农民们使用农业无人机收集的信息来将化肥施

在需要化肥的地方，这就能省钱并减少污染。在使用无人机之前，农民们会在所有区域施同样量的化肥。

无人机还能省时间，因为农民们能在一分钟的时间内检查3公顷的土地。我是玛莎·詹姆斯。

精彩解析

1. He says the technology used is similar to that used by smartphones—except it has wings.

他说这种无人机除了有机翼外，所使用的技术与智能手机的技术很类似。

be similar to 与……相似

例句 Their house is similar to ours.

他们的房子和我们的差不多。

2. As a result, Mr. Bruggeman says there is reduced nitrogen from the fertilizer after the harvest.

布鲁格曼说，因此的结果就是庄稼收割后，来自化肥的氮的含量减少。

as a result 结果，因此

例句 As a result, he won the first prize in the competition.

结果，他在这个比赛中获得了一等奖。

读书笔记

5 美国农业部同意变更肉类标签设计

USDA Agreed to Change the Design of Meat Labels (VOA News)

新闻导读

2013年5月23日，美国农业部（USDA）发布一份最终规则，根据原产国标签（COOL）项目修订分割肉类商品的标签规定。最终规则修订了分割肉标签规定，要求原产地名称包括每个生产步骤（如出生、饲养、宰杀）的发生地点，删除了对分割肉类混合的许可。根据COOL，零售商必须向客户提供有关各种食品，包括水果、蔬菜、鱼类、贝类和肉类的原产地信息。强制性COOL要求将帮助消费者在购买食品之前做出更明智的购买决定。美国农业部AMS将负责COOL法规的实施、管理和执行。

2013年11月23日生效的美国新版肉类原产地标识政策，要求该国市场上的肉类产品必须标注牲畜的出生地、饲养地及屠宰地，美国肉类进口公司不能将来自不同国家的牲畜肉产品包装在一起，这使原本就因旧版COOL而经营困难的经营者处境更加艰难。一些美国公司表示他们无力承担因新规定而增加的对进口肉产品的分类、标识及储藏费用。

新闻热词

industrial [ɪn'dʌstriəl] *adj.* 工业的，产业的

proposal [prə'pəʊzl] *n.* 提议，计划

butcher ['bʊtʃə(r)] *n.* 屠夫

currently ['kʌrəntli] adv. 现在

identify [aɪ'dentɪfaɪ] v. 识别，鉴定

traditionally [trə'dɪʃənəli] adv. 习惯上，传统上

poultry ['pəʊltri] n. 家禽；家禽肉

voluntarily ['vɒləntrəli] adv. 志愿地，自发地

adopt [ə'dɒpt] v. 采取，采用

新闻播报

The United States Department of Agriculture has agreed to meet **industrial proposals** to change the design of meat labels and how meat is described.

Today's common names developed overtime, as meat cutters used terms that described parts of animals, as well as cuts made by **butchers**.

参考译文

美国农业部已经同意变更肉类标签设计和描述以满足行业的建议。

今天的常用名已随着时间有所发展。比如，肉类零售商会使用术语来描述牲畜的部位和屠夫切下来的肉块。

After the new changes, people may have to read more of the label to know what kind of meat they are buying. For example, labels **currently** say "beef" or "pork" on the first line. The new labels will use smaller print and will **identify** the animal on the second line. Also, cuts of meat that were **traditionally** names for beef products like rib steak, will now also being used for pork, that means a rib steak could come from either a cow or a pig.

参考译文

在这次标签变更后，人们可能需要阅读更多的标签内容来了解他们购买的肉类品种。举个例子，标签通常会在第一行标明“牛肉”或“猪肉”。而新标签会在第二行使用更小的印刷字体标明动物名称。此外，传统上用于称呼如肋骨牛排等牛肉制品的“肉块”，现在同样适用于猪肉制品。这就意味着，现在的“肋骨肉排”可能指的是猪肉，也可能是牛肉。

The labels for chicken and other **poultry** will not change, labels for fish will not change either.

The meat industry wants meat producers and supermarkets to **voluntarily adopt** the new description. There are no legal requirements to make the changes. But the Food and Drug Administration is considering new rules that would require complete details on labels about where meat was raised, and processed.

参考译文

鸡肉和其他家禽肉类的标签并未发生变更，鱼肉类标签也跟以前一样。

肉类行业希望肉类生产商和超市自愿采用新标签。当前并没有法律规定必须更改。但美国食品和药品管理局正在考虑出台新的规定，将要求在标签上标注肉类的饲养地和屠宰加工场等完整信息。

精彩解析

1. The United States Department of Agriculture has agreed to meet industrial proposals to change the design of meat labels and how meat is described.

   美国农业部已经同意变更肉类标签设计和描述以满足行业的建议。

   agree to 同意，赞成

例句 It was unwise of you to agree to that.

你同意那件事是不明智的。

2. …will now also being used for pork.
现在同样适用于猪肉制品。

be used for 用于……的，用来做……

例句 The money is to be used for specific purposes.

这笔钱有专门用途。

3. There are no legal requirements to make the changes.
当前并没有法律规定必须更改。

make the change 使发生改变

例句 To be frank, I don't think it is necessary to make the change.

坦率地说，我想没必要改变。

读书笔记

6 美国农业部的国外农业服务正在与饥饿战斗

USDA's Foreign Agriculture Service Fighting Hunger (VOA News)

新闻导读

美国是世界上最发达的国家之一，更是农业强国，同时也是世界头号农产品出口大国。20世纪90年代初期，美国农产品出口大都在400亿美元以上，而90年代中后期其出口值大都超过了500亿美元，1996年曾达到了600亿美元的历史新高。美国农业在20世纪90年代的强势增长，主要得益于农业生产规模经营、机械化水平的提高和农业科学技术的进步。同时，不断完善的政府支持和服务、积极的国际交流与合作对保持和加强美国农业在国际上的竞争力起到了非常重要的作用。

新闻热词

majority [mə'dʒɒrəti] n. 多数，大多数

strengthen ['streŋθn] v. 加强，变坚固

poverty ['pɒvəti] n. 贫穷，缺乏

pledge [pledʒ] v. 保证，抵押，使发誓；许诺拨（款）

assistance [ə'sɪstəns] n. 协助，补助，援助

security [sɪ'kjʊərəti] n. 安全，安全感

initiative [ɪ'nɪʃətɪv] n. 初步行动，主动

infrastructure ['ɪnfrəstrʌktʃə(r)] n. 基础设施

contribute [kən'trɪbjuːt] v. 有助于，捐助

foster ['fɒstə(r)] v. 养育，培养

recipient [rɪ'sɪpiənt] n. 接受者，接受器

sustainable [sə'steɪnəbl] adj. 可持续的

新闻播报

Around the world, some 870 million people go to bed hungry most nights, according to the United Nations Food and Agriculture Organization, or FAO. The vast **majority** of them live in developing countries.

At the G-8 Summit in L'Aquila, Italy, four years ago, President Barack Obama called on global leaders to **strengthen poverty**, hunger and under-nutrition reduction efforts. He **pledged** $3.5 billion in new development **assistance** for food **security** and nutrition.

参考译文

在世界上，大概8.7亿人在晚上睡觉时正在挨饿，据美国食品与农业组织统计，他们大多居住在发展中国家。

四年前在拉奎拉举行的8国首脑峰会上，奥巴马总统号召全球领导人努力减少贫穷、饥饿和营养不良。他许诺拨款35亿美元用于食品安全及营养的新发展援助。

Feed the Future, born out of this commitment, is the U.S. government's global hunger and food security **initiative**. Through Feed the Future, the United States supports partner countries to develop food security strategies, focusing on smallholder farmers and promoting private sector. Feed the Future supports smallholder farmer capacity development, increasing access to better farming techniques and agriculture inputs like seeds; improving access to processing facilities; and improving transportation **infrastructure**. Feed the Future also supports technology access to connect farmers to information, such as weather or crop disease warnings.

参考译文

由这项许诺诞生的计划：保证未来粮食供给，是美国政府的全球饥饿和食品安全倡议。根据此计划，美国支持合作国家发展食物安全策略，关注小型农场并推进私人企业。该计划支持小型农场最大限度的发展，使他们使用更好的种植技术和更多农业投入（例如种子）；改进生产设备和运输设施，当然也包括关于农业的相关信息的技术支持，例如天气和作物病的预警等。

Led by the U.S. Agency for International Development, Feed the Future draws on 10 total US federal agencies to **contribute** to global food security work. The Department of Agriculture, or USDA, is a key partner in this effort.

"In addition to providing much-needed nutritious food, USDA's food assistance programs also **foster** economic growth in the **recipient** countries," said U.S. Secretary of Agriculture Tom Vilsack. "The United States is committed to achieving global food security and supporting **sustainable** agricultural production."

参考译文

在美国国际开发总署的领导下，保证未来粮食供给计划拉动了10个美国联邦政府机构来进行全球食品安全工作。农业部在其中起到关键作用。

美国农业部秘书汤姆·维塞克说道"除了提供急需的营养食物，美国农业部的食品援助项目同样帮助被援助国的经济增长，美国正致力于实现全球食品安全并支持可持续发展农业生产"。

精彩解析

1. Around the world, some 870 million people go to bed hungry most nights...

   每次联邦债务触大概8.7亿人在晚上睡觉时正在挨饿……

   go to bed 睡觉

   例句 I usually go to bed at half past ten.

   我通常十点半睡觉。

2. President Barack Obama called on global leaders to strengthen poverty, hunger and under-nutrition reduction efforts.

   奥巴马总统号召全球领导人努力减少贫穷、饥饿和营养不良。

   call on 号召；呼吁

   例句 We base this call on grounds of social justice and equity.

   我们基于社会正义和公平发出这一呼吁。

3. Feed the Future supports smallholder farmer capacity development, increasing access to better farming techniques and agriculture inputs like seeds.

   该计划支持小型农场最大限度的发展，使他们使用更好的种植技术和更多农业投入（例如种子）。

   access to 接近，有权使用

   例句 Students must have access to a good library.

   学生要有使用好图书馆的便利条件。

4. In addition to providing much-needed nutritious food, USDA's food assistance programs also **foster** economic growth in the **recipient** countries.

   除了提供急需的营养食物，美国农业部的食品援助项目同样帮助被援助国的经济增长。

   in addition to 除……之外

   例句 I minored in literature in addition to art.

   我除了辅修艺术以外还辅修文学。

7 美国农业生产方式的改变

The Changing Landscape of U.S. Farm Production (VOA News)

新闻导读

美国农业的生产方式和生产力水平都处于世界最发达之列。美国农业之所以成功，有其得天独厚的农业资源因素，但更与经历百年的历史演化和市场竞争所形成的农业及相关产业的组织结构和经营机制构成的、有竞争力的生产方式密切相关。美国的农业以家庭农场为主，约占各类农场总数的87%，合伙农场占10%，公司农场占3%。由于许多合伙农场和公司农场也以家庭农场为依托，因此美国的农场几乎都是家庭农场，可以说美国的农业是在农户家庭经营基础上进行的。

新闻热词

landscape ['lændskeɪp] n. 风景；情形，形势

locally ['ləʊkəli] adv. 在附近，在本地

consistency [kən'sɪstənsiː] n. 一致性；稠度

genetics [dʒɪ'netɪks] n. 遗传学

modernize ['mɒdənaɪz] v. 使现代化，使适应现代的需要

intensive [ɪn'tensɪv] adj. 加强的，密集的

新闻播报

Demand for meat, milk and eggs is growing around the world. To meet that demand, the way these products are produced is changing. The change is from small farms to large industrial operations. This has already happened in the United States.

But not everyone is happy with the change. As a result, there is also a growing demand for products growing **locally** on small farms.

参考译文

全球对于肉类、牛奶、鸡蛋的需求正在不断上升。为了满足这些需求，这些产品的生产方式在发生着改变。从小农场到大型工业生产无不发生着改变。美国早已发生了这种变化。

但并不是每一个人都对这种改变表示欢迎。因此，人们对土生土长的小农场提供的农产品的需求也在增强。

In Clinton, North Carolina, some old buildings are all that remain from the days when James Lame raised hogs next to his home. He saw that small farmers were having trouble competing with companies that own large farms.

"They had better **consistency**, better pork quality, and better **genetics**. So after college, in 1998, I decided to try and **modernize**."

He stopped raising hogs in small building and built two industrial-scale hog barns, each of them holds 1,500 hogs. Nearly all pigs are raised this way in the United States now.

参考译文

在北卡莱罗纳州克林顿市，有一些老房子是当年James Lame 在他家附近养猪时所剩下的唯一的东西。他亲眼看到小农户在与那些拥有大农场的公司竞争中所遇到的麻烦。

“因为他们有更稳定的持续性，有质量更优的猪肉，有更好的基因技术。所以，1998年大学毕业后，我决定尝试现代化的养殖模式。”

他没有继续在小建筑中养猪，取而代之的是两个工业级别的猪棚，每个猪棚能够容纳1 500只猪。如今在美国，人们几乎都用这种方式来养猪。

The government says the efficiency of large-scale production in a controlled environment has helped reduce the price of a pork chop by nearly 20 percent since 1998.

These efficient and **intensive** production methods are being used around the world. Many experts say that is a good thing as the demand for meat grows. But livestock expert Carolyn Opio points out that the land, water and feed required to produce it are limited.

参考译文

美国政府表示，在可控环境下大规模生产的效率从1998年开始就帮助政府降低了猪排近20%的价格。

这些有效率有针对性的生产方法在全世界范围内推广开来，许多专家说，这对于不断攀升的肉类需求是件好事。但畜牧专家Carolyn Opio指出，生产所需的陆地、水和饮料是有限的。

精彩解析

1. Demand for meat, milk and eggs is growing around the world.
   全球对于肉类、牛奶、鸡蛋的需求正在不断上升。

   demand for 对……的要求，对……的需求

   例句 The recent demand for houses has perked up the prices.

   最近对住房的需求使房价上涨了。

2. But not everyone is happy with the change.
   但并不是每一个人都对这种改变表示欢迎。

   be happy with 对……感到满意，对……感到愉快

   例句 He won't be happy with the result.

   他对结果不会满意。

3. But livestock expert Carolyn Opio points out that the land, water and feed required to produce it are limited.
   但畜牧专家Carolyn Opio指出，生产所需的陆地、水和饮料是有限的。

   point out 指出，说出

   例句 I should point out that these problems are very tricky.

   我应该指明的是，这些问题是非常棘手的。

读书笔记

8 瑞士牛铃铛有害牛的健康

Swiss Cow Bells Are Harmful to the Cows' Health (BBC News)

新闻导读

瑞士是位于欧洲中南部的多山内陆国。东界奥地利、列支敦士登，南邻意大利，西接法国，北连德国。位于阿尔卑斯山区的瑞士，原本是一个以农牧业为主的小国。每年春天，牧民们将牛群赶到山上草场放牧，到了秋天再将牛群赶下山。有时，牧民们上山察看畜群，为了能比较方便地在山上"听"到自家畜群，牧民们便给牛群挂上牛铃，这就是牛铃的最初功能。听牧民说，给牛群挂牛铃始于何时已无从追溯，但至少也有200~300年历史。早年，牛铃都是用铁皮烧红后手工打制，然后将接缝焊起来即可。各家的牛铃大小不同，铁皮薄厚不同，因而铃声也不同，有的铃声清脆悦耳，有的则低沉浑厚。铃声的高低主要是根据下沿的宽窄，下沿宽，铃声比较浑厚，下沿窄则比较清脆。每个牛铃的音质都不一样。牛铃往往挂在牛群中最强壮的母牛脖子上，这样一来，牧民只要听到熟悉的牛铃声，就能听"铃"识牛。

新闻热词

iconic [aɪ'kɒnɪk] adj. 符号的，标志性的

herd [hɜːd] n. 兽群，牧群

identify [aɪ'dentɪfaɪ] v. 识别，认出

roam [rəʊm] v. 漫游，游荡

collection [kə'lekʃn] n. 收集，采集；收藏品

procession [prə'seʃn] v. 排队前进或列队而行

provoke [prə'vəʊk] v. 激起，挑起

intricate ['ɪntrɪkət] adj. 复杂精细的，错综复杂的

advantage [əd'vaːntɪdʒ] n. 有利条件，优势

新闻播报

It's an **iconic** image of Switzerland **herds** of cows grazing in the mountains with huge bells around their necks. Farmers have been putting them on the cows for two hundred years so that they can **identify** them and find them when they **roam**. Quite how much fun it is for the cow to have a great big bell around its neck however has not been a matter of great concern until now.

参考译文

牛群在山上吃草，脖子上挂着硕大的铃铛——这是瑞士的标志性景观之一。两百年前，农民就开始在牛脖子上系铃铛，方便他们辨认并找到四处游走的牛。然而，没有人在意脖子上挂着大铃铛对牛来说有多少乐趣。如今，情况有了改观。

Farmer is showing off his pride in joy, the huge **collection** of cow bells.

They are all traditional. They are about two hundred years old. Yes. We always use them still. And they make music all together. Can you ring one for me? Sure. That's the normal big one.

There are large bells for the annual **procession** up to the high meadows and smaller ones for every day. Appearing in the mountain farming, it's practical. I hear. If some cow get(s) lost, you can go for days, for days, through the forest.

参考译文

一位农民正在如数家珍般地展示他收藏的牛铃铛。

这些都是祖上传下来的，大约有两百年的历史，对。我们现在还在用，铃铛一起响，会产生美妙的音乐。您能敲一下我听听吗？可以。这是普通的大铃铛。

每年向高山草原挺进的时候用大铃铛，日常放牧用小铃铛。铃铛很适用于山地农业。我时刻在听着，如果哪头牛丢了，我可以追随铃铛的声音，在森林里走好几天。

Environmental health regulations are that nothing louder than 85 decibels is allowed. Cow bells are quite clearly at least twice as loud as that.

Cows wearing bells eat less and sleep less. But her suggestion that bells be abandoned in favor of GPS technology and cows with electronic chips has **provoked** doubt, and not just from farmers.

My name is Roger. Bell maker Roger takes enormous pride in his job. Each bell is individually cast from modes made of sand with **intricate** decorations of scapes, flowers and of course, cows. No two bells are the same.

参考译文

环境卫生法规规定，噪声应控制在85分贝以内。很显然，牛铃铛的声音至少是这个标准的两倍。

铃铛能够导致牛的食欲和睡眠减少。她的建议是舍弃铃铛，使用GPS技术，在牛身上安装电子芯片。但是，该建议引发了来自农民和其他各界人士的质疑。

我叫罗格。罗格是做铃铛的，他对自己的工作感到非常骄傲。每个铃铛都是在沙制模具中浇筑而成的，同时还刻有精致的装饰图案，如花茎、花朵等，当然，还有牛。找不出相同的两个铃铛。

Every bell sounds a little bit different. That's a deep one. And the sound comes from the shape and also the thickness of the wall of the bell. And the high one. The farmer hears which bell is ringing so he can say "Susan is all right and Ilene has a problem." That's a big **advantage** instead of a GPS.

But for animal rights groups, alarm bells are ringing. For us as an animal welfare organization, we can not accept the arguments that the cow bells belong to the images of Switzerland and are look beautiful on the animals.

参考译文

每个铃铛的声音都有点区别。这个铃声比较深沉。铃铛的声音取决于它的形状和厚度。这个铃铛发出的音调比较高。农民们听着铃铛响，就能判定，“苏珊一切正常，艾琳有点问题”。这是相对于GPS来说的一大优势。

但在动物权益保护组织看来，警钟拉响了。作为动物权益保护组织，我们不能接受说牛铃铛是瑞士形象的标志，戴在牛身上很漂亮。

精彩解析

1. The farmer is showing off his pride in joy, the huge **collection** of cow bells.

   一位农民正在如数家珍般地展示他收藏的牛铃铛。

   show off 炫耀，卖弄

   例句 Emily was showing off her engagement ring.

   艾米丽正在炫耀她的订婚戒指。

2. But her suggestion that bells be abandoned in favor of GPS technology...

她的建议是舍弃铃铛，使用GPS技术……

in favor of 以……取代

例句 Price control would gradually disappear in favor of a free market.

价格控制将逐渐被自由市场所代替。

3. We can not accept the arguments that the cow bells belong to the images of Switzerland...

我们不能接受说牛铃铛是瑞士形象的标志……

belong to 属于

例句 The house belongs to my grandfather.

这房子属于我爷爷。

读书笔记

9 山羊竟然吃自行车轮胎

Goats Can Eat Bicycle Tires (BBC News)

新闻导读

山羊（goat），是最早被人类驯化的家畜之一。山羊的觅食力强，食性杂，能食百样草，对各种牧草、灌木枝叶、作物秸秆、菜叶、果皮、藤蔓、农副产品等均可采食，其采食植物的种类较其他家畜广泛。据对5种家畜饲喂植物的试验，山羊能采食的植物有607种，不采食的有83种，采食率为88%，而绵羊、牛、马、猪的采食率分别为80%、64%、73%和46%。在饲草匮乏的情况下，山羊觅食力较强。在荒漠、半荒漠地区，牛不能利用的多数植物，山羊也能有效利用。山羊的采食时间大多集中在白天，日出时开始采食，但并不连续采食，而是在每天的一定时间内摄食量大，而在其他时间进行反刍、休息。据测定，每天清晨和黄昏，山羊的采食量大。因此，在舍饲或半舍饲半放牧时，供给山羊的草料应多样化，且需少食多餐。

新闻热词

digestive [daɪ'dʒestɪv] *adj.* 消化的；助消化的

stomach ['stʌmək] *n.* 胃

enzyme ['enzaɪm] *n.* 酶；酶类

agricultural [ˌægrɪ'kʌltʃərəl] *adj.* 农业的；农用的

microorganism [ˌmaɪkrəʊ'ɔːgənɪzəm] *n.* 微生物

herbivore ['hɜːbɪvɔː(r)] n. 食草动物

bioreactor [baɪəriː'æktər] n. 生物反应器

polymer ['pɒlɪmə(r)] n. 聚合物；多聚体

commodity [kə'mɒdəti] n. 商品

cauliflower ['kɒliflaʊə(r)] n. 花椰菜；菜花

anaerobic [ˌæneə'rəʊbɪk] adj. 厌氧菌的，厌氧菌产生的

新闻播报

Now a story I can vouch for from personal experience. It's about goats and that they can eat just about anything. I used to own one many years ago when I lived in Sudan. We bought it to keep the grass short on our little lawn. But it preferred eating oily rags and bicycle tires if it could get to them. This **digestive** ability of goats may have practical applications. In a study published in the German Science, researchers say fungi in goats' **stomaches** produce **enzymes** that can break down all sorts of things. What exactly can we learn from goats?

参考译文

下面讲一个我亲身经历过的事情。说的是山羊，还有山羊什么都能吃。我很多年前在苏丹的时候养过一只，我们买它是为了把小草坪上的草弄短一点。但山羊更喜欢吃油布和自行车轮胎，能找着就吃。山羊的这种消化能力可能会有实际用途。在德国《科学》杂志发表的一篇论文中，研究人员称山羊胃里的真菌产生的酶可分解各种物质。我们从山羊身上究竟可以学到什么呢？

Goats have been engineered by nature to break down really tough plant waste and **agricultural** waste into sugars for the animal. And what we wanna do is to understand how they are doing that and then translate that ability to **microorganism** so that we can revolutionize bioprocessing of plant waste and food scraps.

参考译文

山羊天生能够将难以咀嚼的植物性废弃物和农业废弃物分解为可供动物吸收的糖。我们想做的就是搞清楚整个过程，然后把这种能力转化为微生物学，从而为植物性废弃物和餐饮垃圾的生物处理带来革命性变革。

Am I right at thinking goats are the best at this or are other **herbivores** equally capable?

That's a great question. So other herbivores are great at this because they have another compartment in their digestive tracts that we don't have called the rumen which is sort of like a little **bioreactor** to break up tough woody things into sugar.

参考译文

山羊是最擅长这个的，我这样理解对吗？还是说其他食草动物都有同样的能力？

这个问题问得好。其他食草动物也很擅长，因为它们的消化道中有我们不具备的一个腔体，叫瘤胃，有点像一个小的生物反应器，它能将不易咀嚼的硬东西分解为糖。

And so it may be that the goats are particularly great at this but we would expect that all animals that have that sort of part of their stomach could actually be just as good. These types of tough woody materials that have a lot of different polymers in them. And these polymers all put together can be broken down into sugar. And so what we wanna do is to unlock the potential of these really tough to degree **polymers** through the action of enzymes. And these are just power houses at breaking up that plant scrap into sugar which then you could convert to other things which might include fuels or chemicals or **commodity** products.

参考译文

所以可能山羊尤其擅长这个，但我们希望胃里有类似部分的动物也同样擅长。这些不易咀嚼的硬物质含有许多不同的聚合物，这些聚合物可以一起被分解为糖。而我们想做的就是通过酶的作用，开发这些坚韧到一定程度的聚合物的潜能。这些就是动力室，将植物碎片分解为糖，然后转化为其他东西，可以是燃料、化学品或商业产品等。

OK. So now and how far down the road are you? Can you…? If I give you, I don't know, if I give you a rotten **cauliflower**, could you turn it into sugar?

So part of what we could do is to feed that rotten cauliflower or corn stover or grasses growing in the great plants of the US to **anaerobic** microorganism.

参考译文

好。那么现在你们进行到哪一步了？你们能……？如果我给你，比方说，我给你一个腐烂的菜花，你能把它转化为糖吗？

我们可以做到的一点就是把那个腐烂的菜花或玉米秸或美国大型植物里长的草喂给厌氧微生物。

精彩解析

1. Now a story I can vouch for from personal experience.

下面讲一个我亲身经历过的事情。

vouch for 证明；证实

例句 He cannot vouch for the accuracy of the story.

他不能证明这一故事的准确性。

2. In a study published in the German Science, researchers say fungi in goats' stomaches produce enzymes that can break down all sorts of things.

在德国《科学》杂志发表的一篇论文中，研究人员称山羊胃里的真菌产生的酶可分解各种物质。

break down （使）（物质）分解

例句 Over time, the protein in the eggshell breaks down into its constituent amino acids.

时间久了，蛋壳中的蛋白质就会分解为其构成成分氨基酸。

3. ...because they have another compartment in their digestive tracts that we don't have called the rumen which is sort of like a little bioreactor to break up tough woody things into sugar.

……因为它们的消化道中有我们不具备的一个腔体，叫瘤胃，有点像一个小的生物反应器，它能将不易咀嚼的硬东西分解为糖。

sort of 有点；有几分地

例句 He's American-bred, with a sort of Irish background somewhere along the line.

他出生在美国，家族的血统里有一部分爱尔兰血统。

读书笔记

卫生健康

1 美国致力于加强全球生物安全性

America Is Strengthening Global Biosecurity (VOA News)

新闻导读

生物安全一般是指由现代生物技术开发和应用对生态环境和人体健康造成的潜在威胁，及对其所采取的一系列有效预防和控制措施。基于生物技术发展有可能带来的不利影响，人们提出了生物安全的概念。生物安全问题引起国际上的广泛注意是在上世纪80年代中期，1985年由UNEP、WHO、UNIDO及FAO联合组成了一个非正式的关于生物技术安全的特设工作小组，开始关注生物安全问题。国际上对生物安全立法工作引起特别重视是在1992年召开联合国环境与发展大会后，此次大会签署的两个纲领性文件《21世纪议程》和《生物多样性公约》均专门提到了生物技术安全问题。

新闻热词

interconnect [ˌɪntəkəˈnekt] v. 互相连接，互相联系

pathogen [ˈpæθədʒən] n. 病菌，病原体

emerging [iˈmɜːdʒɪŋ] adj. 新兴的

devastate [ˈdevəsteɪt] v. 破坏

catastrophic [ˌkætəˈstrɒfɪk] adj. 灾难性的；引起重大灾难的

infectious [ɪnˈfekʃəs] adj. 传染的；传染性的

biological [ˌbaɪəˈlɒdʒɪkl] adj. 生物的；生物学的

partnership [ˈpɑːtnəʃɪp] n. 伙伴关系；合作关系

participate [pɑː'tɪsɪpeɪt] v. 参与；参加

mitigate ['mɪtɪgeɪt] v. 减轻；缓解；缓和

新闻播报

In today's **interconnected** world, a **pathogen** can travel around the globe in as little as 36 hours. Interactions between wildlife, domesticated animals, and humans can give rise to new and **emerging** infections. Spurred by urban density and international air travel, these diseases can spread around the world within days.

参考译文

当今世界里，万事万物彼此联系，因而病原体可在短短36个小时的时间里在全球传播。野生动物、家禽、人之间的接触都可能引发新的感染。在城市人口密集与国际航班频繁的促使下，疾病可以在短短数天内在全球传播。

Biological agents including viruses, bacteria, and toxins, can **devastate** local economies with their potential effects on humans and livestock, wrote Kathryn Insley in a recent blog post. Ms. Insley is the Acting Director of the State Department's Office of Cooperative Threat Reduction, which falls under the Bureau of International Security and Nonproliferation.

参考译文

一些生物因子，如病毒、细菌、毒素可以对人类和家畜产生潜在的诸多影响，继而威胁当地经济的发展，凯瑟琳·因斯雷近日在博客上写道。因斯雷女士是国务院合作减少威胁办公室（Office of Cooperative Threat Reduction）的代理主任，该机构下属于国际安全和核不扩散局（Bureau of International Security and Nonproliferation）。

In addition to potentially **catastrophic** immediate impact, these agents could also set in motion long-term disasters, causing regional instability and challenging international security.

To defeat potential outbreaks should they emerge, it is crucial that the world community is capable of quickly detecting, responding to, and containing **infectious** diseases or other biological pathogens anywhere in the world.

That is why the State Department funds projects around the world that improve the safe handling and responsible use of dangerous **biological** materials. Programs that teach local trainers how to manage possible biorisks within their own country have a multiplier effect.

参考译文

除了可能造成的直接灾难性影响外，这些生物因子也可能引发长期灾害，造成地区动荡，威胁国际安全。

要应对可能出现的灾难，关键是国际社会要对任何地方可能出现的感染性疾病和其他生物病原体疾病有快速监测、应对和抑制的能力。

这就是美国国务院资助了全球各地的多个项目以提升危险生物材料安全处理度和合力使用能力的原因。教导参加培训者如何应对本国内可能出现的生物风险的项目发挥了巨大的积极影响。

The U.S.-Algeria **partnership** to develop biorisk management trainers is one such program. Scientists and professionals within Algeria's public and animal health sectors **participated** in trainings to help them develop the skills necessary to deal with biological pathogens. More importantly, Algerian trainers developed the skills to design new courses tailored to local needs and independently deliver them where they are most needed, writes Acting Director Insley.

参考译文

而美国-阿尔及利亚联手推出的发展生物风险控制培训师就是这样的一个项目。阿尔及利亚公共和动物卫生领域的一些科学家和专业人士参加了这样的培训活动，帮助参加培训者获得应对生物病原体的必要技能。更为重要的是，阿尔及利亚培训师已经能够设计新的课程，来适应当地的不同需要，并在最需要培训的地方独立开展培训活动，凯瑟琳写道。

For scientists with a shared interest in global health security, these projects are a valuable opportunity to share information and learn from each other. They face challenges unique to their varied environments, but collaborating on ways to address threats and prevent disasters is among the most interesting and rewarding parts of their work. The State Department is proud to support efforts that **mitigate** biorisks around the world and strengthen global health security.

参考译文

对于有志于国际卫生安全领域的科学家而言，这样的项目机会难得，可以共享信息，彼此学习。虽然他们各自面临的挑战随具体环境的不同而千差万别，但一起寻找办法来应对威胁并预防灾害是他们工作中最有趣且最具回报的一部分。美国国务院很自豪能够支持致力于消除全球生物风险以及加强全球卫生安全的工作。

精彩解析

1. Interactions between wildlife, domesticated animals, and humans can give rise to new and emerging infections.
野生动物、家禽、人之间的接触都可能引发新的感染。

give rise to 引起，导致；造成

例句 Unhygienic conditions give rise to disease.

卫生条件不好会导致疾病。

2. More importantly, Algerian trainers developed the skills to design new courses tailored to local needs…
更为重要的是，阿尔及利亚培训师已经能够设计新的课程，来适应当地的不同需要……

tailor to 根据……调整

例句 The clinic tailors its treatment to individual need.

这家诊所根据患者不同的病情采取相应的治疗方法。

3. The State Department is proud to support efforts that mitigate biorisks around the world and strengthen global health security.
美国国务院很自豪能够支持致力于消除全球生物风险以及加强全球卫生安全的工作。

be proud to do sth. 很自豪做某事

例句 She's proud to work with you.

她很自豪能与你共事。

2017年世界防治结核病日

World TB Day 2017 (VOA News)

新闻导读

1995年底世界卫生组织（WHO）将每年3月24日作为世界防治结核病日（World Tuberculosis Day），是为了纪念1882年德国微生物学家罗伯特·科赫向一群德国柏林医生发表他对结核病病原菌的发现，以提醒公众加深对结核病的认识。结核病属于慢性传染病，由结核杆菌引起，其中肺结核病最为常见。历史上，结核病曾与天花、鼠疫和霍乱等传染病一样，在全世界范围内广为流行。1882年3月24日，德国科学家罗伯特·科赫宣布发现结核杆菌是导致结核病的病原菌，从而给防治结核病带来突破。此后，随着抗结核药物研制成功，结核病的流行得到有效控制，并在一些地区绝迹。为了纪念科赫的伟大发现，世界卫生组织与国际预防结核病和肺部疾病联盟在1982年决定，将每年的3月24日确定为世界防治结核病日。

新闻热词

commemorate [kə'meməreɪt] v. 纪念，庆祝

bacterium [bæk'tɪəriəm] n. 细菌

awareness [ə'weənəs] n. 察觉，觉悟，意识

epidemic [ˌepɪ'demɪk] n.（疾病的）流行，传播

antibiotic [ˌæntibaɪ'ɒtɪk] n. 抗生素；抗菌素

marginalize ['mɑːdʒɪnəlaɪz] v. 使边缘化；使显得不重要

substandard [ˌsʌb'stændəd] adj. 不够标准的；不合格的

accessible [ək'sesəbl] adj. 易到达的；易进入的

vanquish ['væŋkwɪʃ] v. 击败，战胜

stigmatization [ˌstɪgmətaɪ'zeɪʃn] n. 侮辱

discriminatory [dɪ'skrɪmɪnətəri] adj. 不公平的，歧视的

adoption [ə'dɒpʃn] n. 采取；采纳；采用

affliction [ə'flɪkʃn] n. 病痛；苦恼；折磨

新闻播报

On March 24th each year, nations around the globe observe World Tuberculosis Day, **commemorating** Dr. Robert Koch's 1882 discovery of Mycobacterium tuberculosis, the **bacterium** that causes the disease.

The observance is designed to build public **awareness** about the global **epidemic** of tuberculosis.

Tuberculosis, or TB, is the second leading cause of death from infectious diseases worldwide, infecting almost 9 million people and killing some 1.5 million.

参考译文

每年3月24日，全球各国纪念世界防治结核病日，这一天是为了纪念罗伯特·科赫博士1882年发现了结核杆菌这一引起结核病的病菌。

这个日子是为了让公众意识到肺结核这个全球性流行病。

结核病是全球各类传染性疾病中致死病例第二多的。全球有近900万人患有结核病，因其死亡的病例有近150万例。

Prior to the advent of **antibiotics** in the 1940s, TB was one of the most feared diseases around. Today, the majority of TB deaths occur in the developing world, where the disease is closely linked to poverty, **marginalized** and vulnerable populations, **substandard** housing, and poor nutrition.

This year's theme—Leave no one behind—aims to make TB treatment **accessible** for everyone. This means that, as part of the campaign to **vanquish** TB, we must find a way to end the **stigmatization** of the victims of tuberculosis, and end **discriminatory** practices against them, thus helping these people overcome the barriers that keep them from accessing medical care.

参考译文

在20世纪40年代发现抗生素以前，结核病是人们最害怕的疾病之一。现今，大多数因其致死的病例发生在发展中国家，发展中国家由于贫穷、边缘化及易受冲击的人群、不合标准的房屋、营养不良的问题而一直被结核病困扰。

美国今年结核病的主题是——不让任何人掉队——这个主题是目的是让每个患者都能获得结核病的治疗。这也就意味着，作为消除结核病战斗的一部分，我们必须消除人们对结核病患者的侮蔑，停止对他们的歧视，这样才能帮助他们克服无法获得医治的障碍。

By addressing the health needs of the disadvantaged, the marginalized, and people out of reach of the health system, we not only improve their lives, we also reduce the number of infected people who can, in turn, infect others. And we will improve the access to health services for everyone.

参考译文

通过解决那些弱势的、被边缘化了的、无法获得医疗体系救治的人的健康需求，我们不仅改善了他们的生活，还减少了感染者的数量，继而减少了他们感染别人的几率。我们还将增加每个人获取医疗服务的机会。

The United States is committed to fighting tuberculosis. In

focusing our efforts in countries where the burden of TB is highest, we support programs that save lives, and foster a more secure world. Across the federal government, we have made this fight a priority. We continue to partner with the World Health Organization, the Stop TB Partnership, and the Global Drug Facility, to provide important support for TB control activities worldwide and achieve the world's vision with the **adoption** of the Sustainable Development Goals.

By joining in a global commitment to stop the spread of TB, we can begin to free a new generation from an ancient **affliction**.

参考译文

美国致力于抗击结核病。在将我们工作的重心聚焦在结核病负担最重的国家时，我们在这些国家支持挽救生命的项目，促成一个更加安全的世界。美国整个联邦政府已经将这场战斗作为首要任务。我们继续与世界卫生组织、终止结核病伙伴组织、杜绝结核病全球药品机制合作，为全球结核病控制活动提供重要的支持，并让全球实现可持续发展目标的愿景。

通过加入全球阻止结核病传播的工作，我们可以让子孙后代不受这个长期疾病所扰。

精彩解析

1. The observance is designed to build public awareness about the global epidemic of tuberculosis.
这个日子是为了让公众意识到肺结核这个全球性流行病。

be designed to do sth. 目的是

例句 The experiment is designed to test the new drug.
这个试验是为测试新药。

2. Prior to the advent of antibiotics in the 1940s, TB was one of the most feared diseases around.
在20世纪40年代发现抗生素以前，结核病是人们最害怕的疾病之一。

the advent of ……的出现，问世

例句 Swallows come by groups at the advent of spring.

春天来临时燕子成群飞来。

3. By addressing the health needs of the disadvantaged, the marginalized, and people out of reach of the health system...

通过解决那些弱势的、被边缘化了的、无法获得医疗体系救治的人的健康需求……

out of reach 手够不着，达不到

例句 For a lot of people, those things are slipping out of reach.

对许多人来说，那些东西正在渐渐变得触不可及。

新闻听力加油站

听力训练应培养的能力

在听力训练过程中，往往会碰到听不清或听不懂的情况，原因很多，有时是由于说话人发音不清楚或录音效果不好，有时是因为出现了生词或内容陌生的缘故，这就要靠抓字音及从上下文猜字的能力来解决问题。碰到这样的情况时，首先要记住能听清的声音，然后根据上下文的内容和语法关系提供的线索来进行推测，如果可能的话，还可以根据字音查一下字典，这一能力的培养是听力训练中很关键的一个环节。

排除杂音和各种干扰的能力：为了培养这一能力，要多听新闻广播，听那些看不见说话人口形的录音报告，要逐渐适应人们说话时加上“well”“eh”之类填充语的习惯。

要有适应英国音、美国音及一些主要方言的能力：听力训练可以采取从一种音入手，再逐步过渡至另一种音的办法。为了更快地掌握听好英国音和美国音的能力，学习者可以主动归纳或对比两种英语在发音、语调上的差别，以便更好地渡过这一关。

3 一项新医疗检测或将避免化疗

A New Test May Avoid Unnecessary Chemotherapy (VOA News)

新闻导读

癌症是机体在环境污染、化学污染（化学毒素）、电离辐射、自由基毒素、微生物（细菌、真菌、病毒等）及其代谢毒素、遗传特性、内分泌失衡、免疫功能紊乱等各种致癌物质、致癌因素的作用下导致身体正常细胞发生癌变的结果。常表现为：局部组织的细胞异常增生而形成的局部肿块。癌症是机体正常细胞在多原因、多阶段与多次突变所引起的一大类疾病。

癌细胞的特点是：无限制、无止境地增生，使患者体内的营养物质被大量消耗；癌细胞释放出多种毒素，使人体产生一系列症状；癌细胞还可转移到全身各处生长繁殖，导致人体消瘦、无力、贫血、食欲不振、发热以及严重的脏器功能受损等等。与之相对的有良性肿瘤，良性肿瘤则容易清除干净，一般不转移、不复发，对器官、组织只有挤压和阻塞作用，但癌症（恶性肿瘤）还可破坏组织、器官的结构和功能，引起坏死出血合并感染，患者最终由于器官功能衰竭而死亡。

新闻热词

sample ['sɑːmpl] n. 取样，样本

malignant [mə'lɪgnənt] adj. 恶性的

surgery ['sɜːdʒəri] n. 外科手术

treatment ['triːtmənt] n. 治疗，疗法

chemotherapy [ˌkiːməʊ'θerəpi] n. 化学疗法，化疗

fatigue [fə'tiːg] n. 疲劳，疲乏

infertility [ˌɪnfɜː'tɪləti] n. 不育，不孕症

dementia [dɪ'menʃə] n. 痴呆，痴呆症

unpleasantness [ʌn'plezntnəs] n. 不愉快的事

determine [dɪ'tɜːmɪn] v. 确定，查明

particular [pə'tɪkjələ(r)] adj. 特别的，特定的

resume [rɪ'zjuːm] v. 使重新开始，使继续进行

clinical ['klɪnɪkl] adj. 临床的

新闻播报

When **samples** of breast tissue show the presence of a **malignant** tumor, doctors often prescribe **surgery** followed by a six-month **treatment** of medicine, which could include **chemotherapy** to prevent further spread of cancer cells.

参考译文

当乳房组织样本检测出了恶性肿瘤的存在，随即医生会进行手术，之后接受6个月的药物治疗，其中包括防止癌细胞扩散的化疗。

Chemotherapy kills the remaining cancer cells but also has adverse side effects—nausea, hair loss, **fatigue**, as well as possible **infertility** and damage to some organs.

"We know that some drugs can affect the heart. There's a question about long-term effects of slightly increasing the risks of **dementia** for instance. Apart from that, of course, there's the **unpleasantness** of the four months of treatment that's required, and it'll often take people out of work for six months."

参考译文

化疗能够杀死身体中余下的癌细胞，然而这将伴随着副作用——恶心、脱发、疲惫，还有可能会患有不育症，甚至对脏器构成损害。

"我们知道，一些药物能够对心脏构成影响。长期的副作用还有可能增加患痴呆症的风险。除此之外，这4个月的必要治疗还会给病患带来痛苦，在这6个月的时间里，人们通常不能工作。"

A new test developed in the U.S., called Oncotype DX, **determines** how the patient will respond to chemotherapy.

"Oncotype DX is effectively telling you about the inside workings of the cell, which particular genes have gone wrong to create that **particular** cancer, and, from a reading of those genes, we can then get more information about whether this tumor is the sort that is likely to spread to some other part of the body, or not."

参考译文

在美国，人们研发了一种名叫"Oncotype DX"的检测技术，它能够查明患者对化疗的反应情况。

"Oncotype DX能够告诉你体内细胞的工作情况，它也能够对造成癌细胞的某种基因作出判断，从这些基因中，我们能够对该肿瘤转移到其他脏器的可能性作出评估。"

Avoiding chemotherapy after surgery means that patients like Nia Barton can **resume** their normal lives except for regular checkups to make sure they remain cancer free.

Oncotype DX is one of several gene-based tests that can tell doctors how likely the recurrence of the disease is, and it is most accurate in the early stages. Similar tests, such as Prosigna and Endopredict, are undergoing **clinical** trials in the UK, Germany and Austria.

So far, Oncotype DX is used only in cases of breast cancer, but researchers say similar tests can be developed for other types of cancer.

参考译文

像尼亚·巴顿这样术后不进行化疗的病患，除了对癌细胞进行定期检查外，她可以恢复到正常人的生活。

"Oncotype DX"是多种基因检测中的一种，它能够告诉医生疾病再次复发的可能性，这在早期治疗阶段更为准确。与之相似的还有"Prosigna"以及"Endopredict"，这两种检测正在英国、德国以及奥地利接受临床试验。

到目前为止，"Oncotype DX"仅用于乳腺癌的检测，然而研究人员称，类似检测也能够运用到其他癌症当中。

精彩解析

1. Chemotherapy kills the remaining cancer cells, but also has adverse side effects—nausea, hair loss, fatigue, as well as possible infertility and damage to some organs.

化疗能够杀死身体中余下的癌细胞，然而这将伴随着副作用——恶心、脱发、疲惫，还有可能会患有不育症，甚至对脏器构成损害。

as well as 也，还

例句 He's good at playing basketball as well as playing soccer.

他擅长打篮球，还有踢足球。

2. Apart from that, of course, there's the unpleasantness of the four months of treatment that's required, and it'll often take people out of work for six months.

除此之外，这4个月的必要治疗还会给病患带来痛苦，在这6个月的时间里，人们通常不能工作。

apart from 除……之外

例句 Apart from the cost, it will take a lot of time.

除了成本以外，它还花费很多时间。

3. A new test developed in the U.S., called Oncotype DX, **determines** how the patient will respond to chemotherapy.

在美国，人们研发了一种名叫“Oncotype DX”的检测技术，它能够查明患者对化疗的反应情况。

respond to 对……有某种反应

例句 Did mother's leg respond to treatment?

妈妈的腿治疗后是不是产生效果了？

读书笔记

激光帮助医生锁定脑肿瘤边缘

A New Laser Helps Doctors Find the Outside Edge of Brain Tumors (BBC News)

新闻导读

现在英国医院正在试验激光笔，在手术刀接近肿瘤区域边缘时会发出像停车雷达一样的“哔哔”的声音，让外科医生知道他们已经接近切除边缘。伦敦帝国学院的神经外科医生开始用笔状探针Core，设备会发出近红外光扫描组织后可以区分出肿瘤和健康组织的细微差别。设备能够在一秒内得出区分结果，同时在外科医生接近健康组织时会发出警示音。

目前脑外科手术的主要阻碍之一是正常和肿瘤脑组织很难区分，及时在显微镜下操作也是如此。外科医生只能通过显微外科手术进行细微的组织切割来确保切除的是肿瘤组织。同时组织活检需要90分钟才能将结果反馈给外科医生，再此期间患者必须留在手术台上。

外科医生手握Core即可替代组织样本检验，在探针的顶端会发出激光扫描脑组织化学成分的改变。激光作用下肿瘤分子的震动与健康分子不同，所以反射光线方式也会有差异。探针设备接受反射光线后，信号会通过计算机处理然后即时给出组织是否是癌组织。

新闻热词

disability [ˌdɪsəˈbɪləti] *n.*（身体上的）残疾，伤残

laser ['leɪzə(r)] *n.* 激光

correspondent [ˌkɒrə'spɒndənt] *n.* 记者，通讯员

tumorous ['tjuːmərəs] *adj.* 肿瘤性的

profound [prə'faʊnd] *adj.* 深厚的；意义深远的

surgery ['sɜːdʒəri] *n.* 外科手术

hazy ['heɪzi] *adj.* 模糊的；看不清楚的

analyze ['ænəlaɪz] *v.* 分析；分解

laborious [lə'bɔːriəs] *adj.* 耗时费力的；辛苦的

microscope ['maɪkrəskəʊp] *n.* 显微镜

新闻播报

Surgeons face difficult decisions when dealing with cancer, with brain cancers removing too much too soon can lead to **disability**, taking too little and the disease returns. But scientists say a new **laser** can help doctors quickly find the outside edge of a tumor. Our health **correspondent** James explained why conventional brain surgery is so complicated.

参考译文

若脑癌手术在短时间内切除太多可能导致残疾，但切除太少又导致癌症复发，这让外科医生在对付癌症时面临艰难的选择。然而，科学家称，一种新型激光可有助于迅速找到肿瘤的外边缘。为什么传统脑部手术如此复杂，本台健康记者詹姆斯详细报道。

If you just think of another cancer. You find a **tumorous** growth and then you go "right we've got to get that out." And what you can do is you can just take a section either side. Easy peasy to take it out.

Once you get to the brain, it gets a little bit more difficult because you can't go "Okay, there's the tumor. Let's take you know a nice 5 centimetres around either side. We are just to make sure we've got all of it out" , because if you do that you'll be left with a **profound** disability. So one of the great challenges when it comes to brain **surgery** is only operating on what you have to operate on. It's like a cloud, when it comes to brain surgery. You know where the middle of the tumor is but where the edge of it is gets a little **hazy**.

参考译文

设想一下其他肿瘤，你发现肿瘤生长迹象，然后决定"得切除它"，接下来就可以从任一边开始切除一部分，这个操作非常简单。但是涉及到大脑，手术就变得没那么容易了，你不能说"好，有肿瘤，那就每一边都切除个5厘米吧，得保证切除整个肿瘤"，如果真这么做，将会导致严重的残疾。所以说脑部手术的最大挑战之一就是只能切除必须切除的部分，它就像是一块阴影，你知道肿瘤的中心位置，但它的边缘就有些模糊了。

So tell us about this new method.

The idea of this method is that you use a laser to **analyze** the brain sample for you. And what happens is it changes the properties of the laser depending on what the chemicals are inside the different cells. And a cancer cell is chemically very different to normal brain tissue. So that allows surgeons to very easily spot where the edge of the cloud of that brain tumor is. Now it's only been tested for trying to work out where the edge of a tumor is. So they think it's working quite well. Well, it's really **laborious**. What you have to do is you've taken sample of brain tissue, you have to go away, freeze it, press it down so it's flat, put all kinds of dies on it so that it stains the tissue so you can actually see it and then put it under a **microscope**. And that process can take 40, 50 minutes. And it's one of the reasons why brain surgery can take such a long time.

参考译文

那跟我们讲讲这种新方法吧。

这种方法的实质就是用激光帮助分析脑样本，不同细胞中化学物质的区别会改变激光的特性。癌症细胞的化学性质就与正常脑细胞截然不同，如此一来医生就能很容易地锁定脑瘤阴影的边缘。这种方法目前还在测试当中，观察其能否发现肿瘤边缘。科学家们认为目前效果不错，但确实挺需要下功夫的。做法就是提取脑组织样本，拿去冷冻、压平，在上面放各种模具给脑组织染色便于观察，然后放置在显微镜下。这个过程可能耗费40-50分钟，这就是脑手术耗时长的原因之一。

So as you say, this is, at this state is still just a study. What are the implications then?

Well the grand hope is that not only can you make surgery much quicker but you make sure you are actually getting rid of all of the brain tumor. So the aim really is the aim of all medical research, to make something safer and benefit patients. James.

参考译文

正如你所说，现在只是研究阶段，那么这个研究有什么影响呢?

科学家们最大的愿望是这项研究不仅能使手术速度更快，而且能够摘除所有脑瘤。所以，与一切医学研究的目的一样，这项研究旨在让手术更加安全，患者更加受益。詹姆斯报道。

精彩解析

1. Our health correspondent James explained why conventional brain surgery is so complicated.

   为什么传统脑部手术如此复杂，本台健康记者詹姆斯详细报道。

   brain surgery 脑外科手术

   例句 The doctor recommended him a brain surgery.

   医生推荐他做脑外科手术。

2. So one of the great challenges when it comes to brain surgery is only operating on what you have to operate on.

   所以说脑部手术的最大挑战之一就是只能切除必须切除的部分。

   operate on 给……做手术

   例句 The doctor began to operate on the boy.

   医生开始给那个男孩动手术。

3. What you have to do is you've taken sample of brain tissue, you have to go away, freeze it, press it down so it's flat…

   做法就是提取脑组织样本，拿去冷冻、压平……

   take sample of 采集……样品

   例句 He took sample of the oil and studied it.

   他采集了一些石油样品并进行研究。

新闻听力加油站

听力速度的培养

听力速度直接关系到听力测试的成败，而且是影响学生测试心理的一个重要因素。测试中因为一道题没跟上而顿时慌乱，接连丢失几题的情况并不罕见。

如何训练听力速度？一种方法是“循序渐进法”，即由慢速到快速，逐步提高。这种方法可使初学者逐渐适应有声信息的接受方式，树立起听的信心。但是，人为地将大脑对语速的适应过程分成几个阶段，由慢到快地几经调整，始终处于消极被动的状态。而且，如果信息传播的速度过于缓慢，反而会拉长记忆的距离，造成遗忘，久而久之，大脑的反应速度也就变得迟钝了。

听力测试的语速是英语本族人讲英语的正常速度。为使大脑尽早适应这种语速，宜从一开始就以这种速度进行训练。初期阶段会出现“坐飞机”的现象，但不必担忧，因为在这种语速的不断“轰击”下，耳朵会逐渐敏锐，从开始只能抓住只言片语到能接受一个完整句子，直至大脑完全适应了这种语速，接下来便是行使其记忆与判断的功能了。

在听力速度训练中，要抓住速度这个主要矛盾，采用语法及词汇比较浅显，但语速属于正常的有声材料。

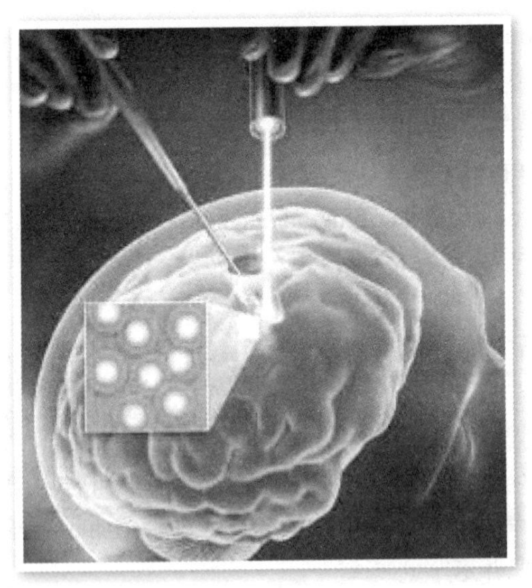

5 美军误将炭疽活菌苗样本外传

American Military Has Mistakenly Sent Samples of Live Anthrax Out (BBC News)

新闻导读

炭疽杆菌属于芽孢杆菌属，是引起某些家畜、野兽和人类炭疽病（人畜共患）的病原菌。发病率最高的是牛羊，猪也可发生，人常因屠宰、食用或与病死畜接触而感染。炭疽杆菌对社会公共卫生和经济发展的危害，迄今仍占相当大的比重。由该菌引起的炭疽病几乎遍及世界各地，四季均可发生。

炭疽杆菌从损伤的皮肤、胃肠粘膜及呼吸道进入人体后，首先在局部繁殖，产生毒素而致组织及脏器发生出血性浸润、坏死和高度水肿，形成原发性皮肤炭疽、肠炭疽、肺炭疽等。当机体抵抗力降低时，致病菌即迅速沿淋巴管及血管向全身扩散，形成败血症和继发性脑膜炎。皮肤炭疽因缺血及毒素的作用，真皮的神经纤维发生变化，故病灶处常无明显的疼痛感。炭疽杆菌的毒素可直接损伤血管的内皮细胞，使血管壁的通透性增加，导致有效血容量减少，微循环灌注量下降，血液呈高凝状态，出现DIC和感染性休克。

新闻热词

official [ə'fɪʃl] n. 官员

military ['mɪlətri] n. 军队，军人

anthrax ['ænθræks] n. 炭疽，炭疽热

lethal ['liːθl] adj. 致命的，可致死的

ingest [ɪn'dʒest] v. 摄取，吸收

warfare ['wɔːfeə(r)] n. 战争，战争状态

batch [bætʃ] n.（食物、药物等的）一批生产的量

bacteria [bæk'tɪəriə] n. 细菌

cordon ['kɔːdn] v. 封锁，用警戒线围住

symptom ['sɪmptəm] n. 症状；征兆

新闻播报

Defence **officials** in the United States say that the **military** has mistakenly sent samples of live **anthrax** to research laboratories in America as well as the one in South Korea. Steve Evans has this story.

参考译文

美国国防官员称军方错误地将炭疽活菌苗样本发给美国和韩国的研究实验室，史蒂夫·伊万斯报道。

Anthrax is **lethal** when inhaled or **ingested**. It's a primary potential weapons in germ **warfare**. According to the Pentagon, a military laboratory in Utah sent **batches** to nine other labs in the U.S. and one in South Korea, under the false impression the **bacteria** were harmless and only for training. When the dangerous truth was realised, labs and bases were **cordoned** off. The military in Korea said twenty-two at the Osan Air Base may have been exposed to the anthrax, but none had shown **symptoms** of illness. World news from the BBC.

参考译文

炭疽活菌被吸入或摄入都会致命，是细菌战中主要的潜在武器。五角大楼称犹他州一个军事实验室将样本发给美国的9个实验

室和韩国的一个实验室，因为他们错误地认为这种细菌是无害的，且只用于培养。当他们意识到危险的真相后，就封锁了实验室和基地。韩国军方称乌山空军基地有22人可能已经接触过炭疽活菌，但没有人表现出疾病症状。BBC世界新闻。

精彩解析

1. When the dangerous truth was realized, labs and bases were cordoned off.

当他们意识到危险的真相后，就封锁了实验室和基地。

cordon off 用警戒线隔离

例句 Police cordoned off part of the city centre.

警察封锁了市中心的部分地区。

2. The military in Korea said twenty-two at the Osan Air Base may have been exposed to the anthrax.

韩国军方称乌山空军基地有22人可能已经接触过炭疽活菌。

be exposed to 遭受，暴露于……

例句 You'd be exposed to less pollution if you moved to a town with pure water and air.

如果你搬到一个具有纯净水和纯净的空气的城镇去，你会接触到更少的污染。

新闻听力加油站

应试英语听力三步骤

1. 听前（pre-listening）

听力考试前必须稳定情绪，做好听音的准备工作。在放音之前，抓紧时间速读书面选择项，对可能涉及的内容作出粗略的猜测和推断，同时也需进行联想，即可能会出现的内容与自己具有的相关知识联系起来，思想介入到要听的内容中去。如若选择项中出现不同的人名、地名、数字、时间或年代以及不同的动词时，必须做好强记的准备。

2. 听时（while-listening）

听音时思想要集中，但情绪不可过度紧张。在听音中要利用预测时得到的潜在信息把握听音的重点，也可利用符号、图示等方法迅速记录要点以促进有效记忆。在听音过程中，必须眼耳并用，也就是一边用耳听，一边用眼浏览选择项进行分析和归纳，做到听与浏览相结合、听与思考及记忆相结合。这一过程必须在短暂的时间内完成。

3. 听后（post-listening）

听完录音后要迅速意念和整理所听懂的内容，并根据书面问题选择或检验答案。要严格控制答题时间，正确答案与听力原文之间的统一性是解题的基本方法。考生要善于根据提问的形式，采用不同的解题方法。

读书笔记

6 首个埃博拉孕妇治疗中心成立

The First Ebola Treatment Center Has Been Set Up (BBC News)

新闻导读

埃博拉病毒是引起人类和灵长类动物发生埃博拉出血热的烈性病毒。“埃博拉”是刚果北部的一条河流的名字。1976年，一种不知名的病毒在这里出现，疯狂地虐杀“埃博拉”河沿岸55个村庄的百姓，致使数百生灵涂炭，有的家庭甚至无一幸免，“埃博拉病毒”也因此而得名。埃博拉病毒主要是通过病人的血液、唾液、汗水和分泌物等途径传播。感染潜伏期为2-21天。感染者均是突然出现高烧、头痛、咽喉疼、虚弱和肌肉疼痛。然后是呕吐、腹痛、腹泻。发病后的两星期内，病毒外溢，导致人体内外出血、血液凝固、坏死的血液很快传及全身的各个器官，病人最终出现口腔、鼻腔和肛门出血等症状，患者可在24小时内死亡。

新闻热词

treatment ['triːtmənt] *n.* 治疗，疗法

pregnant ['pregnənt] *adj.* 怀孕的，妊娠的

extremely [ɪk'striːmli] *adv.* 非常，极其

recover [rɪ'kʌvə(r)] *v.* 恢复健康，复原

suffering ['sʌfərɪŋ] *adj.* 受苦的；患病的

immunity [ɪ'mjuːnəti] *n.* 免疫力

foetus ['fiːtəs] *n.* 胎儿

situation [ˌsɪtʃu'eɪʃn] n. 形势，情况
invariably [ɪn'veəriəbli] adv. 总是，始终如一地
facility [fə'sɪləti] n. 设备，设施
suspect [sə'spekt] v. 怀疑
dangerous ['deɪndʒərəs] adj. 危险的
placenta [plə'sentə] n. 胎盘
focus ['fəʊkəs] n. 重点，焦点
survival [sə'vaɪvl] n. 幸存，存活

新闻播报

The BBC has been given special access to the first ever Ebola **treatment** center specializing in care for **pregnant** women. The death rate for pregnant women is **extremely** high. The BBC's global health correspondent Tulip Mazumdar reports from the Sierra Leonean capital Freetown.

When I arrived, I was bleeding for two hours. No one would touch me. I started to feel much better. Now I am **recovered**. But I need to stay and look after my sister's baby.

参考译文

日前，全球首个埃博拉孕妇治疗中心特别准许BBC进行了参观。孕妇的死亡率极高。BBC健康频道记者图丽普·马宗达，萨拉里昂首都弗里敦报道。

我刚到这儿的时候，血流了两个小时，没人敢接近我。后来我好多了，现在康复了，但我得留下来照顾我姐姐的孩子。

Hello, little one. What's her name? She's **suffering**. How's she been? So weak, she can barely cry. She now has a level of **immunity** to the virus. 6 pregnant women have been admitted to this treatment center since it's opened last month.

Unfortunately, pregnant women are very at risk from dying of Ebola and complications related to Ebola. The reasons seem to be related to delivery or the **foetus** dying earlier in the pregnancy. And there seems to be a concentration of the virus in the foetus. And so even when babies have been born alive, they tend not to survive. And it's an awful **situation**. You have a woman who is at high risk of dying herself and her baby that **invariably** dies as well.

参考译文

你好啊，小不点儿。她叫什么名字？她看着很难受。最近情况怎么样？她太虚弱了，连哭的力气都没有。她现在对病毒产生了一定的免疫力。自上个月开放以来，该治疗中心已接纳了6名孕妇。

不幸的是，埃博拉或并发症导致的孕妇死亡率非常高，原因似乎与分娩有关，或与孕早期胎儿死亡有关。病毒似乎集中于胎儿身上，所以即使胎儿平安降生，往往也活不下来。妇女本身面临着死亡，而孩子也会跟着夭折，这种情况很可怕。

On the other side of town, a new MSF treatment center has just opened. Once it's fully up and running, this will be the first ever **facility** to specialize in treating pregnant women who are **suspected** or confirmed to have Ebola and those who are recovering from the virus.

参考译文

城镇的另一边刚刚成立了“无国界医生组织”治疗中心。开始运转后，它将成为首个专门治疗疑似或确诊感染病毒以及康复中的埃博拉孕妇的机构。

And this will be for pregnant women only here. Suspected, the less suspected, the most probably suspected.

Delivering babies is particularly **dangerous** for health workers. Experts say the viral load of Ebola in both the **placenta** and the foetus, as well as the surrounding fluids is extremely high, even if the woman herself has recovered from the virus.

参考译文

这里将只接收孕妇。疑似患者、轻度疑似患者、重度疑似患者。

对医疗工作者来说，接生具有极大的危险性。专家称，胎盘、胎儿及其周围液体所含埃博拉病毒量极大，即使孕妇本人已经摆脱了病毒的干扰。

Our **focus** is to protect our health staff and then to save the woman, to save the mother and if it's possible to save child, even if the woman, the pregnant woman is killed.

There is still very little known about exactly why the death rate for pregnant women is so high. But it's hoped this new treatment center will help give at least some women the best chance of **survival**.

参考译文

我们的工作重心是保护医护人员，救治孕妇，救治这些母亲，在可能的情况下，即使孕妇已经死亡，也要救治孩子。

孕妇死亡率极高的原因仍然不得而知，但希望这个新的治疗中心能给至少部分女性带来最好的存活的希望。

精彩解析

1. But I need to stay and look after my sister's baby.
但我得留下来照顾我姐姐的孩子。

look after 照顾，照料

例句 I love looking after the children.

我喜欢照顾小孩。

2. And there seems to be a concentration of the virus in the foetus.

病毒似乎集中于胎儿身上。

there seems to be 似乎有，看起来有

例句 There seems to be something wrong with my car.

我的车似乎有毛病。

3. …the surrounding fluids is extremely high, even if the woman herself has recovered from the virus.

……周围液体所含埃博拉病毒量极大，即使孕妇本人已经摆脱了病毒的干扰。

even if 即使，纵然

例句 Even if it rains tomorrow, we won't change our plan.

即使明天下雨，我们也决不改变计划。

读书笔记

7 通过查看空气质量指数保护健康

Check the AQI to Have Better Health (CNN News)

新闻导读

空气质量指数（Air Quality Index），简称AQI，是对每天空气清洁或污染的情况进行追踪记录。AQI也是定量描述空气质量状况的无量纲指数，计算的时候要参考6种主要污染物的浓度，他们分别是细颗粒物（PM2.5）、可吸入颗粒物（PM10）、二氧化硫、二氧化氮、臭氧、一氧化碳。空气质量指数为6类污染物分指数中的最大值，根据指数大小，共分六级，0至50为一级优，51至100为二级良，101至150为三级轻度污染，151至200为四级中度污染，201至300为五级重度污染和300以上为六级严重污染。

1997年，PM2.5第一次纳入美国国家标准，也使美国成为世界上第一个将PM2.5加入国标的国家，当时的PM2.5浓度限值为年平均浓度为15 μ g/m^3，24小时浓度限值为65 μ g/m^{3}来了。直到2000年，美国PM2.5的监测网络才逐步建立。在2006年，美国更改了标准，PM2.5的年平均浓度限值依然为15 μ g/m^3，不过24小时的浓度限值改为了35 μ g/m^3。直到2012年，美国公布了最新的标准，调低了PM2.5浓度限值，24小时的浓度在12 μ g/m^{3}时，空气质量才为优。

新闻热词

index ['ɪndeks] n. 指数

unhealthy [ʌn'helθi] adj. 可能致病的；不健康的

relief [rɪ'liːf] n. 减轻，缓解

polluted [pə'luːtɪd] adj. 受污染的

calculate ['kælkjuleɪt] v. 估算；估计；推算

pollutant [pə'luːtənt] n. 污染物

ozone ['əʊzəʊn] n. 臭氧

sensitive ['sensətɪv] adj. 过敏的；易受影响的

asthma ['æsmə] n. 气喘，哮喘

hazardous ['hæzədəs] adj. 有危险的，有危害的

encourage [ɪn'kʌrɪdʒ] v. 鼓励，鼓舞

consequence ['kɒnsɪkwəns] n. 结果，成果

新闻播报

Wednesday's air quality **index** in Atlanta, Georgia, miles away from any of the fires, was **unhealthy**. In Chattanooga, Tennessee, it was 151. What exactly does that mean?

参考译文

佐治亚州亚特兰大市距离火灾发生地只有数英里远，该市周三的空气质量指数为不良。田纳西州查塔努加市的空气质量指数是151。这是什么意思？

The one thing you need to know is that if you were like many who suffer when the air quality is poor, **relief** could be just a click away.

There's something called the Air Quality Index, or the AQI, and it keeps track of how clean or **polluted** the air is on a day to day basis. The Environmental Protection Agency **calculates** the AQI on five major **pollutants** that are regulated by the Clean Air Act. Ground level

ozone and particle pollution are the greatest threat to human health.

参考译文

有一件事你要知道，如果你和其他人一样在空气质量差的时候感觉难受，想要得到缓解只要点击一下即可。

空气质量指数，简称AQI，是对每天空气清洁或污染的情况进行追踪记录。美国环境保护署通过《清洁空气法》控制的5大主要污染物估算空气质量指数。地表臭氧和颗粒污染物是人类健康的最大威胁。

The Air Quality Index runs from zero to 500, with 500 being the most unhealthy.

Anything over 100 could be considered unhealthy for **sensitive** groups. We're talking about people with **asthma** as well as heart conditions.

Everyone will start feeling the effects of poor air quality when the number reaches 150 or above. Anything over 300 is considered **hazardous** air quality.

参考译文

空气质量指数的范围从0到500，上限500表示空气质量最不健康。

空气质量指数超过100对敏感人群不健康。敏感人群指的是患有哮喘和心脏疾病的人。

当空气质量指数达到150及以上时，所有人都会感受到不良空气质量带来的影响。空气质量指数超过300被认为是有害的空气质量。

It's **encouraged** on these high level days to limit your outdoor activities and stay indoors. Exercising outdoors during one of these high level days could result in serious health **consequences**.

So, before you go outside, check the AQI to protect yourself and to have better health.

参考译文

空气质量指数高的日子应限制室外活动，尽量待在室内。在空气质量指数高的日子进行户外锻炼可能导致严重的健康问题。

所以，在外出以前，大家可以先查看空气质量指数，以保护自己并改善健康状况。

精彩解析

1. There's something called the Air Quality Index, or the AQI, and it keeps track of how clean or polluted the air is on a day to day basis.

   空气质量指数，简称AQI，是对每天空气清洁或污染的情况进行追踪记录。

   keep track of 记录；与……保持联系

   例句 As a doctor, Brooks has to keep track of the latest developments in medicine.

   作为一名医生，布鲁克斯必须了解医学的最新发展动态。

   on a day to day basis 在一天一天的基础上

   例句 You can write about how you eat on a day to day basis.

   你可以写关于每天的日常饮食。

2. Ground level ozone and particle pollution are the greatest threat to human health.

   地表臭氧和颗粒污染物是人类健康的最大威胁。

   ground level 地面，地平面

   例句 The remaining block of woodland is cut down to ground level.

   剩下的那片树林被砍得精光。

专为色盲症设计的一副神奇眼镜

A Pair of Wonderful Glasses Designed for Color Blindness (CNN News)

新闻导读

色盲是指缺乏或完全没有辨别色彩的能力。通常说的色盲多是指红绿色盲。面对五色缤纷的世界，人们到底是如何感知它的呢？原来在人的视网膜上有一种感光细胞——锥细胞，它有红、绿、蓝3种感光色素。每一种感光色素主要对一种原色光产生兴奋，而对其余两种原色光产生程度不等的反应。如果某一种色素缺乏，则会产生对此种颜色的感觉障碍，表现为色盲或色弱（辨色力弱）。色盲又分许多不同类型，仅对一种原色缺乏辨别力者，称为单色盲，如红色盲，又称第一色盲，比较多见；绿色盲，称为第二色盲，比第一色盲少些；蓝色盲，即第三色盲，比较少见。如果对两种颜色缺乏辨别力者，称为全色盲，较为罕见。

色盲又分先天性色盲和后天性色盲，先天性色盲为性连锁遗传，男多于女，双眼视功能正常而辨色力异常。患者常主觉辨色无困难，而在检查时发现。后天性多继发于一些眼底疾病，如某些视神经、视网膜疾病，故又称获得性色盲。单眼色觉障碍见于中央性视网膜变性或视神经病，视觉受累明显，色觉相应受累。双眼色觉障碍也可由药物中毒引起。屈光间质浑浊如角膜白瘢和白内障都可引起辨色力低下。

blindness ['blaɪndnəs] n. 失明

deficiency [dɪ'fɪʃnsi] n. 缺点，缺陷

perceive [pə'siːv] v. 察觉，发觉

distinguish [dɪs'tɪŋgwɪʃ] v. 区分，辨别

unhealthy [ʌn'helθi] adj. 不健康的

definitely ['defɪnətli] adv. 明确地，确切地

struggle ['strʌgl] v. 努力，争取

saturation [ˌsætʃə'reɪʃn] n. 饱和状态，饱和度

absorb [əb'sɔːb] v. 吸收

misnomer [mɪs'nəʊmə] n. 使用不当的名字或名称

overlap [ˌəʊvə'læp] v. 重叠；与……部分相同

significantly [sɪg'nɪfəkəntli] adv. 意味深长地

新闻播报

Color **blindness** is also known as color vision **deficiency**. It's usually inherited and it's more common among men than women. People with the condition **perceive** colors differently than those who don't have it. There's no cure for color blindness, but there are some computer applications that help people **distinguish** between different colors and there are lenses available that are sometimes effective if they're used in bright light.

参考译文

色盲症也被称为色视力缺乏。这种病症通常具有遗传性，男性的患病几率比女性更为普遍。相比普通人，色视力缺乏的人对颜色的感知会截然不同。色盲症没有治愈良方，但也有一些计算机应用能够帮助人们区分不同的颜色，而且在明亮的光线下佩戴相应镜片，有时也能起到帮助。

If I make a steak, I'll bring it in thinking it's totally done and it will be really rare. I just can't see that it's red. It's probably **unhealthy**.

So, I'm out with a couple of CNN producers who also happened to be color blind and that these glasses are supposed to help with that.

OK. I think this kind of work.

参考译文

如果我烹制牛排，我就会想它已经完全熟透，而结果还是血淋淋的生肉。我只是看不到它还是红色的。这道牛排可能不健康。

因此，我和CNN新闻的一些制片人也碰巧是色盲，这些眼镜应该有所帮助。

好的。我认为这会有效。

Let me explain color blindness because it doesn't mean that you see the world in black and white. It means that some colors may seem a little duller and others may just blind together. And it's not as rare as you might think. It affects between 8 percent and 12 percent of men, and up to 1 percent of women in the U.S.

I **definitely** see more shades, like that tree that looks kind of yellow looks actually more orange. That one back there? Yes, that one back there. Yes. And this one right there is a little bit darker than that one.

参考译文

让我解释下色盲症，因为它并不代表你看到的只是黑白的世界。它意味着一些颜色可能有点不鲜亮而其他颜色可能会混淆在一起。而且这并不是你想象的那样罕见。它会对美国8%至12%的男性及1%的女性产生影响。

我肯定看到更多的颜色，比如那棵树看起来有点偏黄，看起来更像橙色。后面的那棵树？是的，后面那棵。好的。这个比那个有点暗。

According to their online tests, Jack's eyes absorb too much green light. He's always **struggled** with the difference between blue and purple. Does it look any different to you?

Things look—I think a little more vivid, like I turn the **saturation** up on the TV almost.

Wendy's eyes on the other hand don't **absorb** enough green light. Before, could you see like the difference between the trunks and the trees and the leaves?

No. And now, I can. Now you can see that? Yes. That's amazing.

参考译文

根据他们的在线测试，杰克的眼睛吸收太多的绿色光线。他总是在区分蓝色和紫色上面临困难。对你而言看起来有什么不同吗？

东西看起来——我想更生动，就像我把电视的饱和度打开一样。

而另一方面，温迪的眼睛没有吸收足够的绿色光线。之前，你能看出像树干、树木及树叶之间的差异吗？

不能。但现在我可以了。现在你可以看到了吗？是的。令人震惊。

They're both forms of what's known as red, green color blindness. The thing is, though, it's kind of **misnomer**, seeing too much or too little green changes the way you see other colors. Purple and blue for example can start to blend together. What color are those flowers behind us now?

Those look purple. They're purple? Yes. Now, take them off. What color do they look like?

They look blue.

参考译文

他们都是所谓的红、绿色盲。是这样的，不过，可能有点用词不当，看到太多或者太少绿色会改变你看其他颜色的方式。比如紫色和蓝色会融合在一起。现在我们身后那些花是什么颜色的?

那些花看起来是紫色的。紫色的是吗?是的。现在,把它们取下来。它们看起来是什么颜色?它们看起来是蓝色的。

The glasses work by shielding your eyes from the part of the spectrum where red and green **overlap** the most.

Brundige, this is a blue purple, but it's definitely purple. I think that's a little more purple with them on. I wouldn't say it's a big change.

The world looks **significantly** different to me. Do you like it better? Yes.

Bottom line, they work pretty well for Wendy, not as great for Jack. But I can tell you, from personal experience, I saw the world in a whole new light.

参考译文

这副眼镜通过保护你的眼睛免受红色和绿色部分重叠频谱的影响。

布伦戴奇,这是蓝紫色,但绝对是紫色的。我觉得紫色更多。我不会说这是很大的变化。

世界在我看来明显不同。你更喜欢这样吗?是的。

结论是这副眼镜很适合温迪,但并不适合杰克。但我可以告诉你,从个人经验来说,我看到了一种新颜色的世界。

精彩解析

1. I'm out with a couple of CNN producers who also happened to be color blind...

我和CNN新闻的一些制片人也碰巧是色盲……

happen to 碰巧

例句 Did you happen to see her leave last Wednesday?

上周三你有没有碰巧看见她离开？

2. He's always struggled with the difference between blue and purple.
他总是在区分蓝色和紫色上面临困难。

struggle with 与……斗争

例句 After struggling with myself for some days, I decided to accept his proposal.

经过好几天的思想斗争，我决定接受他的求婚。

读书笔记

9 我们每晚应该睡几小时

How Many Hours of Sleep Should We Get Every Night? (CNN News)

新闻导读

睡眠（sleep），是高等脊椎动物周期出现的一种自发的和可逆的静息状态，表现为机体对外界刺激的反应性降低和意识的暂时中断。正常人脑的活动，和所有高等脊椎动物的脑一样，始终处在觉醒和睡眠两者交替出现的状态。这种交替是生物节律现象之一。睡眠对于大脑健康是极为重要的。未成年人一般需要有8小时以上的睡眠时间，并且必须保证高质量。如果睡眠的时间不足或质量不高，那么对大脑就会产生不良的影响，大脑的疲劳就难以恢复，严重的可能影响大脑的功能。青少年如果睡眠不足或睡眠质量差，就应适当增加睡眠的时间，比如夏天午睡片刻，并且要设法改善睡眠状况等。一个人的一生当中，有三分之一多的时间是在睡眠中度过的。正当的良好睡眠，可调节生理机能，维持神经系统的平衡，是生命中重要的一环。睡眠不良、不足，第二天就会头晕脑胀、全身无力。睡眠与健康、工作和学习的关系甚为密切。

新闻热词

recommend [ˌrekə'mend] v. 推荐，介绍

function ['fʌŋkʃn] v. 起作用，行使职责

performance [pə'fɔːməns] n. 表现，运行情况

productive [prə'dʌktɪv] adj. 富有成效的；有益的

lamp [læmp] n. 灯，台灯

bulb [bʌlb] n. 电灯泡

artificial [ˌɑːtɪ'fɪʃl] adj. 人造的，人工的

predominantly [prɪ'dɒmɪnəntli] adv. 显著地；占优势地

interfere [ˌɪntə'fɪə(r)] v. 干预，干涉

新闻播报

Time for the "Shoutout." Health experts **recommend** that teenagers should get at least how many hours of sleep every night? Wake up! Is it five, six, seven and a half or nine hours? You've got three seconds, go! To **function** their best, experts say teenagers need at least nine hours of sleep every night. That's your answer and that's your "Shoutout."

参考译文

又到了《大喊答题》节目环节。健康专家建议青少年每天至少应该睡几个小时？醒醒！起来答题了！是5小时、6小时、7.5小时还是9小时？你有3秒钟时间，开始！为了使得身体机能维持最佳状态，专家认为青少年每天至少应该睡9小时。你回答对了吗？这就是本期的《大喊答题》。

But you don't. A number of surveys have found that a relatively small percentage of teenagers, between 13and 15 percent, are getting eight and a half to nine hours of sleep every night. Most get less. That's not good for your grades, your athletic **performance**, how you look and feel.

参考译文

但你可没睡那么久。很多调查发现仅有13%~15%小部分的年轻

人每晚睡8.5~9小时。而更多人睡眠时间则没有这么长。这对你在学校的成绩、运动表现、你的样貌和感觉都没好处。

So, what's keeping all of us up at night? Dhani Jones helps us see the light. Since their introduction, electric lights have helped us live, work and play in what used to be the dark.

But is all of this light a good thing? Or is it actually causing us to lose sleep? And to be less **productive**? We'd have to be more productive, we should actually turn off the lights.

Before gas **lamps** and electric lights people used to work according to the sunlight. When the sun was up, people would toil away, but when the sun set, the work day was pretty much done. Answer, the light **bulb**. Before we knew it, lights were hanging from the factory ceilings. And we can work around the clock. You would think this would mean we could get more work done. But new studies have shown that **artificial** light actually disrupts something called the Circadian cycle. Meaning we'd be getting less sleep.

参考译文

那么，是什么让我们晚上不能安眠呢？戴娜·琼斯帮助我们走进答案。自有了电灯的发明以来，它已经帮助人们在以往的黑暗中生活、工作以及娱乐。

但是所有的光都是好的吗？还是实际上它们真地让我们睡不着吗？而且感到效率不佳？我们必须更有效率，因此实际上我们应该关灯。

煤油灯和电灯之前过去的人们是遵循日出而作、日落而息的规律。当太阳初升，人们会辛苦劳作，而太阳落山时，一天的工作宣告完成。答案是灯泡的发明。在我们知道之前，工厂的天花板上挂着灯。这样我们可以日以继夜地工作。你会认为这意味着我们可以完成更多的工作。但新的研究表明，人造光实际上破坏人类的生理节奏周期。这表示着我们的睡眠时间会减少。

So I talked to a sleep doctor to find out why. Here we are with Dr. Bazil from New York Presbyterian Hospital, Columbia University. You know, doc, what's, preventing us from getting enough sleep?

I think phones are the biggest problem that's new. So, your work is right there, your email is right there. People can text you night and day. Another thing is, your phones and computers emit light, **predominantly** blue light and we think that light can also **interfere** with your ability to sleep.

参考译文

所以我询问睡眠医生希望找出原因。接下来我们有请纽约长老会医院哥伦比亚大学的巴希尔博士。博士，你知道是什么阻止我们得到充足的睡眠吗？

我认为手机是最大的问题。所以，工作时你用手机，你用手机发邮件。人们可能日夜给你发信息。另一件事是，你的手机和电脑发出的光线以蓝光为主，而我们认为这样的光线也会干扰你睡眠的能力。

精彩解析

1. Health experts recommend that teenagers should get at least how many hours of sleep every night?
   健康专家建议青少年每天至少应该睡几小时？

   at least 至少

   例句 He works at least 12 hours everyday.

   他每天至少工作12小时。

2. And we can work around the clock.
   这样我们可以日以继夜地工作。

around the clock 昼夜不停地，毫不疲倦地

例句 The workers work in three shifts around the clock.

工人们昼夜不停地分三班轮流干活。

3. You know, doc, what's, preventing us from getting enough sleep?
博士，你知道是什么阻止我们得到充足的睡眠吗？

prevent from 阻止，防止

例句 His prompt action prevented the fire from spreading.

他的果断行动制止了火势的蔓延。

读书笔记

10 能量饮料的好与坏

Energy Drinks Are Good or Bad for Us? (CNN News)

新闻导读

能量饮料是以补充人体所需能量为主要目的一种特殊用途饮料。人喝了能量饮料后，在饮料中的维生素（一般是B类维生素）和糖分（一般是白砂糖）在相互作用下，转化成人体所需的能量，以达到补充体力、缓解疲劳的目的。广义的能量饮料包括高能量饮料、运动能量饮料、功能饮料。

夏天气温高，再加上剧烈的运动，人体会进行排汗，体内水分流失较多。而人体出汗后适合饮用的是含糖量5%以下，并含有钾、钠、钙、镁等无机盐的碱性饮料。一般运动饮料中水分含量在90%左右，糖分含量8%～12%，无机盐含量为1.6%左右，维生素的含量为0.2%左右。这些成分与人体体液相似，饮用后能更迅速地被身体吸收，及时补充人体因大量运动出汗所损失的水分和电解质（即盐分），使体液达到平衡状态。在补充人体机能的同时，还有助于细胞维持有氧氧化，即使在大运动量时也会减少乳酸产生，减轻运动时人体的心脏负担，对运动中的能量供给和运动后的体力恢复都大有好处。

新闻热词

measure ['meʒə(r)] v. 测量

kilojoule ['kɪlədʒuːl] n. 千焦耳

atmospheric [ˌætməs'ferɪk] adj. 大气的，大气层的

buoyancy ['bɔɪənsi] n. 浮力
ingredient [ɪn'griːdiənt] n. 成分，原料
caffeine ['kæfiːn] n. 咖啡因
stimulant ['stɪmjələnt] n. 兴奋剂，刺激物
inaccurate [ɪn'ækjərət] adj. 不正确的，不准确的
industry ['ɪndəstri] n. 工业；产业
metabolism [mə'tæbəlɪzəm] n. 新陈代谢
insomnia [ɪn'sɒmniə] n. 失眠，失眠症
carbohydrate [ˌkɑːbəʊ'haɪdreɪt] n. 碳水化合物，糖类

新闻播报

Time for the "Shoutout." What is **measured** in **kilojoules**. If you think you know it, shout it out. Isn't it water depth, **atmospheric** pressure, food energy, or buoyancy. You got three seconds. Go! The energy we get from what we eat and drink is measured in kilojoules. That's your answer and that's your shoutout.

参考译文

又到了《大喊答题》节目环节。什么是以千焦耳为单位进行测量的。如果你知道答案，那就大声说出来。是水深、气压、食物能量还是浮力。你有三秒钟考虑时间，开始！我们所食用的食物和摄入的水分是通过千焦耳测算的。你回答对了吗？这就是本期的《大喊答题》。

Energy drinks can have high levels of kilojoules, and some doctors are warning people to put them down. A study in the "Journal of Pediatrics" found their most common **ingredients** include **caffeine**, a **stimulant**, guarana, a stimulant, ginseng, a root that's believed to be stimulating, and lots of sugar. Often, the amounts of caffeine that energy drinks say they have are **inaccurate** and they're not regulated by the Food and Drug Administration. So, how can you get a natural boost.

参考译文

能量饮料的千焦耳含量很高，许多医生警告称要减少能量饮料的摄入量。一篇刊登在“儿科杂志”上的研究发现这种饮料中通常会含有咖啡因，一种兴奋剂，瓜拉那，一种兴奋剂，人参，一种被认为具有兴奋剂作用的根茎以及大量的糖分。通常，能量饮料中说的咖啡因含量是不准确的，并且没有经过食品和药物管理局的监管。那么，我们如何通过自然方法来增加能量。

This may surprise you, but the energy drink **industry** is now a $10 billion a year industry. Think about that, we didn't even have energy drinks just a couple of decades ago. When you think about energy drinks, you're thinking about lots of different things.

参考译文

这或许会让你很吃惊，但是如今的能量饮料市场已经成为了100亿美金的市场。想想吧，几十年前，我们还没有这东西。当你提到能量饮料时，你会想到许多其他的事物。

Obviously, a lot of caffeine, but also stimulants, things that are designed to actually stimulate the body's **metabolism**, would stimulate the body overall. They can lead to all sorts of different things. They can lead to increased heart rate, increased blood pressure, restlessness, anxiety, **insomnia**. There are ways to get really good energy and have that energy last a long time. Think about a couple of things like lean protein and smart **carbohydrates**, almonds, cheese, Greek yogurt. Both those things can make you more productive and could help you live to 100.

参考译文

很显然，大量咖啡因，还有许多能够加快身体新陈代谢的兴奋剂，让全身都兴奋起来。这些物质能够引起各种不良隐患。增加心率、血压上升、焦躁不安、失眠。能量饮料能够增加能量，并且维持很长一段时间。想想这些东西，瘦蛋白、碳水化合物、扁桃仁、奶酪、希腊酸奶。这些都可以让人们精力充沛，让你增加100%的能量。

精彩解析

1. Think about that, we didn't even have energy drinks just a couple of decades ago.

想想吧，几十年前，我们还没有这东西。

a couple of 两个，几个

例句 A couple of days ago, my sister just came by.

前几天，我姐姐刚过来。

2. They can lead to all sorts of different things.

它们能够引起各种不良隐患。

lead to 导致，引起

例句 Eating too much sugar can lead to health problem.

食用过多的糖会引起健康问题。

新闻听力加油站

提高听、说能力

1. 注意区分和模仿正确的语音、语调

在英语里有不少读音相近，但意思却截然不同的词汇，象cure和kill，menu和manure等。设想如果有一个医生想说："I' ll cure you.”（我要治好你的病。）却因发音不好，说成：“I’ll kill you.”（我要杀死你。）那病人会吓成什么样子。因此，我们从一开始就要注意区分和模仿正确的语音、语调。在这个基础上提高听、说，才能收到良好效果。

2. 创造一定的听、说环境

听、说是一种语言交流，没有一个外语环境或一定的听、说条件，只靠单枪匹马很难收效。当然，现代科学为我们提供了录音机这一工具，我们可以把课文，对话和中外成品磁带录制下来反复听和模仿。还可以把自己的口头作文和复述录下来，仔细审听，发现问题。及时纠正。但是，在自然条件下，听与说是不能分的。一个人听的过程实际是另一个人说的过程。

3. 要有不怕听错、说错，不断苦练的精神

练习听、说的学习者，特别是成年人，往往必听错、说错，不敢主支张口练习。然而，语言是一种习惯，没有反复的操练和实践难以产生熟练的技巧。会话重在达意，只要达到交流思想的目的，这种听、说实践就应该说是基本成功的。出了错，注意总结经验，自学改正就是了。

读书笔记

读书笔记

体育娱乐

国际足联主席布拉特被停职

FIFA President Sepp Blatter Was Suspended (VOA News)

新闻导读

国际足球联合会，简称国际足联（FIFA），由比利时、法国、丹麦、西班牙、瑞典、荷兰和瑞士倡议，并于1904年5月21日在法国巴黎成立。协会现有会员209个，是国际单项体育联合会总会成员。工作用语为英、法、西班牙和德语，如有语言冲突时，以英语为准。国际足联下设欧洲、亚洲、非洲、中北美和加勒比地区、南美洲、大洋洲六个地区性组织，其总部于1932年由法国巴黎移至瑞士苏黎世。

2011年5月10日，据国际足联官方消息，FIFA已与国际刑警组织达成一致，余下8年每年出资不少于150万欧元。FIFA官网以“国际足联与国际刑警组织联手打击假球”为题称：“全球致力于打击足坛腐败，今天将成为具有划时代意义的一天。国际足联将成为史上国际刑警组织赞助最多的民间组织，在未来10年中将成立足坛反腐化基金，以此教育和规范全世界球员、裁判员以及足协官员。2015年6月2日晚，国际足联召开发布会，在新闻发布会上，第四次连任的国际足联主席布拉特宣布将辞去主席职务。不过，直到执委会选出新的FIFA主席，布拉特仍将继续执行主席职务。2015年9月25日，瑞士总检察长办公室表示，对国际足联（FIFA）主席布拉特启动刑事诉讼程序。2015年10月7日，国际足联道德委员会召开会议决定，对主席布拉特实施临时停职90天。

新闻热词

suspend [sə'spend] v. 使暂时停职

ethics ['eθɪks] n. 道德规范，伦理标准

attorney [ə'tɜːni] n. 律师

investigation [ɪnˌvestɪ'geɪʃn] n. 调查

capacity [kə'pæsəti] n. 身份，职责，职位

evidence ['evɪdəns] n. 证据

misconduct [ˌmɪs'kɒndʌkt] n. 渎职，不当行为

ban [bæn] v. 禁止，取缔

arrest [ə'rest] v. 逮捕，拘捕

新闻播报

FIFA president Sepp Blatter was **suspended** Thursday for 90 days by an **ethics** committee.

The suspension comes less than two weeks after Swiss **attorneys** opened a criminal **investigation** against Blatter. He is charged with possible involvement in a $2 million payment in 2011 to Michel Platini, the head of the Union of European Football Association.

参考译文

周四，国际足联主席塞普·布拉特被道德委员会停职90天。

国际足联做出停职决定不到两周之前，瑞士律师对布拉特展开了刑事调查。他被控可能于2011年向欧洲足联主席米歇尔·普拉蒂尼行贿200万美元。

FIFA said Blatter is not permitted to represent the organization in any **capacity**.

But Mr. Blatter's lawyers say the FIFA committee failed to follow its own rules by not letting him give **evidence**. They also say the suspension was based on a "misunderstanding" of the case presented by the Swiss.

参考译文

国际足联表示，布拉特不允许在任何范围内代表国际足联。

但是布拉特的律师团表示，国际足联道德委员会并未遵循自己的规定，没让布拉特递交证据。他们还表示，这次停职是因为瑞士递交的案件造成的误解。

Issa Hayatou will serve as acting FIFA president. He served as the head of the Confederation of African Football for many years. He was once punished for **misconduct** by the International Olympic Committee.

The ethics committee also gave a 90-day suspension to FIFA Secretary-General Jerome Valcke. In addition, the committee **banned** former vice president Chung Mong-joon for six years and imposed a $100,000 fine.

参考译文

伊萨·哈亚图将担任国际足联代理主席。他多年来一直担任非洲足球协会主席。他曾因渎职被国际奥委会惩罚。

道德委员会还宣布国际足联秘书长杰罗姆·瓦尔克停职90天。此外，道德委员会还宣布禁止郑梦准参赛六年时间，并处以10万美元的罚款。

In May, 14 FIFA officials were **arrested** in Zurich, Switzerland. They were charged in the United States with nearly 50 counts of corruption. Swiss officials have opened a separate criminal investigation involving the selection of Russia and Qatar as hosts for the 2018 and 2022 World Cup tournaments. I'm Jonathan Evans.

参考译文

5月，国际足联14位官员在瑞士的苏黎世被捕。他们在美国被控以近50款贪腐罪。瑞士官员展开了特别刑事调查，包括选择俄罗斯和卡塔尔作为2018年和2022年世界杯举办国问题。

精彩解析

1. He is charged with possible involvement in a $2 million payment in 2011 to Michel Platini, the head of the Union of European Football Association.

   他被控可能于2011年向欧洲足联主席米歇尔·普拉蒂尼行贿200万美元。

   be charged with 被指控

   例句 He was charged with murder but found innocent later.

   他被控杀人，但后来发现他是无罪的。

2. Issa Hayatou will serve as acting FIFA president.

   伊萨·哈亚图将担任国际足联代理主席。

   serve as 充当，担任

   例句 In the past two years, he served as an assistant for her.

   过去两年的时间里，他担任她的助理一职。

新闻听力加油站

注意单词的发音现象

识别音素很重要。语言信息的表达是通过元音和辅音字母有规律的组合来实现的。如元音字母“a”在不同的组合中有多种发音：bake /eɪ/，bad /æ/，bald /ɔː/，radar /ɑː/，data /ə/。而一个辅音音素可以有多种辅音字母的组合，如/f/：leaf，laugh，philosophy等。

如果说阅读是凭借字母的组合形式去判断词义的话，那么听力则主要依声音去确定词的意思。因此，元音的长、短，辅音的清浊，都对判断有直接影响。

此外，了解连读的一些基本规律，有利于听力测试中抓“准”词句，准确理解。

助动词缩略式连读在听力中最普遍，熟悉这种连读对于正确判断试题的语气和时态十分有用。

相邻音连续，即当前面一个单词的结尾为辅音字母，而紧跟其后的单词又是以元音字母开头时，这两个音连读。

并列连词“or”与其前后的单词连读时，听起来好似/r/。

音的合成连读，即当两个相邻的字母发音相同时，两个音素合并成一个音素。有时，当一个句子中有多处合成连读时，乍一听，似乎有些音素被“吞掉”了。

读书笔记

美国加入庆祝诺鲁孜节

Americans Join in Nowruz Celebration 2017 (VOA News)

新闻导读

诺鲁孜节通常于3月21日庆祝。“诺鲁孜”的意思是“新的一天”，标志着春天的第一天。它是柯尔克孜族、哈萨克族、维吾尔族、塔吉克族、塔塔尔族、乌孜别克族等民族的传统节日。

2010年在阿塞拜疆的倡议下，联合国大会在其第A/RES/64/253号决议中宣布，阿尔巴尼亚、阿富汗、阿塞拜疆、哈萨克斯坦、吉尔吉斯斯坦、前南斯拉夫的马其顿共和国、塔吉克斯坦、土耳其、土库曼斯坦、伊朗伊斯兰共和国、印度共同庆祝诺鲁孜节。

联合国教育、科学及文化组织于2009年将诺鲁孜节列入《人类非物质文化遗产代表名录》，诺鲁孜节是传承下来的庆祝活动，将其视为新的一年的开始。诺鲁孜节，作为文化遗产和悠久传统和睦的象征，对加强各国人民建立在相互尊重、和平及睦邻友好理想基础上的关系发挥着重要作用。

新闻热词

festival ['festɪvl] n. 节日；节庆

celebrate ['selɪbreɪt] v. 庆祝；祝贺

background ['bækgraʊnd] n. 背景

greeting ['griːtɪŋ] n. 祝词，贺词

beginning [bɪ'gɪnɪŋ] n. 开始；开端

community [kə'mjuːnəti] *n.* 社区

generation [ˌdʒenə'reɪʃn] *n.* 代，一代

ancestor ['ænsestə(r)] *n.* 祖先，祖宗

optimism ['ɒptɪmɪzəm] *n.* 乐观；乐观主义

prosperity [prɒ'sperəti] *n.* 繁荣；富足

新闻播报

It's the start of spring, and the ancient **festival** of Nowruz is currently being **celebrated** by peoples from various countries and **backgrounds** around the globe.

U.S. Secretary of State Rex Tillerson sent **greetings** on this holiday, which means "New Day," and also marks the **beginning** of a new year.

参考译文

春季伊始，来自全球不同国家和背景的人都在庆祝由来已久的诺鲁孜节（Nowruz）。

美国国务卿蒂勒森也发出了节日的问候，寓意"新的一天"，同时也标志着新年的开始。

"Millions of people across the world, including **communities** in Afghanistan, Azerbaijan, China, Georgia, India, Iran, Iraq, Kazakhstan, Kyrgyzstan, Pakistan, Russia, Syria, Tajikistan, Turkey, Turkmenistan, Uzbekistan and many other peoples of south and Central Asia and the Persian Gulf celebrate this time of the year with their families and friends," Mr. Tillerson said in a written statement. "Today, many Americans will join in this celebration, sharing with a new **generation** the cherished traditions of their **ancestors**."

参考译文

“来自全球各地的上千万人，包括各地的社群，如阿富汗、阿塞拜疆、中国、佐治亚、格鲁吉亚、印度、伊朗、伊拉克、哈萨克斯坦、吉尔吉斯斯坦、巴基斯坦、俄罗斯、叙利亚、塔吉克斯坦、土耳其、土库曼斯坦、乌兹别克斯坦以及来自南亚、中亚、波斯湾的民众纷纷与家人朋友共庆这一年一度的节日，”蒂勒森在书面声明中写道。“今天，很多美国人都一起庆祝这个节日，与新一代人分享祖先留下的宝贵传统。”

Secretary of State Tillerson said, “Nowruz is a time to look toward the coming year with hope and **optimism**. We look forward to celebrating this new spring together, and hope that this Nowruz brings peace and **prosperity** to all.

参考译文

蒂勒森还说，“诺鲁孜节这一天，我们可以带着希望和乐观的心态去期待明年。我们希望能够一起迎来新的春天，也希望诺鲁孜节能带给所有人和平和繁荣。”

精彩解析

1. U.S. Secretary of State Rex Tillerson sent greetings on this holiday, which means “New Day,” and also marks the beginning of a new year.
美国国务卿蒂勒森也发出了节日的问候，寓意“新的一天”，同时也标志着新年的开始。

the beginning of ……的开始

例句 We’ll talk at the beginning of the next week.

下周初我们再谈吧。

2. We look forward to celebrating this new spring together…

我们希望能够一起迎来新的春天……

look forward to 希望，期望

例句 We look forward to your comments on the above-mentioned proposal.

我们希望听取贵方的意见。

新闻听力加油站

注意起连接作用的词

在组成一篇语言流畅、气势连贯的文章时，起连接作用的词可谓功不可没。这些词有的告诉我们“以下几个问题是并列阐述的”，有的告诉我们“文章意思该转折了”，有的说“下面该举几个例子了”，有的则说“以下的事情是提前发生的”…… 如果我们抓住这些小词，带着准备去听，听力就会更有成效。

1. 表示并列、递进关系的词有：and, also, moreover, in addition, besides, what is more等。

2. 表示转折关系的词有：but, however, otherwise, nevertheless, on the contrast, although, even though, in spite of, despite等。

3. 表示因果关系的词有：because, since, as, now that, for, therefore, so, due to, as a result, result in, cause, lead to, consequently, hence等。

4. 表示时间关系的词有：before, are, ago, earlier, previously, meanwhile, at the same time, next, then, finally等。

5. 表示举例，可以用：for example, such as, for instance, as follows 等。

6. 表示条件关系，可以用：if, incase, so long as, in the event that, supposing that等。

注意这些小词，及时把握作者思路，就会更加容易理解文章。

特奥会为运动员提供展现自己的舞台

Special Olympics Provide a Platform for the Athletes (VOA News)

新闻导读

世界特殊奥林匹克运动会（Special Olympics），简称特奥会，是专门为智能低下、言语不清的神经和精神障碍患者甚至是生活不能自理的儿童举办的国际性运动竞赛活动。特奥运动项目非常丰富，从最基本的机能活动到最高级的竞赛，适合所有年龄和能力等级的特奥运动员。特殊奥林匹克运动会（简称特殊奥运会或特奥会）包括本地、国家、洲际和世界等不同级别。其中，世界特殊奥运会每两年举办一届，夏季和冬季交替举行。国际特奥会共举办过13届夏季特殊奥运会、10届冬季特殊奥运会。

通过参加特奥运动，智障人可以增强身体机能、动作技能、自尊、自信、培养友谊以及得到家庭成员的支持。特奥运动员将这些益处带入他们的日常生活、工作、学习和社区活动中。家庭成员可以变得更加亲密，社区志愿者可以和运动员成为好朋友，每个人都可以看到智障人的价值。

新闻热词

athlete ['æθliːt] n. 运动员

medal ['medl] n. 奖章，奖牌

division [dɪ'vɪʒn] n. 分组，级别

practice ['præktɪs] n. 练习；训练

program ['prəʊgræm] n. 项目

dividend ['dɪvɪdend] n. 回报，红利

globally ['gləʊbəli] adv. 在全球范围内

motivate ['məʊtɪveɪt] v. 激发，激励

pride [praɪd] n. 自豪，骄傲

aquatic [ə'kwætɪk] adj. 水上的，水中的

新闻播报

From table tennis to handball. Special Olympics **athletes** have given it their best, and some will take home **medals**. Irish athlete Carole Catling earned a gold for table tennis, and Olowoyuni Sunday won a gold in his **division**. His coach, Olawuyi Amoo, says it took **practice**.

参考译文

从乒乓球到手球。特奥会运动员们在赛场上竭尽自己所能，有些人会将奖牌带回家。爱尔兰运动员卡罗尔·卡特琳夺得了乒乓球的金牌，而奥罗云尼·苏尼达在个人项目中赢得金牌。他的教练奥拉乌尼·阿莫表示这枚金牌代表着他不懈努力的结果。

"We come from Nigeria. And you know, before we came for this **program**, we made a provision where these athletes came for five weeks to train them toward these world games. And I think this is the **dividend** of the training."

"我们来自尼日利亚。你知道，在我们参加比赛之前，我们做出规定，这些运动员会为了这次赛事进行为期5周的训练。而且我认为这是艰苦训练的成果。"

A 27-year-old Panamanian bowler, Casandra Barletta, is here with her family. Her brother says she has the skill and focus to excel in her sport.

"Thankfully, she's very good at it. She has competed in a lot of competitions around the world, and also in Panama, national and **globally**, and she has done very well."

参考译文

27岁的巴拿马投球手卡桑德拉·巴勒塔正和她的家人在一起。她哥哥说她拥有赢得比赛的技能和专注力。

"幸运的是，她很擅长。她已经参加了世界各地的比赛，而且巴拿马也同样如此，无论是自己国家还是全世界范围，她已经做得很好。"

But it's not all about winning. Canadian bocce coach Dona Cade says what **motivates** these athletes with intellectual disabilities is the thrill of competition and sense of **pride**.

"They've worked hard the whole year to get here, getting themselves as fit as they can. And it just means everything to be representing your country."

More than 6,000 athletes from 165 countries have participated in sports from **aquatics** to power lifting, and this week of competition has let them show the world what they can do.

Mike O'Sullivan, VOA NEWS, LOS ANGELES.

参考译文

但这项赛事并不只是为了赢得胜利。加拿大室外滚球教练多纳·凯德表示问题运动员的参与赛事的动力是竞争的刺激和自豪感。

"他们为了来到这个赛场已经努力了整整一年，让自己尽可能适应。参加比赛代表着你是为了自己的国家。"

来自165个国家的6 000多名运动员参加从游泳到举重的比赛，而本周的赛事提供给他们向世界展示自己的机会。

迈克·奥沙利文，VOA新闻，洛杉矶。

精彩解析

1. Her brother says she has the skill and focus to excel in her sport.
她哥哥说她拥有赢得比赛的技能和专注力。

excel in 在……出众

例句 They each excel in their respective fields.

他们在各自领域里都是出类拔萃的。

2. More than 6,000 athletes from 165 countries have participated in sports from aquatics to power lifting...
来自165个国家的6 000多名运动员参加从游泳到举重的比赛……

participate in 参加

例句 In the ancient Greek Olympics, only men were allowed to participate in it.

在古希腊奥运会中，只允许男人参加比赛。

读书笔记

伊拉克少儿在音乐中获得慰藉

Iraqi Kids Find Refuge in Music (VOA News)

新闻导读

伊拉克地处美索不达米亚，是世界古文明的发祥地之一。伊拉克的主要乐器有弦乐器乌德、交扎、卡龙、拉巴布、桑图尔和坦布尔等；管乐器有纳伊、米兹玛尔、祖尔纳和米特巴季等；打击乐器有达夫和代尔布卡鼓等。民间器乐形式主要是合奏和为声乐伴奏。古典音乐的器乐形式需遵从固有的传统和演奏规则；独奏带有即兴性。随着伊拉克社会经济的发展，传统音乐发生了较大变化。西方音乐在伊拉克的流传越来越广，许多人到欧美学习音乐，并运用西方音乐的创作技巧来创作本民族的音乐。同时，在伊拉克还成立了国家交响乐团。

新闻热词

dominate ['dɒmɪneɪt] v. 支配，影响

surround [sə'raʊnd] v. 包围，围绕

motto ['mɒtəʊ] n. 座右铭；格言

extremism [ɪk'striːmɪzəm] n. 极端主义

behavior [bɪ'heɪvjə] n. 行为，举止；态度

stimulus ['stɪmjələs] n. 刺激物；刺激因素

tension ['tenʃn] n. 紧张关系；紧张局势

exclusion [ɪk'skluːʒn] n. 排斥；拒绝

envision [ɪn'vɪʒn] v. 设想；想象；预想

enrollment [ɪn'rəʊlmənt] n. 登记；注册

instructor [ɪn'strʌktə(r)] n. 指导者，教师

approach [ə'prəʊtʃ] n. 方法；手段

新闻播报

All too often, in Iraq and many other places in the world, this can **dominate** the sounds gabbed you. But here, children are **surrounded** by a different sound.

"The Children's Orchestra"—the brainchild of Adnan Sahi, head of the music department at the University of Basra's Faculty of Arts. The **motto** of this project is "Culture fights backwardness and **extremism**."

参考译文

伊拉克和世界上许多其他地方的孩子们生活中经常环绕的声音是这样的。而这里的孩子听到的却是不一样的声音。

"少儿乐团"的点子是阿德南想出来的。阿德南是伊拉克巴士拉大学艺术学院音乐系主任。而这个项目的宗旨是"用文化抗击落后和极端"。

"Human **behavior** in general, and children's, is a response to a **stimulus**—a reflection of their environment. What we're trying do is keep the Iraqi child from the negative environmental effects caused by the surrounding violent **tensions**. We try to keep our children away from the language of violence, the language of **exclusion**."

参考译文

"总体上来说，人的行为，包括孩子们的行为，都是对外界刺

激的一种回应——是对周遭环境的反应。而我们想要做的就是让伊拉克孩子远离由周围暴力因素引起的负面环境影响。我们力图让孩子们远离暴力的语言和排斥的语言”。

This is his work of art. He **envisions** the “Children’s Orchestra” as a safe haven for these children. Kids as young as five can join the program to learn a set of skills they would never pick up, if they were left to play in the streets.

Enrollment in this music school is free, but students have to buy their own instruments.

For all of these kids, playing instruments is a unique experience.

参考译文

而这就是他的作品。他构想出了“少儿乐团”作为孩子们的安全保护地。五岁及以上无家可归的孩子都可以加入这个项目，学习一些从未习得的技能。

而加入这所音乐殿堂是免费的，但学生们需要自费买乐器。

对于少儿乐团的所有孩子们来说，演奏乐器是一种独特的体验。

I haven’t seen a piano before, only on TV, but now we are playing with one in addition to the guitar and violin, so it’s way better than playing with toy guns and that sort of stuff.

Instructors volunteer to work with kids because they believe music can shield children from the violence around them and provide them with a fun and positive summer experience before going back to school.

参考译文

除了在电视上看到之外，我以前从未见过钢琴。而现在，除了钢琴之外，我们还可以接触到吉他和小提琴。所以这体验简直比玩儿玩具枪之类的东西好太多了。

孩子们的指导老师们都是自愿来到这里的，因为他们相信音乐能够庇护孩子们，让他们远离暴力，并能让他们在重返学校之前拥有积极有趣的暑假经历。

Basra's "Children's Orchestra" is not the first attempt to help kids heal and thrive through arts. Other projects included an art program in an Iraqi orphanage in Bagdad, and a ballet school in Arbeel.

Different **approaches** to the same end; using art to change Iraqi children's lives, so they can change their world.

参考译文

巴士拉大学的"少儿乐团"并非第一家通过艺术来治愈并培养孩子们之作。还有巴格达伊拉克孤儿院的艺术项目和Arbeel的芭蕾学校。

这些尝试殊途同归，都希冀用艺术来改变伊拉克孩子们的生活，并通过这些孩子改变世界。

精彩解析

1. We try to keep our children away from the language of violence, the language of exclusion.

我们力图让孩子们远离暴力的语言和排斥的语言。

keep away from 不接近；避开

例句 Keep the children away from the machine.

别让孩子们接近机器。

2. He envisions the "Children's Orchestra" as a safe haven for these children.

他构想出了"少儿乐团"作为孩子们的安全保护地。

safe haven 避难所；庇护所

例句 Are emerging markets a safe haven in the current crisis?

新兴市场是逃避当前危机的避难所吗？

新闻听力加油站

影响听力的因素

1. 发音不准，造成理解障碍

如果长期读不准单词的发音，听音也肯定不会准确。另有部分学生习惯了听字字清晰的英语，当说话者以正常语速和语调讲话时，他们的理解也会大打折扣。

2. 知识面过窄

由于头脑中存储的知识面窄，从而影响了听力。这些知识包括：词汇量、语法、句法、社会文化知识、科普知识等，在听的过程中，如不能把原来存储于大脑的语音、语法与所听到的信息进行比较和利用，对声音就不能做出积极反应。

3. 母语影响了听力的反应速度

许多学生听到一段语言信息后，习惯用中文逐句翻译出来，而不是直接将语言转化成一个情景，因而影响了听力理解程度。

针对以上问题，我们在练习听力的同时，应做到：1. 纠正发音，培养正确的辨认和运用英语语音、语调、重音、连读等能力。对一些容易发错的音素进行辨析，突破语音关，同时注意培养朗读习惯。2. 听写，听写是听力训练的重要形式，它贯穿于听力训练的全过程，常运用的听写内容是课文的句子和概括课文大意的短文。

总之，听更能突出英语交际功能，只有听好，才能把握英语真正的活力和生命力。

5 科幻电影为新晋科学家助力

Martian Science Fiction Film Hopes to Inspire New Scientists (VOA News)

新闻导读

科幻电影是以建立在科学上的幻想性情景或假设为背景，在此基础上展开叙事的电影。科幻电影所采用的科学理论并不一定被主流科学界接受，例如外星生命、外星球、超能力或时间旅行等等。科幻电影常常使用可能的未来世界作为故事背景，用宇宙飞船、机器人或其他超越时代的科技等元素彰显与现实之间的差异。许多科幻电影会表现出对于政治或社会议题的关注，以及哲学方面如人类处境的探讨。一些科幻电影是从科幻文学作品改编而成，但科幻电影会注重撷取其中的文学或人文方面的元素，而无视科幻文学比较注重的科学严谨性和逻辑性。科幻电影是电影类型的一种，其特色的情节包含了科学奇想。乔治里叶的《月球之旅》是电影史上最早的一部科幻片。

新闻热词

astronaut ['æstrənɔːt] n. 宇航员

planet ['plænɪt] n. 行星，星球

botanist ['bɒtənɪst] n. 植物学家

aspiring [ə'spaɪərɪŋ] adj. 有抱负的，有志向的

commander [kə'mɑːndə(r)] n. 指挥官，司令官

enthusiast [ɪn'θjuːziæst] n. 热心者，爱好者

educational [ˌedʒuˈkeɪʃənl] adj. 教育的，与教育相关的
positive [ˈpɒzətɪv] adj. 积极的，肯定的
engineering [ˌendʒɪˈnɪərɪŋ] n. 工程，工程学
accomplish [əˈkʌmplɪʃ] v. 完成，达到
obstacle [ˈɒbstəkl] n. 障碍，障碍物
filmmaker [ˈfɪlmˌmeɪkə] n. 电影制作人
headquarters [ˌhedˈkwɔːtəz] n. 总部，总公司
diversity [daɪˈvɜːsəti] n. 多样化，多元性

新闻播报

In *The Martian*, Mark Watney is a U.S. **astronaut** who has to survive alone on Mars after his crew leaves the **planet** without him, thinking he died in a storm that swept him away.

The **botanist** played by Matt Damon is not a typical Hollywood hero, but he is one of several role models in the film for **aspiring** scientists. Another is Mars mission **commander** Melissa Lewis, played by Jessica Chastain.

参考译文

在《火星救援》中，马克·沃特尼是一位美国宇航员。他必须要在火星上独自设法生存下来。他的同伴们以为他在一场风暴中死去，便抛下他离开了这个星球。

这位由马特·戴蒙饰演的植物学家并不是典型的好莱坞英雄，但他为那些立志成为科学家的年轻人树立了一个榜样。另一个榜样是由杰西卡·查斯顿饰演的火星任务指挥官梅莉莎·刘易斯。

It's a performance that excites Costa Rican space **enthusiast** and student Montserrat Cordero, who appeared on HashtagVOA via

Skype.

Jessica Chastain's character is amazing. We also have the computer programmer who is also a woman. This is not what we tend to see. So I'm really excited to see this kind of thing, hope to see a lot more of it.

参考译文

她的表演让哥斯达黎加的太空爱好者、学生蒙特塞拉特·科德罗兴奋不已，她通过Skype参加了美国之音的节目。

杰西卡·查斯顿扮演的角色棒极了。电影里还有一名女性电脑程序员。这是我们不常在电影里看到的，所以当我看到她们的时候特别激动，希望能有更多这样的角色。

Cordero is also a graduate of an international summer school run by the Foundation for International Space Education in Houston, Texas.

It's director of **educational** programs told HashtagVOA via Skype that *The Martian*'s role models will have a **positive** influence.

参考译文

科德罗毕业于位于德克萨斯州休斯敦的国际太空教育基金会的一个国际暑期学校。

这个基金会教育项目的主管通过Skype告诉美国之音，电影里的这些角色会带来积极影响。

The more women we have involved in science, technology, **engineering** and math, the better a society we have, and the better we'll be able to **accomplish** those missions and do things like go to Mars.

In the film, NASA, the U.S. government space agency, tries to overcome great **obstacles** to bring Watney back to Earth.

参考译文

在科学、技术、工程和数学领域有越多的女性参与，这个社会就会变得越好，我们也就能更好地完成这些使命，完成登录火星任务等等。

在电影中，美国太空署设法克服各种阻碍让沃特尼返回地球。

That's not just science fiction. The science and technology seen in the movie is based on real-life work by NASA, which acted as an adviser to the **filmmakers**. And that work been done here at NASA **headquarters** in Washington includes preparations for an actual manned mission to Mars.

As part of that effort, NASA's Jet Propulsion Laboratory has been operating rovers to collect Martian soil samples.

参考译文

这一切并不只是科幻。人们在电影里看到的科学技术都是以美国太空署真正的研究成果为依据。美国太空署也为这部电影的制作担当顾问。而在华盛顿的美国太空署总部正在做的工作中就包括为人类登上火星的任务做准备。

作为登陆火星工作的一部分，美国太空署的喷气推进实验室一直在使用探测器收集火星上的土质样本。

Speaking to HashtagVOA via Skype, the laboratory's Mars engineering manager, said his team needs **diversity** to succeed.

People who see the world from different angles to come in and bring their creative ideas with them, to come here and to help us out. So what we do here is really, in many respects, an international effort.

NASA hopes *The Martian* will help that effort by inspiring young scientists everywhere to bing humans to Mars by 2030.

参考译文

这个实验室的火星工程项目负责人通过Skype告诉美国之音，他需要一个多样化的团队才能成功。

我们需要能从不同角度看世界的人加入我们，并且带给我们创新的想法，来帮助我们成功。我们所做的工作很多方面带有国际性。

美国太空署希望《火星救援》能激励全球各地的年轻科学家们一起努力在2030年以前把人类送上火星。

精彩解析

1. The botanist played by Matt Damon is not a typical Hollywood hero, but he is one of several role models in the film for aspiring scientists.

   这位由马特·戴蒙饰演的植物学家并不是典型的好莱坞英雄，但他为那些立志成为科学家的年轻人树立了一个榜样。

   role model 榜样，模范

   例句 He becomes such a good role model for young people.

   他成为年轻人的典范楷模。

2. This is not what we tend to see.

   这是我们不常在电影里看到的。

   tend to 趋向，倾向于

   例句 Prices tended to rise year by year, but at a modest rate.

   物价年年上涨，但涨幅不大。

3. The more women we have involved in science, technology, engineering and math…

   在科学、技术、工程和数学领域有越多的女性参与……

   involve in 参与，卷入

   例句 He wouldn't like to involve in this serious trouble.

   他不会想卷入这个大麻烦当中的。

一些快速蹿红榜单的歌曲

Some Fast-rising Songs on the Chart (VOA News)

新闻导读

《公告牌》（Billboard）是创办于1894年的美国音乐杂志，当时名为“公告牌公告”，内容包含许多音乐种类的介绍与排行榜，其中最重要的排行榜为公告牌单曲榜（Billboard Hot 100）（单曲排行）与Billboard 200（专辑排行）。1894年11月1日，美国俄亥俄州辛辛那提市的一个小酒馆里，两个专门为马戏团、展览会设计告示牌的年轻人威廉.H.唐纳德森（William H.Donaldson）和詹姆士.F.亨宁汉（James F. Henningham）酒后兴起，萌生了办刊物的念头，《公告牌》就这样诞生了。不过那时，它还叫做“Billboard Advertising”，这份月刊只有8页，售价10美分，内容以州内大事、狂欢节日、娱乐、演出为主。1897年，杂志更名为“The Billboard”，同时做出一系列调整。唐纳德森买下了亨宁汉的股份、将月刊转变为周刊、在纽约以及芝加哥设立办公室。杂志内容则逐步娱乐化：增添唱片界的新闻与广告、电影介绍、歌曲评论、专栏专区等等。直到1913年，《公告牌》出现首份榜单“上周最畅销的前十名流行歌曲”，成为第一本拥有排行榜的杂志。

新闻热词

track [træk] n. 歌曲，乐曲

specifically [spə'sɪfɪkli] adv. 确切地说

rapper ['ræpə(r)] n. 说唱乐手，说唱歌手

slot [slɒt] n. 位置

platinum ['plætɪnəm] n. 铂，白金

perform [pə'fɔːm] v. 表演

remixer [ˌriː'mɪksə(r)] n. 混音师

新闻播报

We have some fast-rising songs on the chart...but thcy just haven't arrived yet. So this week, we have the same five **tracks** as last week, in slightly different order.

Let's open in fifth place, where Wiz Khalifa and Charlie Puth drop two slots with "See You Again." What does Charlie miss the most about his native New Jersey? You gotta find out at the moment.

参考译文

在本期的榜单中我们有一些快速蹿红的歌曲……但它们还没有进入。因此本周我们的5首歌曲和上周一致，只是排名略有出入。

我们首先关注排名第5的歌曲，维兹·卡利法和查理·普斯的前冠军单曲*See You Again*下降2个名次。查理最想念新泽西的什么呢？你马上就会知道。

Charlie grew up in New Jersey but is now based in Los Angeles. He says he misses the Jersey Shore...**specifically** the pizza. Charlie claims he hasn't had good pizza in nearly a year. Maybe Kendrick Lamar can point Charlie in the right direction.

The Los Angeles **rapper** holds at number four with Taylor Swift and "Bad Blood". Taylor sure has her fans, and one may surprise you. Hold on for more.

Taylor Swift and Kendrick Lamar stay put their number four with their ex champion "Bad Blood." Chuck D of Public Enemy says he likes Taylor Swift…for one specific reason. He tells the New York Post that Taylor leads the pack when it comes to understanding streaming services as they exist today.

参考译文

查理在新泽西长大但现在住在洛杉矶。他说自己想念泽西海岸……尤其是那里的披萨。查理曾坦言称他已经快一年没有享受到美味的披萨。也许肯德里克·拉马尔可以为查理指引正确的方向。

这位洛杉矶的说唱歌手同泰勒·斯威夫特及*Bad Blood*牢牢占据第4名的位置。泰勒肯定有她的粉丝，而且这一个可能会让你大吃一惊，请别走开，还有更多精彩内容。

泰勒·斯威夫特和肯德里克·拉马尔以*Bad Blood*保持第四名位置。公敌的Chuck D说他喜欢泰勒·斯威夫特……而且是因为一个特别的原因。他告诉《纽约邮报》，当流媒体服务来临时泰勒就已经占据主导地位。

Silento lives up to his song title, as "Watch Me" jumps two **slots** to third place. It's now a bona-fide sales hit.

Silento jumps two slots to third place with the "Watch Me." Not only is everybody dancing to the 17-year-old rapper's song, they're also buying it.

Last week, The Recording Industry Association of America certified it **platinum**, meaning "Watch Me" has now sold more than one million units. It went to number one on the Billboard Streaming Songs subchart, and at this rate, it's headed for the Hot 100 title.

参考译文

Silento没有辜负他的歌曲取名，就像*Watch Me*一样，排名上升2位，现在位居第三。现在真可谓红得发紫。

Silento的*Watch Me*上升2位，位居第三。不仅是每个人都随着这位17岁说唱歌手的歌曲舞动摇摆，而且人们也竞相购买。

上周，这首歌曲获得美国唱片工业协会白金认证，意味着*Watch Me*现在已经售出超过一百万。它在Billboard歌曲的subchart榜单中跃居第一位，以这种速度，很有可能跻身100首最热门单曲之列。

Not today, though…and The Weekend didn't hit the bulls-eye, either. He remains close, though, as "Can't Feel My Face" holds in the runner-up slot.

The Weekend remained toiled to strike, "Can't Feel My Face" holds in the second place. We're three weeks away from his next album "Beauty Behind the Madness".

And this week we got a look at the track list, and Lana Del Rey guests on one song, "Prisoner." The album drops on August 28. Two days later, The Weekend **performs** at the MTV Video Music Awards.

参考译文

但今天尽管The Weekend乐队没有位居第一。不过，他仍然已经距冠军非常接近，*Can't Feel My Face*位居第二名。

The Weekend乐队奋力争取，*Can't Feel My Face*还是位居第二名。距离他的下一张专辑*Beauty Behind the Madness*还有3个星期时间。

这周我们看到了曲目列表，和拉娜·德雷客串的一首歌*Prisoner*。这张专辑在8月28日出炉。两天后，The Weeknd 在MTV音乐录影带大奖中表演。

Up at number one for a third week we have OMI with "Cheerleader." This hit was eight years in the making. Stay with me.

OMI is your hot 100 rulers for the third week with "Cheerleader". The Jamaican singer tells Rolling Stone magazine that about eight years ago, he woke up with the melody running through his head. At the time he was completely unknown.

"Cheerleader" first became a Jamaican hit, then broke worldwide after German **remixer** Felix Jaehn got his hands on it.

Will The Weekend grab the gold next week? Join me us seven days and find out!

参考译文

第三周我们的冠军单曲是OMI的*Cheerleader*。这首歌曲8年前就已经开始酝酿。

OMI的*Cheerleader*是第三周我们的冠军单曲。这位牙买加歌手告诉《滚石》杂志，大约8年前，他有一次醒来的时候，这首歌的旋律就在他的耳边萦绕。当时的他竟浑然不知。

*Cheerleader*首先成为牙买加的冠军单曲，而凭借德国混音师福利克斯·约恩，这首歌曲成为全世界最热单曲。

The Weeknd会重新夺回冠军宝座吗？下周让我们拭目以待！

精彩解析

1. Charlie grew up in New Jersey but is now based in Los Angeles.
   查理在新泽西长大但现在住在洛杉矶。

   grow up 长大，成长

   例句 She grew up in a small town.

   她在一座小城镇长大。

2. …and at this rate, it's headed for the Hot 100 title.
   ……以这种速度，很有可能跻身100首最热门单曲之列。

   head for 朝……进发，向……发展

   例句 It looks as if the firm is heading for another record year.

   看来今年公司又要创纪录。

7 《爱乐之城》赢取最佳影片奖

La La Land Wins the Best Film Award (BBC News)

新闻导读

《爱乐之城》是由达米恩·查泽雷执导，艾玛·斯通、瑞恩·高斯林、J·K·西蒙斯等主演的喜剧歌舞片。该片讲述一位爵士乐钢琴家与一名怀揣梦想的女演员之间的爱情故事。第70届英国电影学院奖在伦敦皇家艾伯特大厅揭晓，《爱乐之城》成为最大赢家，获得5项大奖，包括最佳影片、最佳导演、最佳女主角、最佳摄影和最佳原创配乐5项大奖。

新闻热词

ceremony ['serəməni] n. 典礼，仪式

musical ['mjuːzɪkl] n. 乐剧；音乐歌舞片

star [stɑː(r)] v. 担任主角，主演

nomination [ˌnɒmɪ'neɪʃn] n.（奖项的）提名

singer ['sɪŋə(r)] n. 歌手；歌唱家

announce [ə'naʊns] v. 宣布；公布

exhaustion [ɪg'zɔːstʃən] n. 精疲力竭；疲惫不堪

新闻播报

A **ceremony** has begun at the Royal Albert Hall in London to hand out the British Academy Film Awards, or BAFATs. The American

musical La La Land, **starring** Ryan Gosling and Emma Stone, has 11 **nominations**, and is the favorite to take the Best Film Award.

参考译文

皇家艾尔伯特音乐厅举行了一场盛大的典礼，颁发英国电影学院奖。瑞恩·高斯林和艾玛·斯通主演的美国音乐剧《爱乐之城》获得11项提名，同时获得最佳影片奖。

The award-winning Jazz and Pop **singer** Al Jarreau has died in a Los Angeles hospital, just days after **announcing** he was retiring due to **exhaustion**. He was 76. BBC News.

参考译文

获奖爵士和流行歌手艾尔·贾诺在洛杉矶一家医院去世，享年76岁。就在几天之前，他刚刚宣布由于精力衰竭而退休。BBC新闻。

精彩解析

1. A ceremony has begun at the Royal Albert Hall in London to hand out the British Academy Film Awards, or BAFATs.
   皇家艾尔伯特音乐厅举行了一场盛大的典礼，颁发英国电影学院奖。

   hand out 分发；给予

   例句 Will you help me to hand out the materials for the lecture?

   你可以帮我分发演讲材料吗？

2. ...just days after announcing he was retiring due to exhaustion.
   ……就在几天之前，他刚刚宣布由于精力衰竭而退休。

   due to 由于；因为

   例句 It was a real prize due to its rarity and good condition.

   因为稀有并且品相完好，它价值连城。

8 伦敦旅馆发现已逝雷鬼教父磁带

Some Recordings of Reggae's Deceased Superstar Found in a London Hotel (BBC News)

新闻导读

雷鬼音乐是一种由斯卡（Ska）和洛克斯代迪（Rock Steady）音乐演变而来的牙买加流行音乐，也译作雷吉，雷盖。Regge是一种风格独特的牙买加音乐，但它起源于New Orleans的R&B，Reggae的直接根源是Ska，这是一种起源于住在美国的牙买加人的一种极富韵律的音乐。其依靠的是吉他轻快的演奏及切分的节奏，Ska是在60年代早期十分流行的R&B的一种方式，在Ska的基础上，Reggae酝酿而生。Reggae同Blues一样，是一种丰富多彩的音乐，它综合了旋律摇滚和民谣摇滚等众多的音乐元素，使Reggae被赋予多样化的诠释，从而在主流区域日见明亮。而“Reggae Sunsplash”艺术节和UR40乐队的出现，使Reggae音乐更趋向于流行化。同时，Reggae音乐的权威人物Bob Marley和Perry对Folk、Rock和Dance音乐的影响也是不可估量的，他们对流行音乐的贡献也是巨大的。

新闻热词

revere [rɪ'vɪə(r)] v. 尊敬；崇敬

admire [əd'maɪə(r)] v. 钦佩；欣赏

superstar ['suːpəstɑː(r)] n. 超级明星

restore [rɪ'stɔː(r)] v. 修复

appalling [ə'pɔːlɪŋ] adj. 骇人听闻的，令人震惊的

drench [drentʃ] v. 使湿透；使浸湿

sprinkler ['sprɪŋklə(r)] n. 洒水器，喷洒器

rewind [ˌriː'waɪnd] v. 倒回；倒带；倒片

contaminant [kən'tæmɪnənt] n. 污染物，致污物

rubbish ['rʌbɪʃ] n. 垃圾；废弃物

horrible ['hɒrəbl] adj. 讨厌的；糟透的

gunk [gʌŋk] n. 黏糊糊的东西

新闻播报

36 years after his death, Bob Marley is still **revered** as a national hero in Jamaica and **admired** by music fans the world over. Now some previously lost recordings of Reggae's first global **superstar** have been uncovered in a London hotel. The **restored** material features many tracks like Jammin and No, Woman No Cry. 13 master tapes with original live recordings of concerts in Paris and London in the 1970s were found in a basement. They were found by Martin Nichols, a recording engineer at White House Studios in the west of England. James asked him what state the tapes were in when he first saw them.

参考译文

在逝世36年后，鲍勃·马利依然被奉为牙买加的民族英雄，并且受到全球音乐迷的追捧。日前，伦敦一家旅馆发现了这位教父级雷鬼世界巨星早期遗失的一批录音带，修复好的材料中包含Jammin和No，Woman No Cry等多首歌曲。地下室发现的这13盘母带是20世纪70年代鲍勃·马利巴黎和伦敦演唱会的原版现场录音带，由来自英国西部White House录音公司的录音师马丁·尼克尔斯发现。詹姆斯问马丁见到这些录音带时它们处于什么状态。

Oh, frankly they were **appalling**. I almost didn't have the heart to tell the boys how bad they were because they were obviously so eager to get something off them. They'd obviously been **drenched** in water at some point. And I suspect it was from a **sprinkler** system cuz it was dirty water. They'd been left to dry out which is obviously very bad news. It needs to be dried off pretty quickly and these hadn't been.

参考译文

噢，老实说挺惊人的。小伙子们显然太想从这些录音带中得到点什么，所以我都不忍心告诉他们录音带破成什么样子了。带子明显是在水里泡过的，还是脏水，所以我怀疑是自动灭火喷水系统造成的。麻烦的是它们沾上水后自动干透了，原则上应该立即烘干，而情况并非如此。

So is your initial thought "I don't really think I'll be able to do anything"?

I wasn't too hopeful. Unfortunately no. Someone had tried to **rewind** the rails. So it was very much a question of how to rescue what was there without doing any more damage.

参考译文

所以你开始就想"我真无能为力了"？

我没报太大希望，实在是没办法。也有人试图倒带，关键的问题是在不继续损伤磁带的前提下补救现存的部分。

And how did you go about rescuing it?

Well, the first job was to try and free them up. And because the water had been the **contaminant**, the only way really to do that was to soak them into still water for a long period of time and hopefully dissolve away some of the **rubbish** that was sticking them together.

Then pulling the rails out and wiping off all the surface to remove the bits that is stuck. There was all sorts of rubbish on there. Literally inch by inch because that we are talking about half-an-hour rails here, tapes that would play for half an hour, which will give you 2,500 feet I think in total. And I could clean about 6 inches at a time. Move it on. Clean it. Dry it. Move it on. Clean it. Dry it. And so on. So yes a **horrible** job. And my back took quite a while to recover, I have to say.

参考译文

那你是如何着手补救的？

嗯，首要工作就是清理磁带。由于水是污染源，唯一的办法就事将磁带长时间静置于水中，但愿能溶解掉一些黏着的杂质。然后拉出带子，擦拭表面，去除粘在上面的东西，各种各样的杂质。这些录音带能播放长达半小时，我估计总共应该有2 500英尺（762米）长，所以真的要一点一点地清理。我一次大约能清理6英寸（15. 24厘米）。往前送，擦拭，烘干，往前送，擦拭，烘干……重复这个程序。所以，确实是份苦差事，说实在的，我后背疼得好久才缓过劲儿。

And how did you clean off the **gunk**?

Well, by hands. Literally with lots of you know cleaning cloths, literally damping them, wiping off, removing what I could, turning the tape on...

参考译文

怎么擦去那些泥状物质呢？

用手喽，用各种抹布先打湿再尽可能擦掉，打开磁带……

精彩解析

1. I almost didn't have the heart to tell the boys how bad they were because they were obviously so eager to get something off them.

小伙子们显然太想从这些录音带中得到点什么，所以我都不忍心告诉他们录音带破成什么样子了。

be eager to 盼望，渴望

例句 You'll be eager to jump into holiday activities.

你将会迫不及待地想要参加节目活动。

2. Then pulling the rails out and wiping off all the surface to remove the bits that is stuck.

然后拉出带子，擦拭表面，去除粘在上面的东西。

wipe off 擦去，拭去

例句 I'm afraid this paint won't wipe off.

我怕这种涂料是擦不掉的。

NBA大明星访古巴进行篮球外交

Some NBA's Biggest Stars Visited Cuba for a Little Basketball Diplomacy (CNN News)

新闻导读

NBA（美职篮），全称美国男子职业篮球联赛（National Basketball Association），是一个国际体育及媒体集团，由三个职业体育联盟组成：美国男子职业篮球联盟（NBA）、美国女子职业篮球联盟（WNBA）以及NBA发展联盟（NBA Development League）。其中NBA是世界上水平最高的篮球联赛、美国四大职业体育联赛之一。

NBA产生了迈克尔·乔丹、魔术师约翰逊、科比·布莱恩特、姚明、勒布朗·詹姆斯等世界巨星。该协会一共拥有30支球队，分属两个联盟：东部联盟和西部联盟；而每个联盟各由三个赛区组成，每个赛区有五支球队。30支球队当中有29支位于美国本土，另外一支来自加拿大的多伦多。从2009-10季后赛开始，因广电总局的相关规定，在电视转播中，解说员不再说“NBA”，而是极为别扭的用NBA的全称：美国男子职业篮球联赛，简称“美职篮”。

NBA正式赛季于每年11月的第一个星期的星期二开始，分为常规赛和季后赛两部分。常规赛为循环赛制，每支球队都要完成82场比赛；常规赛到次年的4月结束，东西部联盟的前八名，包括各个赛区的冠军，将有资格进入接下来进行的季后赛。季后赛采用七战四胜赛制，共分四轮；季后赛的最后一轮也称为总决赛，由两个联盟的冠军争夺NBA的最高荣誉——总冠军。

新闻热词

diplomacy [dɪ'pləʊməsi] n. 外交，外交手段

rivalry ['raɪvlri] n. 竞争，敌对

communist ['kɒmjənɪst] adj. 共产主义的，共产党的

neighbor ['neɪbə] n. 邻居，邻国

thaw [θɔː] v. 解冻，融雪；变缓和

retirement [rɪ'taɪəmənt] n. 退休，退职

ideological [ˌaɪdiə'lɒdʒɪkl] adj. 思想的，意识形态的

athlete ['æθliːt] n. 运动员

serenade [ˌserə'neɪd] n. 组曲，小夜曲 v. 为……唱曲

powerhouse ['paʊəhaʊs] n. 权势集团，强国

phenomenal [fə'nɒmɪnl] adj. 非凡的；不寻常的

exposure [ɪk'spəʊʒə(r)] n. 报道；宣传

embargo [ɪm'bɑːgəʊ] n. 禁运，贸易禁令

overcome [ˌəʊvə'kʌm] v. 战胜，克服

新闻播报

Basketball is not the most popular sport in Cuba. Baseball gets top honors there. But some of the NBA's biggest stars recently traveled to the Caribbean nation, shooting for a little basketball **diplomacy**. The U.S. and Cuban governments are moving toward better relations following decades of cold war **rivalry**. Political divisions remain.

In January, Cuba warned the U.S. not to interfere with its **communist** government. But as far as sports go, the NBA is helping build a bridge between the U.S. and its south eastern **neighbor**.

参考译文

篮球在古巴并不是最受欢迎的运动。棒球在那个国家才享有最高的声望。但最近一些NBA大牌明星前往这个加勒比海国家开展一场小小的篮球外交。数十年的冷战僵局过后美国和古巴两国政府正朝着更好的关系发展。但政治分歧依然存在。

今年1月，古巴方面曾警告美国方面不要干涉其政府。但对体育运动而言，NBA正帮助在美国及其东南的邻居之间架起一座桥梁。

Hoop dreams come to Havana, along with some of basketball's living legends. As U.S.-Cuba relations slowly **thaw**, for the first time, the NBA hosts a basketball training camp in Cuba.

Towering legends of the game came out of **retirement** to practice a little basketball diplomacy. Following the Cuban Revolution, sports became part of the **ideological** struggle with capitalism, as Fidel Castro declared Cubans would play for the love of the game, not the sky high salaries that he said corrupted American **athletes**.

参考译文

篮球梦现身哈瓦那，随之而来的还有一些篮球界的传奇人物。随着美国与古巴的关系慢慢破冰，NBA首次在古巴办起了篮球训练营。

篮球界的顶尖传奇巨星们走出退役生活开展小小的篮球外交。古巴革命后，体育运动成为与资本主义斗争的意识形态的一部分，当时菲德尔·卡斯特罗宣布古巴人会因着热爱而进行这项运动，而非因着腐化美国运动员的高薪。

Politics couldn't stop Cubans, though, from addressing U.S. sports stars. The visiting players were given awards by the Cuban government and **serenaded** by a tune not often heard in communist-run Cuba, the U.S. national anthem. Cuba, they say, has the potential to be a basketball **powerhouse**.

参考译文

但政治不能阻止古巴人民接受美国体育明星们。来访的球员们接受了古巴政府的嘉奖而且他们的伴奏曲子美国国歌在共产主义古巴可不会经常听到。球员们表示古巴有着成为篮球强国的潜力。

Cuba has a great history of producing **phenomenal** athletes. You know, it's-it's a-the-what they-what I think what Cuba needs is **exposure**.

The U.S. economic **embargo** and Cuban government restrictions make it difficult for a Cuban player to compete in the NBA. Many of Cuba's top athletes still defect in order to play in the US. But becoming the best, the visiting players say, is all about **overcoming** the odds.

I think it helps the young women and the young men to know that anything is possible. And if it happened to me, it can happen to them.

参考译文

古巴的伟大历史中曾诞生过很多卓越的球员。你知道，这是我认为面对外界古巴所需要的。

美国的经济禁运及古巴政府本身的限制使得古巴球员很难在NBA的激烈竞争中大展拳脚。为了能够在美国本土打上比赛古巴的许多顶尖球员仍然选择叛逃。但来访的球员表示成为最好的球员就意味着要克服所有困难。

我认为这让年轻一代了解一切皆有可能。如果能在我身上发生，也会发生在他们身上。

精彩解析

1. In January, Cuba warned the U.S. not to interfere with its communist government.

今年1月，古巴方面曾警告美国方面不要干涉其政府。

interfere with 干预，阻挠

例句 The noise interferes with my work.

这噪声妨碍我的工作。

2. But as far as sports go, the NBA is helping build a bridge between the U.S. and its southeastern neighbor.
但对体育运动而言，NBA正帮助在美国及其东南的邻居之间架起一座桥梁。

as far as 就……来说

例句 As far as I'm concerned, I don't mind that you wear this mini-skirt.

就我个人而言，我不介意你穿这件迷你裙。

3. Cuba, they say, has the potential to be a basketball powerhouse.
球员们表示古巴有着成为篮球强国的潜力。

have the potential to do 有潜力做……

例句 She has the potential to become a big star.

她有潜力成为大明星。

读书笔记

10 地震学家对《末日崩塌》的评价

Seismologist's Remark About *San Andreas* (CNN News)

新闻导读

地震又称地动、地振动，是地壳快速释放能量过程中造成振动，期间会产生地震波的一种自然现象。地球上板块与板块之间相互挤压碰撞，造成板块边沿及板块内部产生错动和破裂，是引起地震的主要原因。地震开始发生的地点称为震源，震源正上方的地面称为震中。破坏性地震的地面振动最烈处称为极震区，极震区往往也就是震中所在的地区。地震常常造成严重人员伤亡，能引起火灾、水灾、有毒气体泄漏、细菌及放射性物质扩散，还可能造成海啸、滑坡、崩塌、地裂缝等次生灾害。

震级是地震大小的一种度量，根据地震释放能量的多少来划分，用“级”来表示。震级的大小可划分为超微震、微震、弱震（或称小震）、强震（或称中震）和大地震等。弱震震级小于3级。如果震源不是很浅，这种地震人们一般不易觉察。有感地震震级等于或大于3级、小于或等于4.5级。这种地震人们能够感觉到，但一般不会造成破坏。中强震震级大于4.5级、小于6级。属于可造成破坏的地震，但破坏轻重还与震源深度、震中距等多种因素有关。强震震级等于或大于6级。其中震级大于等于8级的又称为巨大地震。

新闻热词

tsunami [tsuː'nɑːmi] *n.* 海啸

skyscraper ['skaɪskreɪpə(r)] *n.* 摩天大楼

blockbuster ['blɒkbʌstə(r)] n. 轰动一时的电影

seismologist [ˌsaɪzmə'lɒdʒɪst] n. 地震学家

magnitude ['mæɡnɪtjuːd] n. （地震）级数

generate ['dʒenəreɪt] v. 造成，引起

collapse [kə'læps] v. 倒塌，塌下

premier ['premiə(r)] n. 首映式

approach [ə'prəʊtʃ] v. 接近，走近

friction ['frɪkʃn] n. 摩擦

新闻播报

A **tsunami** bearing down on a Golden Gate Bridge, **skyscrapers** collapsing. Can't fault an earthquake **blockbuster** for going a little overboard. And before it falls through the cracks, CNN and the film studio are both owned by Time Warner.

How does a **seismologist** size up "San Andreas" ? I would definitely give it two thumbs up. It had me on the edge of my seat. And the tsunami really had scientists rolling their eyes.

参考译文

海啸逼近金门大桥，摩天大楼即将倒塌。这部地震大片有点离谱。在上映之前，CNN及电影制片厂都属于时代华纳旗下。

《末日崩塌》的地震规模如何？我肯定会给它最高的评价。它让我非常激动。而且海啸真的让科学家们感到震撼。

Oh, it's way too big. It's all a question of **magnitude**, 9.6, according to the movie. But the San Andreas Fault isn't deep or long enough to **generate** that big of a quake. Two cities get hit. Could you lose both cities, San Francisco and L.A.? I think it's highly, highly,

highly unlikely.

Could the Hoover Dam **collapse**? No. I think the Hoover Dam is safe. You know, we all laughed at that scene and said, "There is water behind the Hoover Dam?" That's a little dry humor about the drought. Seismologist Dr. Lucy Jones posed with the Rock at the **premier** and live-tweeted scientific inaccuracies.

参考译文

哦，太震撼了。是关于震级的问题，电影称震级是9.6级。但圣安地列斯断层的深度和长度都无法产生那样大的地震。两坐城市受到影响。你能失去这两座城市，旧金山和洛杉矶吗？我认为这非常，非常，非常不可能。

胡佛水坝会倒塌吗？不。我认为，胡佛水坝很安全。你知道的，看到那个场景我们都笑了，而且还说，“胡佛水坝后面有水？”这是一个关于干旱的冷笑话。地震学家露西·琼斯博士在首映时评价其中的岩石断层并且现场发布推特称这是科学错误。

When the Rock **approaches** the gaping fault like, Dr. Jones tweeted, "OMG! A chasm? If the fault could open up, there'd be no **friction**. With no friction, there'd be no earthquake." But there's one thing the scientists love. The movie repeats the "duck, cover and hold on" mantra experts recommend. And if it makes people prepare, what is a little earthquake earth quakery.

So, maybe there's a little cinematic here and there that seemed too special effective for seismologist who decides it didn't size up. But as long as the science is deafening, it's certainly something Hollywood approve of.

I'm Carl Azuz. Keeping it real to real for CNN STUDENT NEWS.

参考译文

当岩石到达张开的断层时，琼斯博士，在推特上说："我的天！裂缝？如果断层可以打开，就没有摩擦。没有摩擦，就没有地震。"但有一件事是科学家们所钟爱的。这部电影一直在强调的"伏倒、掩护和抓住"原则是专家们推崇的。如果它让人有所准备，这就是小的地震会引发大地震。

所以，也许有点艺术效果，只是对于认为其言过其实的地震学家来说有些过头。但只要不在乎科学事实，这还是一部好莱坞标准的大片。

我是卡尔·阿祖兹。CNN学生新闻让这部电影变得更加真实。

精彩解析

1. A tsunami bearing down on a Golden Gate Bridge, skyscrapers collapsing.

海啸逼近金门大桥，摩天大楼即将倒塌。

bear down on 冲向，向……逼近

例句 The enemy warship tried to bear down on our small airboat.

敌舰企图逼近我们的小汽艇。

2. How does a seismologist size up"San Andreas"?

《末日崩塌》的地震规模如何？

size up 估量，估计

例句 It isn't easy to size up the situation.

这个形势不好估量判断。

3. But as long as the science is deafening, it's certainly something Hollywood approves of.

但只要不在乎科学事实，这还是一部好莱坞标准的大片。

as long as 只要

例句 I'll stay in New York as long as my money holds on.

只要我的钱还能维持一天，我就在纽约待一天。

读书笔记

教育热点

1 支持尼日利亚的初等教育

Supporting Primary Education in Nigeria (VOA News)

新闻导读

尼日利亚联邦共和国（Federal Republic of Nigeria），位于西非东南部，非洲几内亚湾西岸的顶点，邻国包括西边的贝宁，北边的尼日尔，东北方隔乍得湖与乍得接壤一小段国界，东和东南与喀麦隆毗连，南濒大西洋几内亚湾。尼日利亚是非洲第一人口大国，总人口1.73亿，占非洲总人口的16%，同时也是非洲第一大经济体。尼日利亚于1976年起实行小学免费教育。但由于经济困难，自1985年起改为收费。1999年9月尼政府出台全国基础教育计划，恢复小学免费义务教育。学制为小学6年，初中3年，高中3年，大学4年。全国21%的人口只受过小学教育，成年人36.7%为文盲。全国现有大学88所，著名大学有艾哈迈德·贝罗大学、拉各斯大学、伊巴丹大学、尼日利亚大学和伊费大学等；中等专业学校近200所；师范学校近250余所；商业学校80所；普通中学12 610余所；小学59 340余所。大多数学校教学设施陈旧，师资不足。

新闻热词

memorandum [ˌmeməˈrændəm] n. 备忘录

commitment [kəˈmɪtmənt] n. 承诺；责任；义务

framework [ˈfreɪmwɜːk] n. 架构；体系

preliminary [prɪˈlɪmɪnəri] adj. 预备的；初步的

currently ['kʌrəntli] adv. 目前地；当前地
approximately [ə'prɒksɪmətli] adv. 大约地；大概地
extraordinary [ɪk'strɔːdnri] adj. 非凡的；特别的
opportunity [ˌɒpə'tjuːnəti] n. 机会；时机
partnership ['pɑːtnəʃɪp] n. 伙伴关系；合作关系

新闻播报

The U.S. government, through the Agency for International Development, or USAID, announced its continuing support to the education sector in Bauchi, Nigeria.

This five-year **memorandum** of understanding, or MOU, sets out the shared and individual **commitments** for collaboration in the education sector made by both USAID and the government of Bauchi and provides a **framework** for mutual accountability for education activities in Bauchi State. The MOU supports the Bauchi state government's education goals and establishes a **preliminary** plan for joint monitoring and evaluation of progress.

参考译文

美国政府通过美国国际开发署宣布其会继续支持尼日利亚包奇州的教育事业。

这一为期5年的谅解备忘录阐述了美国国际开发署和包奇州政府在教育领域合作方面所承担的共同和各自的责任，为包奇州教育活动的相互问责制提供了框架。这份谅解备忘录支持了包奇州政府的教育目标，为共同监督和进度评估设立了初期方案。

USAID supports Nigeria's efforts to improve the quality of and access to basic education. **Currently**, USAID implements three activities that support Bauchi State efforts to improve the education sector: Northern Education Initiative Plus, Education Crisis Response, and the Leadership, Empowerment, Advocacy and Development. These activities build state and local government capacity and systems that will teach **approximately** 2 million primary school children how to read and allow nearly 55,100,000 children the opportunity to attend classes in community-based learning centers by the year 2020.

参考译文

美国国际开发署支持尼日利亚为提升基础教育质量、拓宽基础教育渠道所做出的努力。目前，国际开发署实行了3项活动来支持包奇州改善教育行业：北部教育+行动，教育危机应答活动，领导、自强、倡导、发展活动。这些活动构筑了包奇州政府和当地政府的能力，建立了教育体系，让近200万小学儿童学会如何识字，也在2020年之前让近5 510万名儿童得以有在社区学习中心念书的机会。

"The United States commends Bauchi State for its **extraordinary** efforts to provide greater learning **opportunities** for its children," said USAID Mission Director Michael Harvey. "This MOU will expand the **partnership** between USAID and Bauchi State to improve primary education in Bauchi."

The United States is proud to work with its partner Nigeria to provide a better future for the children of Nigeria.

参考译文

"美国赞扬包奇州为孩子们提供更好的学习机会所做出的卓绝努力，"国际开发署专项负责人迈克尔·哈维说。"这份谅解备忘录将拓展国际开发署与包奇州之间的伙伴关系，提升包奇州的基础教育。"

美国很骄傲能与其合作伙伴尼日利亚一道，为其儿童提供一个更加美好的明天。

1. This five-year memorandum of understanding, or MOU, sets out the shared and individual commitments for collaboration in the education sector made by both USAID and the government of Bauchi…

   这一为期5年的谅解备忘录阐述了美国国际开发署和包奇州政府在教育领域合作方面所承担的共同和各自的责任……

   set out 陈述，阐述，说明

   例句 He has written a letter to *The Times* setting out his views.

   他已经给《泰晤士报》去信阐明自己的观点。

2. The United States commends Bauchi State for its extraordinary efforts to provide greater learning opportunities for its children.

   美国赞扬包奇州为孩子们提供更好的学习机会所做出的卓绝努力。

   commend for 因……赞扬

   例句 We commended them for their enthusiasm.

   我们称赞他们的热心。

2 华盛顿史密森学会致力文化保护培训

Smithsonian Institution Provides Training on Protecting Cultural Sites (VOA News)

新闻导读

美国华盛顿史密森学会（Smithsonian Institution），是唯一由美国政府资助、半官方性质的第三部门博物馆机构。由英国科学家詹姆斯·史密森遗赠捐款，根据美国国会法令于1846年创建于首都华盛顿。学会下设14所博物馆和1所国立动物园。

14所博物馆中，有弗里尔美术馆，阿瑟·M.萨克勒美术馆，国立美国历史博物馆，国立自然历史博物馆，国立美国艺术博物馆，国立肖像馆，国立航空和航天博物馆，赫什霍恩博物馆和雕塑园，美术和工业大厦，伦威克美术馆，阿纳卡斯蒂亚地区傅物馆，库柏-休伊斯博物馆等。

新闻热词

religious [rɪ'lɪdʒəs] adj. 宗教的；信教的

preserve [prɪ'zɜːv] v. 保护；保存；维护

effective [ɪ'fektɪv] adj. 有效的

stack [stæk] n. 一堆；一叠 v. 将……码放整齐

fresco ['freskəʊ] n. 壁画

dissipate ['dɪsɪpeɪt] v. 消失；消除；驱散

tragically ['trædʒɪkli] adv. 悲剧地，悲惨地

artifact ['ɑːtɪfækt] n. 人工制品，手工艺品，加工品

outreach ['aʊtriːtʃ] n. 外展服务；扩大服务

mosaic [məʊ'zeɪɪk] n. 马赛克；镶嵌图案；拼花图案

新闻播报

The U.S. State Department partnered with the Smithsonian Institution to engage **religious** minority groups directly, providing them with training and information on **preserving** cultural sites and objects that are at risk. Some of these preventative methods are simple, but **effective** said Special Advisor Thames:

参考译文

美国国务院与华盛顿史密森学会合作以达到直接与宗教少数群体接触的目的，为他们提供有关保护濒危文化遗址和文物的培训和信息。这些预防性措施中有一些简单又有成效，特别顾问泰晤士说：

"There was a training that went on in northern Syria, where churches were trained about how to **stack** sand bags in front of ancient **frescos** and murals so that if a mortar shell were to land, the explosive force would be **dissipated** by the sand bags—it wouldn't hurt the mural. And they had these very striking before and after pictures of a room full of sandbags, the bomb **tragically** hit, the sand bags are exploded but the mural is fine."

参考译文

"我们曾在叙利亚北部做过一次培训，教那里的各个教堂如何在古老的壁画前堆砌沙袋，这样就能在迫击炮弹坠落后，通过沙袋来消散爆炸的冲力——从而保护壁画。他们确曾经历过这种惊心动魄的场景，在将沙袋满满地堆砌在房间中的壁画前后，在炸弹不幸

坠落后，这些沙袋虽然分崩离析，但壁画完好无损。”

Trainings also include information on protecting movable **artifacts** by creating digital documentation of the items that can be stored remotely. The Smithsonian Institute has created a special **outreach** program in Erbil, Iraq, that is dedicated to the effort.

参考译文

培训还包括传授关于保护可挪动的人工作品的信息，教学方法是制作可以远程储存的物品的电子文件。华盛顿史密森学会在伊拉克的埃尔比勒已经创建了一个特殊的外展计划，该计划就是致力于这个方面的。

“These communities that are so unique, that create this **mosaic** of culture and religion,” said Special Advisor Thames. “They can be pieced back together and protecting their common culture can be a way to do that.”

参考译文

“这些社群都是独一无二的，正是他们创造了文化和地区的美好画面，”泰晤士说。“他们可以一片片拼凑完整，而保护它们的共有文化正是拼凑完整的途径之一。”

精彩解析

1. …providing them with training and information on preserving cultural sites and objects that are at risk.

……为他们提供有关保护濒危文化遗址和文物的培训和信息。

at risk 有危险

例句 An estimated seven million people are at risk of starvation.

估计有700万人面临着饿死的危险。

2. …where churches were trained about how to stack sand bags in front of ancient frescos and murals so that if a mortar shell were to land, the explosive force would be dissipated by the sand bags…

……教那里的各个教堂如何在古老的壁画前堆砌沙袋，这样就能在迫击炮弹坠落后，通过沙袋来消散爆炸的冲力……

so that 以便；结果

例句 I had the house decorated quickly so that my parents could move in.

我很快地把房子粉刷了一遍，这样我的父母就能搬进来了。

3. The Smithsonian Institute has created a special outreach program in Erbil, Iraq, that is dedicated to the effort.

华盛顿史密森学会在伊拉克的埃尔比勒已经创建了一个特殊的外展计划，该计划就是致力于这个方面的。

dedicate to 献（身）于……；把（时间、精力等）用于……

例句 He dedicated his life to the cause of education.

他将自己的一生献身于教育事业。

3 硅谷传奇学校别出心裁打造企业家

Silicon Valley School Uses Unconventional Methods to Train Entrepreneurs (VOA News)

新闻导读

德雷普英雄学院（Draper University of Heros），是美国硅谷的一家民办高校，也是一个硅谷7周的创业培训项目，由德丰杰的创始人蒂姆·德雷普（Tim Draper）创办，并宣称是哈利·波特上的霍格沃茨魔法学院的硅谷现实版。蒂姆·德雷普建造这座学校的原因是因为“这个世界需要更多英雄”——更多的创业者，去解决我们实际存在的问题。德雷普英雄学院的最大特色是，每个学员在加入时都要签保密协议，保证打死都不会告诉别人到底在里面学了什么。外面的人万一问起，都要一脸神秘的回答“不能说，但绝对改变你的人生。”

新闻热词

billionaire [ˌbɪljə'neə(r)] n. 亿万富翁；巨富

unexpected [ˌʌnɪk'spektɪd] adj. 想不到的，料不到的

blindfold ['blaɪndfəʊld] v. 蒙住……的眼睛；遮住……的视线

conventional [kən'venʃənl] adj. （行为、观念等）传统的，符合习俗的

extraordinary [ɪk'strɔːdnri] adj. 非凡的；优秀的

tenacity [tə'næsəti] n. 坚韧；坚毅

immune [ɪ'mjuːn] adj. 免疫的；有免疫力的

startup ['stɑːtʌp] n. 新兴公司

succeed [sək'siːd] v. 达到目的；成功做成

consistent [kən'sɪstənt] adj. 一致的，吻合的，不矛盾的

新闻播报

Most of the students did not expect jumping into a chilly pool with a **billionaire** investor would be their first step at Draper University. But the **unexpected** is the norm at Draper, and Aima Ohiwerei from Nigeria is experiencing it first-hand.

参考译文

大多数学生都未曾料想到，他们在德雷普英雄学院学到的第一课竟是跟着一位身价过亿的投资人一起跳进冰冷的水池里。不过，在这所学校里，意料之外的事情才是常态，而来自尼日利亚的学生Aima Ohiwerei正切实感受着这一点。

It's not like your regular school. Kind of like pushes you to try and imagine more than you can actually think you can imagine. Such as crossing the street **blindfolded** with only the help of verbal instructions. Thinking about doing something beyond the **conventional** is what Draper University tries to teach, says the school's founder and venture capitalist Tim Draper.

参考译文

这所学校不像你们脑海里的常规学校。它有点儿类似于推动着你去尝试并想象超乎你认为自己所能想象的事情，比如蒙着眼睛、在他人的口头引导下试着横穿街道。考虑做打破常规的事情正是德雷普英雄学院力图实现的目标，该校创始人兼投资人蒂姆·德雷普

说到。

People need to be able to step out, apart from the crowd, and try **extraordinary** things and now that we're all interconnected, and all communicating with each other throughout the entire world, it's even more important for people to be able to step out and do something a little different.

参考译文

我们需要走出去，远离人群，尝试做一些出格的事情。而且在这样一个全世界人彼此联系、彼此沟通的世界里，跨出去一步、做与众人略不相同的事情就更重要了。

Draper says for entrepreneurs to step outside their comfort zones takes a certain mindset and emotional **tenacity**.

I'm trying to get into people's heads that starting a business is very difficult. You will be up against a lot of pressures and we want you to, after going through this program, we want you to be able to be **immune** to the pressures that are going to be coming against you.

参考译文

德雷普说，对企业家来说，要想走出舒适区，没有一定的思维模式、没有锲而不舍的韧性，是做不到的。

我想让人们明白创业维艰。你会面临许多压力，而我们就是希望能通过学校里这样的项目来让你能够对未来可能遭受的压力产生抗体。

That's exactly what Ohiwerei hopes to learn in this seven-week course. Just push through all the negative thoughts and all the negative comments towards your **startup**, toward you, just push through that's what I want to learn.

I would like to know how to be fearless, just go full speed without stopping.

参考译文

那就是Ohiwerei希望在这为期7周的课程中学到的东西——排除创业路上向你扑面而来的负面想法和负面评论，不要去管他们，这就是我想学到的东西。

我的初衷是想知道如何做到无畏——就是全速前进不要停。

Hundreds of students from more than 70 countries have attended this entrepreneurship course. Students between 18 and 28 years old learn to be emotionally prepared for entrepreneurship by listening to Silicon Valley startup founders who have **succeeded** and those who have failed. They also experience some unusual training, like a volleyball game they play where the rules keep changing.

参考译文

来自70多个国家的上百名学生参加了这个企业家课程。通过聆听硅谷创业者们或成功或失败的经验，这些18至28岁的学生们学会了怎样为创业做好心理上的准备。他们还参加了一些非同寻常的培训，比如适应规则不断变化的排球比赛。

Different things start to happen and their brains start to open up and they start thinking, "Hey, anything is possible".

Consistent with the uniqueness of the school, the graduates become superheroes. They get a cape and mask as they are sent out as entrepreneurs to change the world with their unique ideas.

参考译文

他们的身上有了不一样的地方，他们的头脑开始变得开放，开始思考，“嘿，一切其实都有可能”。

德雷普英雄学院的学生们传承了学校特色，成了超级英雄。在毕业离校、奔往世界各地去用自己独特的想法改变世界时，他们已如拥有了金钟罩和铁布衫。

精彩解析

1. People need to be able to step out, apart from the crowd, and try extraordinary things…

   我们需要走出去，远离人群，尝试做一些出格的事情……

   apart from 除去，撇开……来说，离开

   例句 Apart from some spelling mistakes, the composition is fairly good.

   除了一些拼写错误，这篇文章写得很不错。

2. Draper says for entrepreneurs to step outside their comfort zones takes a certain mindset and emotional tenacity.

   德雷普说，对企业家来说，要想走出舒适区，没有一定的思维模式、没有锲而不舍的韧性，是做不到的。

   comfort zone 舒适区，安逸的环境

   例句 In order to grow, I must stretch beyond my comfort zone.

   为了成长，我必须离开眼前的安逸。

3. Consistent with the uniqueness of the school, the graduates become superheroes.

   他们的身上有了不一样的地方，他们的头脑开始变得开放，开始思考。

   consistent with 与……一致，并存

   例句 His action is always consistent with his words.

   他始终言行一致。

美国学生通过星谈计划学习俄语

US Students Learn Russian Through STARTALK (VOA News)

新闻导读

美国星谈计划（STARTALK）是美国国家安全局资助，美国马里兰州立大学的全国外语中心管理的一个项目。星谈计划的使命是让更多美国市民学习、说、教授迫切需要的外语。星谈计划向学习这些语言的学生（K–16）和教授这些语言的教师提供富有创造性和参与性的暑期学习经历，力求成为语言教育和语言教师专业发展的实践典范。美国国家情报总监办公室（ODNI）在2006年推出星谈计划，并授权美国国家安全局监督执行。国家安全局又与马里兰大学（UMD）国家外语中心（NFLC）签订协议，让其作为该计划的实施和管理专家。

新闻热词

immersion [ɪ'mɜːʃn] n. 浸没；浸泡

colleague ['kɒliːg] n. 同事；同僚

presidency ['prezɪdənsi] n. 总统职位

participant [pɑː'tɪsɪpənt] n. 参加者，参与者

diplomat ['dɪpləmæt] n. 外交官；外交家

mysterious [mɪ'stɪəriəs] adj. 神秘的

symbolic [sɪm'bɒlɪk] adj. 象征的，象征性的

literature ['lɪtrətʃə(r)] n. 文学；文学作品

politician [ˌpɒləˈtɪʃn] n. 政治家；政客

新闻播报

Here Americans only speak Russian and they only respond to Russian names.

Such language **immersion** helps American students make progress in studying the Russian language in just a few weeks. And for American Russian teachers, this is a chance to meet their **colleagues** and improve language skills.

This is one of many foreign language courses within STARTALK, a program launched during George W. Bush's **presidency** as part of a U.S. national security strategy. Arabic, Chinese, Hindi, Persian, and Russian were named "critical-need" foreign languages.

参考译文

这里的美国人只说俄语，也只会对俄语名字作出回应。

这样的语言浸透模式帮助这群美国学生在短短几周的时间里，在学习俄语方面取得了巨大进步。而对美籍俄罗斯教师来说，这也是与同事们会面并提升语言技能的机会。

这是STARTALK众多外语学习课程中的一个，是在布什担任美国总统期间创立的栏目，作为美国国家安全策略的一部分。在美国，阿拉伯语、汉语、北印度语、波斯语、俄语都被视为“重要”外语。

Charles Byrd, professor of Russian at the University of Georgia and a STARTALK program **participant**, says that American students are interested in Russian but many find it very hard to learn and master. For Byrd himself, Russian was once "forbidden fruit."

"My parents were American **diplomats**, and they always wanted to go to Russia, but they were not allowed to," he said. "Because they could not travel to Russia, I always wanted to go there. I remember during my childhood I often heard about the Evil Empire. I had always the impression that Russia is a **mysterious** riddle."

参考译文

查尔斯·伯德是乔治亚大学的教授和STARTALK项目参与者。他表示，美国学生对俄语很感兴趣，但觉得很难学习掌握。对于伯德教授本人来说，俄语曾是"禁果"。

查尔斯说："我父母都曾是美国外交家，他们一直很想去俄罗斯，但一直不被允许。因为他们想去而不能去，所以俄罗斯也是我很想去的地方。我记得小时候对俄罗斯的听闻是，那里是邪恶帝国。所以，在我的印象中，俄罗斯一直像谜一样神秘。"

19-year-old Joseph Doran has been to Russia, he says he ate borscht seven times a week and took walks along the Volga, a **symbolic** river in Russian culture. At STARTALK, Doran is an assistant teacher, students call him the Russian name, Joseph Timofeyevich.

"I love Russian culture, language. I love reading Russian classical **literature**," said Doran. "It is a very interesting language. Russian people are very nice. I love the opportunities that open to me because I know Russian."

参考译文

19岁的约瑟夫·多伦曾去过俄罗斯，他说在俄期间，他一周喝7次罗宋汤，也总沿着伏尔加河散步，那是一条象征俄罗斯文化之河。Doran在STARTALK担任助教老师，学生们叫他的俄罗斯名字Joseph Timofeyevich。

约瑟夫说，“我爱俄罗斯文化和语言。我爱读俄罗斯古典文学。俄语是一门很有意思的语言。俄罗斯人民都很友好。我了解俄罗斯，我爱它对我敞开的机会之门。”

Betsy Sandstrom, a program director of Discovery Russia at STARTALK, says that, for many students, learning a foreign language is an important first step into their future careers.

"They have different interests — one person wants to become a Russian language teacher, another wants to be a **politician**," she said. "Knowledge of any foreign language is needed. And Russia is the largest country in the world."

According to Forbes magazine, Russian is among the top 10 most popular languages for American college students.

参考译文

贝琪是STARTALK发现俄罗斯的项目负责人，他认为，对很多学生来说，学习外语对将来的职业生涯是重要的第一步。

“他们有不同的兴趣——有的想成为俄语老师，有的想当政治家。了解任何一门外语都有必要。况且俄罗斯是世界上最大的国家。”

《福布斯》杂志的数据显示，俄语是美国大学生之中最受欢迎的10门语言之一。

精彩解析

1. Such language immersion helps American students make progress in studying the Russian language in just a few weeks.
这样的语言浸透模式帮助这群美国学生在短短几周的时间里，在学习俄语方面取得了巨大进步。

make progress in 在……方面取得进步

例句 We continue to make progress in all fields.

我们在各领域继续取得进展。

2. I remember during my childhood I often heard about the Evil Empire.
我记得小时候对俄罗斯的听闻是，那里是邪恶帝国。

hear about 得悉，听说

例句 Have you ever heard about the movie?
你听说过这部电影吗？

5 伊斯兰合作组织通过教育促进和平

Organization of Islamic Cooperation on Peace Through Education (VOA News)

新闻导读

伊斯兰合作组织（Organization of Islamic Cooperation），原名伊斯兰会议组织，2011年6月改为现名。是由伊斯兰国家组成的国际组织，为联合国常驻机构；该组织由遍及中东、中亚、西非、北非和印度次大陆的57个国家组成（2013年止），覆盖的人口约为13亿。秘书处设在沙特阿拉伯王国的吉达市。组织的宗旨是促进各成员国之间在经济、社会、文化和科学等方面的合作；努力消除种族隔离和种族歧视，反对一切形式的殖民主义；支持巴勒斯坦人民恢复民族权利和重返家园的斗争；支持穆斯林保障其尊严、独立和民族权利的斗争。

新闻热词

minister ['mɪnɪstə(r)] n.（政府）部长，大臣

prosperity [prɒ'sperəti] n. 繁荣；兴旺

radicalization [ˌrædɪkəlaɪ'zeɪʃn] n. 激进化，激进

ideology [ˌaɪdi'ɒlədʒi] n. 意识形态；思想体系；思想方式

dignitary ['dɪgnɪtəri] n. 高官，要员

facilitate [fə'sɪlɪteɪt] v. 促进，助长

adopt [ə'dɒpt] v. 采用，采取，采纳

unemployment [ˌʌnɪm'plɔɪmənt] n. 失业；失业率

populace ['pɒpjələs] n. 百姓；平民

democracy [dɪ'mɒkrəsi] n. 民主；民主制度

innovation [ˌɪnə'veɪʃn] n. 革新；创新

pluralism ['plʊərəlɪzəm] n. 多元化；多元性

enhance [ɪn'hɑːns] v. 提高，增加

advance [əd'vɑːns] v. 促进，推动

新闻播报

In mid-October, the foreign **ministers** of the Organization of Islamic Cooperation member countries met in Tashkent, Uzbekistan to find new ways to promote peace and **prosperity**, and fight **radicalization** and reign in violent extremism.

In the belief that education is an important tool to promote peace and economic development and to combat the **ideology** of terrorism and violent extremism, the **dignitaries** adopted the theme "Education and Enlightenment: The Path to Peace and Creativity." To **facilitate** the process of countering violent extremist ideology online, the Organization also launched the Center for Dialogue, Peace and Understanding.

参考译文

10月中旬，伊斯兰合作组织各成员国的外交部长于乌兹别克斯坦首都塔什干会晤，以寻求促进和平繁荣、打击激进化、控制暴力极端化的新途径。

秉持着教育是促进和平与经济发展、打击恐怖主义与暴力极端化意识形态的重要利器的信念，各国外交部长将本次会晤主题定为"教育与启蒙——通往和平与创造的正途"。为促进线上打击暴力

极端主义意识形态的进程，伊斯兰合作组织还成立了对话、和平与理解中心。

The ministers **adopted** the Tashkent Declaration, which, among other goals, strives to promote peace and combat violent extremism by addressing problems caused by under-performing economies and high **unemployment**, through increased investments in human capital, training and quality education. Such investments should result in a well-educated **populace** that values and works toward achieving **democracy** and toward modernizing and improving their home countries.

The theme of this year's ministerial—education and enlightenment—appropriately focuses on the solution to many of the ongoing challenges facing OIC members and the international community, said Acting U.S. Special Envoy to the Organization of Islamic Cooperation, Arsalan Suleman.

参考译文

各国外长采用了《塔什干宣言》，该宣言的宗旨之一就是通过解决由疲弱经济、高度失业造成的诸多问题，并通过提升对人力资本、培训、素质教育的大量投资，来力图促进和平、打击暴力极端主义。这些投资将实现广大人口的素质教育，使人们尊重民主，并为实现民主、实现现代化以及改善祖国状况而不断努力。

本期部长级会议的主题是——教育与启迪，基本上专注于寻求伊斯兰合作组织成员国以及整个国际社会目前所面临诸多挑战的解决方法，美国驻伊斯兰合作组织代理特使阿尔萨兰·苏莱曼这样表示道。

Education and **innovation** are the currency of the modern

global economy. A well-rounded education is what has enabled our global civilization to achieve such great advances in all areas, from technology and health to tolerance and **pluralism**. It is what helps us break down the mental barriers that divide us.

We must work together more closely to jointly address global challenges like the refugee crisis and climate change. We must also recognize the urgent need to **enhance** global efforts to protect the rights of minorities, including religious minorities, said Special Envoy Suleman.

参考译文

教育与创新就是现代全球经济的货币。全方位的教育才能让全球各国实现各个领域的巨大进步，从科技、健康到包容与多元化，不一而足。全方位的教育才是帮助我们打破将彼此分隔的精神障碍的正道。

我们必须更加紧密地合作，以共同解决诸多全球性挑战，如难民危机与气候变化。同时，我们必须认识到亟需加强全球的共同努力，保护少数群体的权益，包括宗教少数群体，特使阿尔萨兰·苏莱曼说道。

The United States is proud of the progress in **advancing** U.S.-OIC cooperation in a number of areas, including on political crises, humanitarian affairs, health, countering violent extremism, women's rights, entrepreneurship, and human rights. We look forward to working with all of you to further enhance US-OIC partnerships and cooperation.

参考译文

美国非常骄傲能够提升美国与伊斯兰合作组织之间在诸多领域的合作，其中包括政治危机、人道主义事宜、健康、打击暴力极端主义、女性权益、企业家精神、人权。我们期待与所有人一道，共同加强美国与伊斯兰合作组织的合作伙伴关系。

精彩解析

1. The ministers adopted the Tashkent Declaration, which, among other goals, strives to promote peace and combat violent extremism by addressing problems…

   各国外长采用了《塔什干宣言》，该宣言的宗旨之一就是通过解决由疲弱经济、高度失业造成的诸多问题……

   strive to 力求，力图

   例句 They strive to retain access to more resources.

   他们力求获取更多资源。

2. The theme of this year's ministerial—education and enlightenment—appropriately focuses on the solution to many of the ongoing challenges facing OIC members and the international community...

   本期部长级会议的主题是——教育与启迪，基本上专注于寻求伊斯兰合作组织成员国以及整个国际社会目前所面临诸多挑战的解决方法……

   focus on 对(某事或做某事)予以注意

   例句 Today we're going to focus on the question of homeless people.

   今天，我们主要讨论无家可归者的问题。

3. The United States is proud of the progress in advancing U.S.-OIC cooperation in a number of areas…

   美国非常骄傲能够提升美国与伊斯兰合作组织之间在诸多领域的合作……

   be proud of 对……感到骄傲，自豪

   例句 You should be proud of your excellent work.

   你应该对你出色的工作感到自豪。

在线女子学校提供新的学习机会

Online Girls' School Provides a New Chance to Study (VOA News)

新闻导读

网络课堂是基于互联网络的远程在线互动培训课堂。一般系统采用音视频传输以及数据协同等网络传输技术，模拟真实课堂环境，通过网络给学生提供有效地培训环境。其标准使用状况是：学员在连接互联网的计算机上安装网络课堂客户端软件或直接使用浏览器，再使用由网络课堂管理者提供的学员账号登陆客户端，即可参加由培训学校提供的在线培训课程。网络课堂的核心就是教学资源共享、协同浏览。标准的网络课堂系统拥有文档播放、视频语音交互、背景音乐、电子教鞭、电子白板、屏幕共享、网页共享、文字交互、课程录制、虚拟课堂等功能；还应有众多个性化细节设计，如：公聊、私聊、答疑、禁止某个学员发言、踢出、锁定课堂、学员搜索、申请发言、指定学员进入提问席、在线投票等等。常见的网络课堂系统具备完善的教学管理平台，可实现对培训机构、讲师、学员和课堂的管理。一些网络课堂软件甚至提供了课堂数据统计和下载，如：学员列表、聊天记录、投票结果等。

新闻热词

pursue [pə'sjuː] v. 寻求，追求

psychology [saɪ'kɒlədʒi] n. 心理学

placement ['pleɪsmənt] n. 实习工作，实习课；安置

Advanced Placement 美国大学预修课程

regular ['regjələ(r)] adj. 正常的，常见的，普通的
project ['prɒdʒekt] n. 项目，计划
otherwise ['ʌðəwaɪz] adv. 否则，另外
produce [prə'djuːs] v. 产生，造成
confidence ['kɒnfɪdəns] n. 信心，信任
exemplary [ɪg'zempləri] adj. 典型的，示范的
attendance [ə'tendəns] n. 出席，出勤
capitalize ['kæpɪtəlaɪz] v. 利用

新闻播报

Marlborough School student Xochitl Green wants to **pursue** a career in the field of **psychology**. Her high school only offers one psychology course, and that's not enough for her. "Because I wanted to take a more in-depth class, they told me there was an option to do an online course, and so I looked into it."

参考译文

马尔伯勒学校的学生希克特里·格林一直梦想着从事心理学领域的职业。但她的高中只提供了一种心理学课程，这对格林而言是远远不够的。“我想去上更为深入的课程，因此他们告诉我上在线课程是不错的选择，所以我就来了。”

In addition to her classes in school, Green took an online Advanced **Placement** psychology course through Online School For Girls. She said the experience was different from a **regular** classroom. "I actually thought it was a lot easier to say your thoughts because there weren't any eyes looking at you like there are in a classroom. You got to be completely 100 percent yourself. There were a lot of

projects, though, where we had to video chat with girls or you had to text girls."

参考译文

除了学校的课程之外，格林还进行在线女子学校上预修心理学课程的学习。她表示网络课堂体验和一般课堂完全不同。“我认为网络课堂更容易表达你自己的想法，因为不像教室那样会有人盯着你。你可以成为100%的自己。有很多课程，我们女孩间都是视频聊天或互相发短信。”

Marlborough School's Stuart Posin said partnering with Online School for Girls gives students opportunities they **otherwise** wouldn't have. "There are a lot of APs, a lot of STEM courses that we just don't have the interest or the mass of students to be able to **produce** those classes, and so by partnering with other schools around the nation and getting the best teachers around the nation, we're giving girls the opportunity they just otherwise wouldn't have."

参考译文

马尔伯勒学校学生斯图尔特·博赛因表示与在线女子学校合作为学生们提供了前所未有的机会。“有很多先修课程和STEM课程，之前由于没有学生有兴趣或学生数量不足而无法开设，现在通过与全国其他学校协作，获得全国最好的师资力量，我们给女孩们提供前所未有的机会。”

Brad Rathgeber, Executive Director for the Online School for Girls. "What we're trying to do in these single gender settings is really build an enormous amount of **confidence** in the girls so they can find great success they go onto college and beyond."

A single sex education is not what makes a student successful, though, says Diane Halpern of the Minerva Schools at Keck Graduate Institute. She spoke to VOA in a Skype interview. “Often people will point to **exemplary** single sex schools and say ’look here’s an example that it works,’ but they tend to be highly selective in terms of the students they admit. Parents are wealthier, especially in the U.S., where people have paid they tend to be very academically focused.”

参考译文

在线女子学校执行董事布拉德·拉特格博说道。“我们之所以尝试设置单性别学校是想要为这些女孩树立极大的信心，这样她们进入大学可以获得更大的成就。”

不过单性教育不会让一名学生取得成功，凯克研究所密涅瓦学校戴安·哈尔普恩说道。在通过Skype接受的采访时她对美国之音说道。“人们经常会指着某些模范单性别学校说‘看这里有一个运作良好的范例，’但是他们往往在招收学生时有很高的选择性。父母更为富裕，尤其是在美国，那些愿意花钱的人更关注学术。”

But there is growing interest in an all girls’ online school. Since it began five years ago, the Online School for Girls has seen an increase in **attendance**, and the number of high schools partnering with Online School for Girls has grown from 4 to 85. Rathgeber said his online girls’ school provides students with a strong sense of community that helps them learn.

参考译文

但人们对于所有女子在线学校的兴趣正在逐渐增加。从5年前开始，在线女子学校人数增加，而且与这种学校合作的高中数量已从4所增加到85所。拉特格博表示他的在线女子学校为学生提供了一种帮助自己学习的强烈社区意识。

"If you're creating a small cose knit community and you're trying to really bond students with their teachers and students with each other, gender can matter at some level. And we think we can create a learning environment that **capitalizes** on a single gender experience." Rathgeber is now working on building an online school for boys.

参考译文

"如果你希望创建一个紧密团结的社区并且你想真正让学生们，师生之间心连心，性别在某种程度上会至关重要。我们认为利用单性别经验可以创造这样的一种学习环境。"拉特格博现在的一所在线男子学校正在构建当中。

精彩解析

1. In addition to her classes in school, Green took an online Advanced Placement psychology course through Online School For Girls.

除了学校的课程之外，格林还进行在线女子学校上预修心理学课程的学习。

in addition to 除……之外，还……

例句 She gets various perquisites in addition to her wages.

她除工资以外，还有各种津贴。

2. ...but they tend to be highly selective in terms of the students they admit.

……但是他们往往在招收学生时有很高的选择性。

in terms of 依据，按照；在……方面

例句 In terms of law, they are equally authentic.

按照法律条款，它们具有同等的效力。

7 最新联合国报告显示小学教育不容乐观

A New UN Report Said Primary Education Isn't Optimistic (BBC News)

新闻导读

联合国教科文组织在教育领域的计划旨在实现所有级别持续一生的全民教育目标。事实上，教育对个人发展、经济增长和社会团结至关重要。这也是在与贫困做斗争和维持可持续发展中起决定性作用的一项工作。2000年在达喀尔（塞内加尔）举办的国际教育论坛为在实现这些目标方面取得进步制定了一个行动框架：加强对幼儿阶段的关注和教育；普及全民初级教育；增加年轻人和成年人的受教育机会；将成年文盲的比率减少一半；努力实现两性平等；在各个方面改善教育质量。在这些目标中，两个主要的、并且也是联合国千年发展目标中所包括的目标是：普及初级教育和消除两性间在受教育方面的不平等现象。正是在这个框架内拟订了教科文组织的中期战略（2002—2007年），战略所依据的三个主要目标是：增进教育这一基本人权；通过内容和方式的多样化改善教育质量；在这一领域促进试验、创新、公布、交流和分享数据及更好的方法，并且鼓励围绕教育政策进行对话。

新闻热词

selection [sɪ'lekʃn] *n.* 可供选择的事物；挑选出来的人或事

literacy ['lɪtərəsi] *n.* 读写能力，识字

motivate ['məʊtɪveɪt] v. 激发，激励
refuge ['refjuːdʒ] n. 避难（所），庇护（处）
vulnerable ['vʌlnərəbl] adj. 脆弱的，易受伤害的
numeracy ['njuːmərəsi] n. 识数，计算能力
challenge ['tʃæləndʒ] n. 挑战，难题
progress ['prəʊgres] n. 进步，前进
gender ['dʒendə(r)] n. 性，性别
massive ['mæsɪv] adj. 巨大的，庞大的
particularly [pə'tɪkjələli] adv. 特别地

新闻播报

This is Maddy Savage bringing you a **selection** of highlights from across BBC World Service News. Coming up, a new report says poor teaching is leaving hundreds of millions of children without basic maths and **literacy**. "Many teachers are highly **motivated** but they are not all to teach children how to read, for example, the right fundamentals of education system."

参考译文

我是麦蒂·萨维奇，通过BBC“全球服务”栏目，为您带来今天的新闻要点。这次新闻的主要内容有：一项新的调查报告显示，教学质量低下导致数亿儿童缺乏基本的算术和读写能力。“许多老师积极性都很高，但是并不是所有人都教会了孩子们最基本的东西，比如阅读。”

In his State of the Union address, President Obama warns congress, "I'm eager to work with all of you, but America does not stand still and neither will I." Also, Britain says it will give **refuge** to a few hundred of the most **vulnerable** people fleeing war in Syria. And why Emanuel Bach should be just as celebrated as his more famous father? "His music, I mean, it's... it's incredibly intellectual. It's human. It's, I mean it's just, it's incredible music."

参考译文

奥巴马在他的国情咨文演讲中这样警示国会："我热切希望与你们诸位合作，但是美国不会停滞不前，我也不会如此。"另外，英国表示将为叙利亚战争中逃亡的数百位最困难人员提供避难所。为什么伊曼纽尔·巴赫会和他知名度更高的父亲一样值得尊敬？"他的音乐，非常地有才华，有人情味，是非常棒的音乐。"

First, we start with that new UN report on education which is grim reading. It says at least a quarter of a billion children leave school without basic literacy and **numeracy** skills. And it says it will be another 70 years before all boys and girls all have access to primary education. The **challenges** for the poorest countries in Africa are especially tough. As a primary school teacher in a government school in Malawi has been explaining — "There are a lot of problems in most of our government schools because some of them still learn under trees, learning under trees where there are no desks in most schools in government."

参考译文

首先，我们来看一项新的联合国教育报告，这份报告着实令人担忧。报告显示，至少2.5亿儿童在不具备基本读写和算术能力的情况下离开了校园。而且，要让所有男孩和女孩都接受小学教育，还需要70年的时间。对于非洲最贫穷的国家来说，挑战尤为艰巨。一名马拉维的公立小学教师解释道。我们的公立小学还存在很多的问题，学生们仍然在大树下学习，大多数公立学校没有桌椅，学生们只能在大树下学习。

"Over the past decade we've actually seen great **progress** in getting more girls into school, so one of the success stories of education goals is actually narrowing of this **gender** gap. However, when we look at more details, we see that the poorest rural girls are far far behind. They are the ones that are really getting left behind. So on average in Africa, the poorest rural girls have spent about three years in school, compared to nine years for the richest urban boys. So it's a **massive** gap."

参考译文

"在过去的10年中，我们确实看到在女童入学方面巨大的进步，因此，性别差距的缩小是教育目标的成功案例之一。然而，经过仔细观察，我们发现，最贫困的农村女孩在这方面远远落后。她们是真正落后的人。在非洲，平均起来说，最贫困的农村女孩只有3年的学龄，而最富裕的城市男孩有9年学龄。所以说，这个差距不小。"

"So where are you talking about exactly?" "The biggest problem is in west African countries, in countries like Senegal and Mali and Burkina Faso and so on. These are countries that still need to make far more progress and **particularly** in getting more girls into school. We find that many teachers are highly motivated and they go into profession for the right reasons, but that they don't always have the skills that they need to do their job."

参考译文

"您说的具体是哪些地区？" "最大的问题出在西非国家，例如，塞内加尔、马里、布基纳法索，等等。这些国家仍然需要取得更大的进步，尤其是在女童入学方面。我们发现，许多老师积极性很高，从业动机也很端正，但是并不能够具备必要的工作技能。”

精彩解析

1. So on average in Africa, the poorest rural girls have spent about three years in school, compared to nine years for the richest urban boys.
在非洲，平均起来说，最贫困的农村女孩只有3年的学龄，而最富裕的城市男孩有9年学龄。

on average 平均起来

例句 On average he watches three movies a week.

他平均每周看三场电影。

2. The biggest problem is in west African countries, in countries like Senegal and Mali and Burkina Faso and so on.
最大的问题出在西非国家，例如，塞内加尔、马里、布基纳法索，等等。

and so on 等等，诸如此类

例句 This shop sells clothes, shoes, hats and so on.

这商店卖衣服、鞋、帽子等等。

读书笔记

8 让儿童爱上古典音乐

Getting Children Interested in Classical Music (BBC News)

新闻导读

古典音乐（classical music）是指那些从巴洛克时期开始一直到20世纪早期，在欧洲文化传统背景下创作的，有别于通俗和民族的经典音乐。它是一个独立的流派，艺术手法讲求洗练，追求理性地表达情感。广义的古典音乐是指西洋古典音乐，那些从西方中世纪开始至今的、在欧洲主流文化背景下创作的音乐；狭义的古典音乐是指古典主义音乐，是1750—1820年这一段时间的欧洲主流音乐，又称维也纳古典乐派。此乐派三位最著名的作曲家是海顿、莫扎特和贝多芬。事实上，很多西方古典音乐最早都是来自于为宗教仪式庆典而写的音乐。

欧洲古典音乐，不能不提到中世纪伊丽莎白时期，格里高利时期的音乐，其中，占主导地位的是宗教音乐。当时的人们对基督的信仰与崇拜，直接影响到了当时社会的政治与音乐，当时的音乐，只是纯粹的宗教用途，只限于在教堂中演唱，没有乐器，但是，却对今后的音乐发展起到了重要的作用。

新闻热词

ambitious [æm'bɪʃəs] adj. 有雄心的，有野心的；规模宏大的

initiative [ɪ'nɪʃətɪv] n. 积极的行动

launch [lɔːntʃ] v. 发动，开展

ambassador [æm'bæsədə(r)] n. 大使，使节

extraordinary [ɪk'strɔːdnri] adj. 非凡的，优秀的

specialist ['speʃəlɪst] n. 专家，行家

automatically [ˌɔːtə'mætɪkli] adv. 自动地，自然而然地

potential [pə'tenʃl] adj. 潜在的，有可能的

orchestra ['ɔːkɪstrə] n. 管弦乐队

trumpet ['trʌmpɪt] n. 小号，喇叭

concert ['kɒnsət] n. 音乐会

exciting [ɪk'saɪtɪŋ] adj. 使人兴奋的，令人激动的

choice [tʃɔɪs] n. 选择，选择权

engage [ɪn'geɪdʒ] v. 吸引（人），引起（注意、兴趣）

新闻播报

The BBC is launching an **ambitious** project to get Britain's children interested in classical music. They selected 10 pieces, some very well-know and some not so. And the **initiative** will be **launched** on October 6th. There will be cinema screening with workshops in schools, DVDs and so on. There will also be 10 pieces **ambassadors**. So what made her interested in classical music as a child?

参考译文

为增加英国儿童对古典音乐的兴趣，BBC正在筹备一个大型项目。该项目精选10出剧目，有非常著名的，也有鲜为人知的。项目启动时间为10月6日。届时将会有工作室在校园播放电影、DVD等，10部剧的代表也会出现。下面这位小女孩为何对古典音乐如此感兴趣呢？

I just knew that I love the sound of it. And it's just **extraordinary** to me. Is it true that music isn't widely taught in many British schools now?

I think it's not. I mean, an increasing number of schools in Britain don't have **specialist** music teachers any more. Music is not **automatically** part of the curriculum. And I think there is a bit of feeling among young people and indeed among some teachers that classical music is a bit dull and dry. So this project I think really does have the **potential** to excite people because it makes classical music seem incredibly exciting. The BBC has produced wonderful film, soundtrack provided by the BBC National **Orchestra** of Wales that can't help but bring young children, primary school children, age between 5 and 11 into the exciting world of fine music.

参考译文

我就是喜欢古典音乐的声音，因为它很特别。音乐课是不是在英国的学校不太普及?

我觉得是这样。英国许多学校都不再雇佣专业的音乐教师了，音乐课不再是课表上自动出现的课程。而且我觉得许多年轻人甚至一些老师都感觉到古典音乐有些乏味。所以我认为这个项目会让人激动，因为它使古典音乐变得激动人心。BBC已经剪辑出很棒的影片，BBC威尔士国家交响乐团提供了原声音乐，把5至11岁小学生带入激动人心的音乐世界。

And I think it is needed. Both of my young children play the **trumpet**, clarinet. But when you talk to them about classical music and I discuss this with them, they do think it's dull and you know, just jazz they want to play.

Or pop music. Yeah. And yet you know, we were talking on my

program this morning about first time that people went to a **concert** hall and heard a live orchestra. And I was saying I wish I could that experience again. I remember doing it when I was 7 or 8 and just being blown away by the sound of full scale hundred piece orchestra, exciting to watch as well as listen. So we can just get young people to get that experience, even if it's not first-hand. That's very exciting.

参考译文

我认为很有必要。我的两个小孩学在学习喇叭和单簧管，但讨论起古典音乐的时候，他们会觉得古典音乐很枯燥。他们只想玩爵士乐。

或者流行乐。是的。今天早上我们在节目中讨论起第一次去音乐厅听现场交响乐的感觉，我想说我希望再体验一次。我记得第一次听交响乐是在7、8岁的时候，当时就被百人交响乐的声音震撼了，那绝对是一场视听盛宴。所以我们可以让年轻人也拥有这样的体验，即使不是亲临现场。那是非常震撼的。

Let's hear some of the pieces then, some very well-known. That's great. That is **exciting**.

Well, absolutely. See, I think that's one of the things that makes it clear this is a project for British school children. It does have some very British things on it. Well, I guess it would be a very different top 10 list if it was being done in the United States, for example, where Bernstein or Copland might play a role in it. But I think they've come up with a great **choice** of 10 reflecting different ages, different musical styles. And there really is something I think for all children there to **engage** them with music.

参考译文

我们来听一下一些古典音乐的片段，其中一些非常著名。太棒了，非常激动人心。

确实。这也清楚地展现了我们的初衷，即这个项目是为英国学龄儿童准备的，它确实包含了一些英国特色的东西。我想，如果美国启动这一项目，那么他们的10佳剧目一定是不一样的，可能会包含伯恩斯坦和科普蓝。但是我觉得BBC选出的这10个剧目反映了不同的年代和不同的音乐风格，这些音乐里确实有些东西值得所有孩子欣赏和学习。

精彩解析

1. So what made her interested in classical music as a child?

下面这位小女孩为何对古典音乐如此感兴趣呢？

be interested in 对……感兴趣

例句 I am interested in playing basketball.

我对篮球运动感兴趣。

2. So we can just get young people to get that experience, even if it's not first-hand.

所以我们可以让年轻人也拥有这样的体验，即使不是亲临现场。

even if 即使，尽管

例句 I wouldn't lose courage even if I should fail ten times.

即使要失败十次，我也绝不灰心。

读书笔记

9 纽约画廊让学生实现梦想

New York's Art Galleries Make Students' Dream Come True (CNN News)

新闻导读

纽约现代艺术博物馆（The Museum of Modern Art），坐落在纽约市曼哈顿城中，位于曼哈顿第53街（在第五和第六大道之间），是当今世界最重要的现当代美术博物馆之一，与英国伦敦泰特美术馆、法国蓬皮杜国家文化和艺术中心等齐名。博物馆最初以展示绘画作品为主，后来展品范围渐渐扩大，包括雕塑、版画、摄影、印刷品、商业设计、电影、建筑、家具及装置艺术等项目。现在艺术品数量已达15万件之多。

纽约现代艺术博物馆（The Museum of Modern Art），在经过两年的休馆改建后，终于在2004年11月20日正式揭开它的面纱。由于大片落地窗的设计，自然光轻易地流进有着六层展览厅，高约 34 米的主展馆室内，而大量白墙的运用，更可让 MOMA 尽情地展示无价收藏。在二楼大厅，莫内的知名画作睡莲（Water Lilies）就在白墙上延伸超过 50 公尺，越往上层你将越被更壮观的艺术品所慑服，例如普普艺术家詹姆士·罗森奎斯特（James Rosenquist）在 1965 年的画作 F-111 战斗机（F-111 Fighter Jet）所占据的六楼白墙长度，又更甚于莫内的睡莲。现代艺术博物馆扩充了视觉和听觉的艺术表现，更积极投入艺术教育，它像是扩大的图书馆、档案室、阅览室、大讲堂、剧场、工作室，让艺术爱好者有更多的学习机会，如痴如醉地留连于如此多功能的空间中。

新闻热词

serious ['sɪəriəs] adj. 严重的，危急的

doodling ['duːdlɪŋ] n. 涂鸦

eventually [ɪ'ventʃuəli] adv. 终于，最后

discover [dɪ'skʌvə(r)] v. 发现

occasion [ə'keɪʒn] n. 时刻，时候，场合

confident ['kɒnfɪdənt] adj. 自信的，充满信心的

showcase ['ʃəʊkeɪs] v. 展示

contemporary [kən'temprəri] adj. 当代的，现代的

boldly ['bəʊldli] adv. 大胆地，显眼地

新闻播报

When he was a student in India, Adarsh Alphons got in some **serious** trouble for **doodling**. But he kept on drawing and **eventually** found himself commissioned to do a painting for Pope John Paul II. When he moved to New York, Alphons was trouble to find that almost 30 percent of public schools didn't have a full time art teacher. So, he opened up free classes.

参考译文

当他还是个印度的学生时，阿德斯·阿尔方斯就因为胡乱涂鸦惹上过不少麻烦事。但他继续作画，最终自己受到委托为教皇约翰·保罗二世作画。当他搬到纽约，在他发现近30%的公立学校没有全职美术老师后，他感到担忧。因此他开放了免费课程。

Art has a power to let children discover who they are. Every child needs to have a space for them to create.

When I moved to New York City, I noticed that access to our education was lacking. I decided we need to be the ones to put art in the hands of kids. We open our classes in public libraries that are near the schools that need us most.

参考译文

艺术能够让孩子们发现他们是谁。每个孩子都需要有一个创作的空间。

当我搬到纽约，我注意到我们缺乏相关的教育课程。我决定需要以我们之手让孩子们接受艺术教育。我们在学校附近最需要我们的公共图书馆开放我们的课程。

Our goal is not to create artists. Our goal is to let kids **discover** themselves.

I use art as an escape. I do look forward to coming here every week, and on most **occasions**, I persuade them to let us stay longer. See how you can take it, right?

After we bring art into their lives, they become more **confident**. The changes are quite remarkable. At the end of every semester, we **showcase** this students' artwork in **contemporary** art galleries in New York's art district.

参考译文

我们的目标不是创造艺术家。我们的目标是让孩子们发现自己。

我将艺术视为一种逃避。我期待每周来这里，而且在大多数情况下，我说服他们让我们呆更长时间。看看你如何处理，可以吗？

在我们把艺术带进他们的生活后，他们变得更加自信。变化非常显著。每学期结束时，我们在纽约的艺术区当代艺术画廊展示学生们的作品。

I tried to use water to make it darker and tuned for the water. When I saw my artwork in a real gallery, I feel proud of myself. That's amazing.

I hope it sets a spark that it's OK to chase after your dreams, but you should go after it **boldly** and fearlessly, and that anything is possible.

参考译文

我试图使用水表现使它变得更暗，所以使用了水。当我在一间真正的画廊看到我的作品，我为自己感到骄傲。这令人感到吃惊。

我希望这能够燃起火花，没问题，去追逐你的梦想，但你应该大胆、勇敢地追求，一切皆有可能。

精彩解析

1. Alphons was troubled to find that almost 30 percent of public schools didn't have a full time art teacher.

在他发现近30%的公立学校没有全职美术老师后，他感到担忧。

full time 专职，全部时间

例句 He has a full time job as a Chinese teacher.

他的专职工作是中文老师。

2. ...and on most occasions, I persuade them to let us stay longer.

……而且在大多数情况下，我说服他们让我们呆更长时间。

persuade sb. to 劝告某人……

例句 My husband persuaded me to come to the party.

我的丈夫劝我来参加聚会。

10 千禧一代担忧贷款债务

Millennials Worry About Their Loan Debts (CNN News)

新闻导读

美国最重要的助学贷款有两种：一种叫做帕金斯贷款助学金。这种贷款助学金直接来自于政府，而不是银行。学校拿到政府发放的资金后，贷款给家庭经济状况困难的学生。学生在校期间，政府支付利息，利率为5%。一个本科生总共可以借1.5万美元，研究生可以借3万美元。学生毕业9个月后开始还款，还款期限一般为10年。另一种叫做斯坦福贷学金，这是美国目前最盛行的助学贷款。斯坦福贷学金分两种形式：一种形式是资金直接来自于政府，政府承担风险；另一种形式是由银行或其他金融机构提供贷款，由州政府进行担保，联邦政府进行再担保。如果学生违约没有归还贷款，或者由于死亡、疾病等原因无法还贷，州政府和联邦政府将向银行赔付95%的拖欠贷款。这对银行来说是一颗定心丸。斯坦福贷学金的利率上限是8.25%，具体的利率都在每年7月1日根据当年中央银行的基础利率进行调整。由于美国过去几年一直降息，所以斯坦福贷学金的利率目前非常低，2004—2005年的利率是在校期间2.77%，毕业后3.37%。一个本科生最多可以借4.6万美元，一个研究生可借13.85万美元。学生从学校毕业6个月后开始还款，还款期限一般为10年，最长可以延长到30年。在取得斯坦福贷学金的学生中，家庭经济状况困难的学生还能得到政府的利息补贴，自己不用支付大学期间的贷款利息。

新闻热词

financial [faɪ'nænʃl] adj. 金融的，财务的

generation [ˌdʒenə'reɪʃn] n. 代，一代

millennial [mɪ'lenɪəl] adj. 一千年的

average ['ævərɪdʒ] adj. 通常的，普通的；平均的

reluctant [rɪ'lʌktənt] adj. 勉强的

purchase ['pɜːtʃəs] v. 购买，采购

payment ['peɪmənt] n. 付款，支付

basement ['beɪsmənt] n. 地下室

savvy ['sævi] adj. 有见识的，具有实际知识的；见识，悟性

customizable ['kʌstəmaɪzəbəl] adj. 可定制的

dramatically [drə'mætɪkli] adv. 戏剧性地，引人注目地；急剧地

tuition [tju'ɪʃn] n. 学费

新闻播报

Hope you had a great weekend. I'm Carl Azuz and I'm pumped to welcome you to the special edition of CNN STUDENT NEWS.

We're taking an in-depth look at the country's young labor force, its **financial** picture, its student loan debt, advice for when it comes time to look for a job in the online area. We've teamed with CNN Money to focus today's show on some of the financial challenges facing this newest **generation** of American workers.

参考译文

希望你周末过得愉快。我是卡尔·阿祖兹，欢迎收看本期特别版的CNN学生新闻。

我们正深入了解这个国家现在的年轻劳动力，关注他们的财务状况，学生贷款债务并且为互联网时代找工作的人提出建议。我们联手CNN金融栏目关注美国年轻一代劳动力所面临的金融难题。

A good place to start is to define. We're talking about people born in the 1980s and 1990s. It's time to meet the **millennials**.

Hey, millennials. What makes you so special anyway? Well, for starters, that generation is the biggest in American history. There are at least 80 million people age 18 to 35. They're the most educated generation ever and they have the student loan debt to show for it. The **average** student loan balance for someone under 30 years old, more than $21,000.

I currently have $46,000 in debt. I have about $54,000. $95,000 in student debt. Scarred by the Great Recession, millennials have been **reluctant** to buy a house. I don't think I plan to buy a home at any point. Never occurred to me that I would **purchase** a home. I really believe in a sharing economy.

参考译文

我们首先从定义开始。我们正在谈论的是20世纪80年代及90代出生的人，他们正是千禧一代。

嘿，千禧一代，是什么让你们如此特别呢？嗯，首先，这一代有着美国历史上最大的人数。18至35岁至少有8 000万人。他们是受教育最多的一代，而且身上有学生贷款的债务。30岁以下的平均学生贷款额为21 000多美元。

我现在身背46 000美元的债务。我的债务大约是54 000美元。我的债务是95 000美元。受大萧条影响，千禧一代们一直不愿买房子。我在任何时候都没打算买房。我从来没想过会买一套房子。我真地相信分享型经济。

Thirty percent still living with their parents, but most millennials say they want to buy and some are starting to take the plunge.

My goal for a down **payment** is $20,000, and I'm actually achieving that goal and I'm going to get there quicker than I actually thought.

Living in the mom and dad's **basement** means fewer millennials are tying the knot. Their parents probably got married in their early 20s. This generation, 30 is the new normal. And they're waiting to have kids, too.

I don't want to bring a child into the world until, you know, I know that I can afford that.

参考译文

30%的人仍与父母同住，但大多数千禧一代表示他们想买房，而且有些人正开始冒这个风险。

我的目标首付是20 000美元。我会达成这一目标而且会比自己所预期的更早实现。

在父母地下室居住意味着很少有千禧一代步入婚姻的殿堂。他们的父母可能在20岁出头的时候就已经结婚。这一代30岁是新常态。而且他们也在翘首期盼要个孩子。

我不想要孩子，你知道，直到我具有一定的经济能力才行。

Millennials are the first generation born online.They're tech **savvy**, which makes them quick learners and smart shoppers.But they care about much more than just the bottom line. So, companies have to adjust to make their products more sustainable, higher quality and **customizable**. That's what millennials want.

The ethics are very important to me.I'm looking for authenticity. It's good to know that it will go to a good cause if it goes to a good company.

Ready or not, millennials are **dramatically** changing expectations and shaping the world.

参考译文

千禧一代是互联网时代出生的第一代人。他们精通技术，很快能够掌握各种技能而且是购物高手，但他们关心的不仅仅是这些基本问题。因此各大公司必须调整使自家的产品更持续、质量更高及能够定制。这才是千禧一代想要的。

道德对我来说至关重要。我在寻找真实。很高兴知道如果去一家不错的公司供职的话会有份不错的事业。

不管你是否准备好，千禧一代正极大颠覆人们的观念及改变这个世界。

OK. You just heard it, the average student loan balance for millennials, saving lost in the Great Recession, a weak job market for young people, the cost of college, these are some reasons why students have loan debt.

According to the College Board, the average **tuition** and fees for a public four-year college in America, more than $9,000 a year for in-state students, $23,000 a year for out of state students. Average tuition at a private school, more than $31,000 a year.How much money college students borrowed depends, but they are expected to pay it back.

参考译文

好的。你刚刚听到过关于千禧一代的报道，这一代的平均学生贷款余额，拯救陷入大萧条的人们，对于年轻人疲软的就业市场，大学的费用，这是一些学生贷款债务的理由。

大学理事会显示美国公立4年制大学州内学生的平均学费和费用

每年超过9 000美元，州外学生每年23 000美元。而对于私立学校而言，平均学费每年超过31 000美元。大学生借多少钱视情况而写，但他们预期会偿还。

精彩解析

1. We're taking an in-depth look at the country's young labor force…
我们正深入了解这个国家现在的年轻劳动力……

labor force 劳动力

例句 The farm labor force is running down steadily.

农场里的劳动力在不断减少。

2. Well, for starters, that generation is the biggest in American history.
首先，这一代有着美国历史上最大的人数。

for starters 首先，一开始

例句 For starters, he didn't consider himself an intellectual.

首先，他并没有把自己当成一个知识分子。

3. But they care about much more than just the bottom line.
但他们关心的不仅仅是这些基本问题。

bottom line 底线，最低条件

例句 She says £95,000 is her bottom line.

她说95 000英镑是她的底线。

读书笔记

读书笔记

科技前沿

1 VR头显或成未来手机市场主流配置

Virtual Reality Goggles May Be Next Must-Have (VOA News)

新闻导读

虚拟现实头戴式显示设备，简称VR头显，是一种利用头戴式显示设备将人的对外界的视觉、听觉封闭，引导用户产生一种身在虚拟环境中的感觉。其显示原理是左右眼屏幕分别显示左右眼的图像，人眼获取这种带有差异的信息后在脑海中产生立体感。一般来说，VR头显可分为三类：外接式头显、一体式头显、手机盒子头显。一体式头显，无需借助任何输入输出设备就可以在虚拟的世界里尽情感受3D立体感带来的视觉冲击。手机盒子头显，结构简单、价格低廉，只要放入手机即可观看，使用方便。

新闻热词

subscriber [səb'skraɪbə(r)] *n.* 消费者；用户

manufacturer [ˌmænju'fæktʃərə(r)] *n.* 生产商；制造商

differentiate [ˌdɪfə'renʃieɪt] *v.* 区分；区别；辨别

touchscreen [tʌtʃɪzk'riːn] *n.* 触摸屏

modular ['mɒdjələ(r)] *adj.* 组合式的；模块化的

assortment [ə'sɔːtmənt] *n.* 各式各样；五颜六色；什锦

function ['fʌŋkʃn] *n.* 功能；作用

gigabyte ['gɪgəbaɪt] *n.* 千兆字节

potentially [pə'tenʃəli] *adv.* 潜在地；可能地

goggles ['gɒglz] n. 护目镜

mingle ['mɪŋgl] v. 应酬；交际

connectivity [ˌkɒnek'tɪvɪti] n. 连接性；连通性

satellite ['sætəlaɪt] n. 卫星；人造卫星

consumer [kən'sjuːmə(r)] n. 消费者，顾客

headset ['hedset] n.（头戴式）耳机，耳麦

新闻播报

The real-time counter on the GSMA Intelligence website shows the constant rise of mobile phone **subscribers** worldwide. The market is huge and there's plenty of money to be made, but there's a design challenge for **manufacturers**.

"How do you **differentiate** a rectangular block with a **touchscreen**, a battery and a camera? And what we've seen at Mobile World Congress is some of the manufacturers addressing that with some of the launches they've delivered."

参考译文

GSMA移动智库上的实时统计显示，全球的移动手机用户数量在持续增加。虽然市场很大，也有很多盈利的空间，但制造商也同时面临着设计方面的挑战。

“你会怎样通过触摸屏、电池、摄像头来区分不同手机的呢？我们在世界移动通信大会上，看到一些制造商展示了自己推出的一些产品，解决了这一问题。”

For Sony, it's all about the camera. Its Xperia X phone has a camera that is ready to take a picture in less than 0.6 second. LG's new G5 has a **modular** design and an **assortment** of attachments that add battery life and upgrade the phone's camera **function**. Samsung's Galaxy the S7 has a larger battery, and you can add memory as much as 200 **gigabytes**. But these gadgets cost a lot, so manufacturers in China and India are coming out with cheaper smartphones.

参考译文

索尼专注于做手机的摄像头。它的Xperia X款手机的摄像头照相仅需不到0.6秒。LG新出的G5配有标准化设计和各种附件，以延长电池寿命并升级手机的摄像头功能。三星的Galaxy S7则是电池更大，能增加10亿字节的记忆存储。上述配件的成本都很高，所以中国和印度的制造商开始生产成本更低的智能手机。

"We are seeing a swing from developed markets to developing markets. So, more Chinese brands. More Indian brands. And I think, **potentially**, also more African brands in the future, as well."

But with cameras that can shoot 360 degrees, another opportunity is opening up: virtual reality. Samsung is already pairing its phone with VR **goggles**.

参考译文

"我们看到市场开始从发达国家的市场转向了发展中国家的市场。我是说，越来越多的中国手机品牌和印度手机品牌。而且我预测，未来也会有更多的非洲品牌出现。"

不过，能进行360° 无死角拍摄的摄像头的出现为我们打开一个新的契机：虚拟现实。三星已经在为手机配置相应的头显了。

"These are the devices that are going to generate loads of content, and user-generated content is going to be key to driving the market."

Manufacturers are hoping that, very soon, almost everybody will want a set of VR goggles for gaming, exploring distant places or

mingling with friends and family who are not physically present. And **connectivity** may soon be available to new areas.

参考译文

“这些部件能产生很多信息，而从客户产生出来的信息对于推动市场具有重要意义。”

制造商希望，不出多久，每个人都能人手一套VR头显来玩游戏、探索遥远地带、跟不在身边的朋友和家人相聚。这些新领域的连通性将很快得以实现。

“We are, this year, going to launch our first **satellite** over Africa in order to be able to work with operators to extend connectivity and beam down Internet there.”

CCS Insight predicts that by the end of this year, **consumers** will buy as many as 13 million virtual reality **headsets**.

参考译文

“今年，我们将会向非洲上空发射第一颗卫星，这样我们就能跟运营商合作，扩展非洲的连通性，让非洲的互联网发达起来。”

市场研究机构CCS Insight预测，今年年底之前，VR头显的购买量将高达1 300万。

精彩解析

1. LG’s new G5 has a modular design and an assortment of attachments that add battery life and upgrade the phone’s camera function.
LG新出的G5配有标准化设计和各种附件，以延长电池寿命并升级手机的摄像头功能。

modular design 模块化设计，标准设计

例句 The platform is built by a modular design, with good reusability.

该平台采用模块化设计方法，具有良好的复用性。

an assortment of 各式各样的

例句 There's an assortment of jewelry there.

那里有各式各样的首饰。

2. Samsung is already pairing its phone with VR goggles.
三星已经在为手机配置相应的头显了。

pair with 与……配对

例句 The parents finally agreed to pair their daughter with that young man.

父母最终同意女儿同那位年轻人结婚。

3. …almost everybody will want a set of VR goggles for gaming, exploring distant places or mingling with friends and family who are not physically present.
……每个人都能人手一套VR头显来玩游戏、探索遥远地带、跟不在身边的朋友和家人相聚。

mingle with 参加，加入（某团体）

例句 One of the hostess's duties is to mingle with the guests.

女主人的职责之一是与客人们交际。

美国助力亚美尼亚IT行业发展

U.S.-Armenia IT Cooperation (VOA News)

新闻导读

亚美尼亚共和国，通称亚美尼亚（The Republic of Armenia），是一个位于亚洲与欧洲交界处的外高加索地区的共和制国家。亚美尼亚近十多年来，IT行业发展非常快。2008年至2010年亚美尼亚IT业收入达到1.5亿美元，增长15.6%。2011年，亚美尼亚IT公司年营业额达2亿美元。IT行业从业人员将近5 500人，如果加上电信公司工作人员则总数超过1万人。目前，亚美尼亚共有197家IT企业，其中72家是外资公司。IT业的收入的61.2%来自外资公司。亚美尼亚IT业的收入主要来自软件设计、服务外包和网络服务。

新闻热词

support [sə'pɔːt] v. 支持；帮助

premise ['premɪs] n. 前提

specialist ['speʃəlɪst] n. 专家；行家

strengthen ['streŋθn] v. 加强，巩固

potential [pə'tenʃl] adj. 潜在的；可能的

collaboration [kəˌlæbə'reɪʃn] n. 合作，协作

representative [ˌreprɪ'zentətɪv] n. 代表；代理人

faculty ['fæklti] n.（大学、学院或院系的）全体教员

modernize ['mɒdənaɪz] v. 使现代化

artificial [ˌɑːtɪ'fɪʃl] *adj.* 人造的
priority [praɪ'ɒrəti] *n.* 优先，优先权
establishment [ɪ'stæblɪʃmənt] *n.* 成立；建立
capstone ['kæpstəʊn] *n.* （尤指成就的）顶点

新闻播报

The Innovative Solutions and Technologies Center, or ISTC has been **supporting** the development of Armenia's information technology sector since 2014. It recently opened a new 1,000 square-meter state-of-the-art **premises** on the Yerevan State University campus.

参考译文

自2014年以来，创新方案和技术中心就一直在支持亚美尼亚IT行业的发展。最近，创新方案和技术中心又在埃里温国立大学校园内新开设了一个占地1 000平方米的先进事务所。

The ISTC—a joint project of the Government of Armenia, the Enterprise Incubator Foundation, IBM, USAID, and Yerevan State University—helps meet the demand for quality **specialists** to work in Armenia's IT sector. ISTC will help develop and **strengthen** the education and research **potential** of Armenian universities in the areas of IT and hi-tech.

参考译文

创新方案和技术中心是由亚美尼亚政府、企业孵化器基金会、IBM、美国国际开发署和埃里温国立大学联合创办的项目，该项目助力满足有意愿在亚美尼亚IT行业发展的优质专家的工作要求。创新方案和技术中心将会助力发展并加强亚美尼亚各所大学在IT和高

技术领域的教研潜力。

“I am proud of the fact that this uniquely designed partnership promotes the education of one of Armenia’s most valuable resources—its youth. The **collaboration** between the private sector and universities creates economic opportunities for younger generations of Armenia,” said U.S. Ambassador to Armenia Richard Mills, who was joined at the opening of the new facility by more than 100 Armenian tech and business **representatives**.

参考译文

“我很骄傲地看到，这一设计别出心裁的合作项目提升了为亚美尼亚最宝贵的资源之一——年轻人提升了教育。私企与大学之间的合作为亚美尼亚的青年一代创造了许多经济机会，”美国驻亚美尼亚大使理查德·米尔斯说。理查德和100多名亚美尼亚科技领域和商圈代表共同参加了新事务所的开幕式。

The ISTC serves students and university **faculty**, providing them with the latest hardware and software for training and research. Since the project’s launch, the ISTC has already assisted more than 100 professors from nine major Armenian universities to improve their training courses. Thanks to these efforts, more than 1,500 students already received training through 30 **modernized** curricula in the areas of **artificial** intelligence, business process management, cloud computing, and cyber security among others.

参考译文

创新方案和技术中心为大学师生服务，为他们提供最新的硬件和软件设施，以供其进行培训和研究。自创新方案和技术中心的项目创建伊始，该项目已协助亚美尼亚9个主要高校的100多名教授提升了其培训课程。正是由于上述努力，1 500多名学生已经接受到了30个现代化课程的培训内容，具体领域如：人工智能、业务流程管理、云计算、网络安全等。

Supporting the development of Armenia's IT sector has long been a **priority** of the U.S., Ambassador Mills said. "USAID support to the IT sector began a decade ago. Since that time, USAID has played an important role in laying the foundation for a strong and vibrant IT sector in Armenia," he said during the opening.

"We see the **establishment** of the Innovative Solutions and Technologies Center as a **capstone** achievement in our efforts to partner with you to develop and strengthen IT in Armenia."

参考译文

长期以来，支持亚美尼亚IT行业的发展都是美国的首要任务之一，大使米尔斯说。"美国国际开发署早在10年前就开始支持其IT行业了。从那时候起，美国国际开发署就一直在为打造强大而又有活力的亚美尼亚IT业基础方面起到了重要的作用，"米尔斯在开幕式上说。

"我们将创新方案和技术中心项目的创立视为我们与亚美尼亚合作以发展并壮大其IT业的巅峰成就。"

精彩解析

1. The ISTC—a joint project of the Government of Armenia, the Enterprise Incubator Foundation, IBM, USAID, and Yerevan State University—helps meet the demand for quality specialists to work in Armenia's IT sector.

   创新方案和技术中心是由亚美尼亚政府、企业孵化器基金会、IBM、美国国际开发署和埃里温国立大学联合创办的项目，该项目助力满足有意愿在亚美尼亚IT行业发展的优质专家的工作要求。

   meet the demand 满足需要，符合要求

例句 We will never have enough resources to meet the demand.

我们永远都不会有足够的资源来满足需求。

2. Thanks to these efforts, more than 1, 500 students already received training through 30 modernized curricula…

正是由于上述努力，1 500多名学生已经接受到了30个现代化课程的培训内容……

thanks to 幸亏，多亏，由于

例句 Thanks to your help, we were successful.

由于你的帮助，我们得以成功。

3. Since that time, USAID has played an important role in laying the foundation for a strong and vibrant IT sector in Armenia.

从那时候起，美国国际开发署就一直在为打造强大而又有活力的亚美尼亚IT业基础方面起到了重要的作用。

lay the foundation 奠基，打基础

例句 Medical consumables lay the foundation for clinical diagnosis and treatment.

医用耗材是医院医疗诊治工作的物质基础。

3 1.7亿年前的海洋鱼龙骨架

The Skeleton of Sea Monster with 170 Million Years Old (VOA News)

新闻导读

鱼龙是一种类似鱼和海豚的大型海栖爬行动物。它们生活在中生代的大多数时期，最早出现于约2.5亿年前，比恐龙稍微早一点（2.3亿年前），约9 000万年前它们消失，比恐龙灭绝早约2 500万年。有些鱼龙身体十分渺小，但还有些鱼龙身体很大。

鱼龙的起源，当前尚缺少可靠的线索，已知最早的早三叠世晚期的化石，就已高度地特化。因此它们的祖先应出如今三叠纪以前。由形态构造推测，鱼龙可能起源于杯龙类。侏罗纪的鱼龙属（ichthyosaurus）是典型的鱼龙。它们的外形酷似一些大型快速游泳的鱼类，纺锤形的身体，皮肤裸露，三角形的头向前伸出似剑的长吻，嘴内长满锥状的牙齿，牙齿有迷路构造。鱼龙类的身躯构造说明，它们完全失去了上陆的能力。关于鱼龙的生殖方式，当前多认为属卵胎生。

新闻热词

discover [dɪ'skʌvə(r)] v. 发现
paleontologist [pælɪɒn'tɒlədʒɪst] n. 古生物学者
skeleton ['skelɪtn] n. 骨架；骨骼
ichthyosaur ['ɪkθɪəsɔːə] n. 鱼龙
reptile ['reptaɪl] n. 爬行动物

squid [skwɪd] n. 乌贼，墨鱼

ecosystem ['iːkəʊsɪstəm] n. 生态系统

spectacular [spek'tækjələ(r)] adj. 引人注目的；惊人的；壮观的

dinosaurs ['daɪnəsɔː(r)] n. 恐龙

capture ['kæptʃə(r)] v. 俘虏，擒获，占领，夺取

eventually [ɪ'ventʃuəli] v. 最后，终于

新闻播报

The bones of the sea monster are 170 million years old and were **discovered** in Scotland's Isle of Skye. **Paleontologists** are excited by the almost-complete **skeleton**.

"There's over 100 bones there, so a whole bunch of the skeleton, and now we get to get down to the fun business of actually studying it, figuring out what it is," said Stephen Brusatte, a paleontologist at the University of Edinburgh.

参考译文

从这只海兽的骨架来看，应该有1.7亿年历史了，是在苏格兰的天空岛（Isle of Skye）发现的。古生物学家被为具近乎完整的骨架所震惊。

"这具骨架有100多根骨头，也就是说，整个骨架完好无损。那么我们现在就要真的开始着手研究它，看看它是怎么回事了"，斯蒂芬·布鲁萨特如是说道。斯蒂芬是爱丁堡大学的古生物学家。

What the scientists do know is that the sea monster is more than 4 meters long. It is from a class of ancient marine creatures called **ichthyosaurs**, which resembled dolphins. The **reptile** could swim fast, and with its hundreds of cone-shaped teeth, fed on fish and **squid**.

The scientists hope to gain a better understanding about the creature's **ecosystem** and more about the Middle Jurassic period that lasted from about 160 to 180 million years ago. Since so few fossils have been discovered from that age, the sea monster is a **spectacular** find.

参考译文

这些科学家目前确凿可知的是，这头海兽有4米多长，属于一种名为鱼龙的古代海洋生物，类似海豚。这类爬行动物游速很快，因为有成百上千颗圆锥形牙齿，并且以普通鱼类和鱿鱼为食。

科学家希望更好地理解鱼龙的的生态系统以及中侏罗纪时期也就是1.6亿-1.8亿年前的情况。由于中侏罗纪时期的化石比较罕见，所以该鱼龙骨架的发现十分喜人。

"It's one of the only good skeletons of one of these ocean reptiles from the middle part of the Jurassic Period. This was a time that was a really interesting moment in evolution. You had all kinds of new groups of **dinosaurs** and ocean reptiles getting their start, starting to spread around the world," said Brusatte.

Like other ichthyosaurs, this sea monster faded into extinction 95 million years ago, about 30 million years before the dinosaurs disappeared.

参考译文

"这是中侏罗纪时期海洋爬行动物中所存不多的完好骨架。这段时期是进化史上十分有趣的点，因为这段时期中，各种恐龙和海洋爬行动物的新群体都开始衍生，并分布全球"，布鲁萨特如是说道。

不过，这头骨架的主人和其他鱼龙一样，也在9 500万年前灭绝，比全部恐龙的灭绝时间早3 000万年。

"It looks like it was changes in the oceans, in the chemistry and in the ecology of the oceans, and so you had a long-term willowing away of these ichthyosaurs as they became less and less common, less and less diverse, until they trickled away to extinction, and then that is when groups like sharks and ultimately whales and dolphins moved on in," said the paleontologist.

Sea monsters have often **captured** people's imaginations. The skeleton of this one will **eventually** be put on display for the public to see.

参考译文

"好像是由于海洋发生了很多变化，比如海洋的化学和生态发生了变化，于是在很长一段时间内，这种鱼龙逐渐消失，越来越不常见，种类越来越少，直到一点点灭绝。而鲨鱼以及后来的鲸鱼等生物群体也正是在这个时候出现"，史蒂芬说道。

海兽总是能激发人们的联想。这只鱼龙的骨架最终将为公众展示。

精彩解析

1. There's over 100 bones there, so a whole bunch of the skeleton, and now we get to get down to the fun business of actually studying it, figuring out what it is.

   这具骨架有100多根骨头，也就是说，整个骨架完好无损。那么我们现在就要真的开始着手研究它，看看它是怎么回事了。

   get down to 开始干，着手做

   例句 Let's get down to the specifics.

   我们下面谈谈具体的吧。

   figure out 弄明白；解决

   例句 I simply couldn't figure out his intention.

   我简直揣摩不透他的用意。

2. The skeleton of this one will eventually be put on display for the public to see.
   这只鱼龙的骨架最终将为公众展示。

   put on display 展出；展览

   例句 The birds were put on display at the zoological society.

   这些鸟类在动物协会展出。

可喷涂太阳能电池或能代替硅基太阳能板

Paintable Solar Cells May Someday Replace Silicon-Based Panels (VOA News)

新闻导读

太阳能电池又称为“光电池”，是一种利用太阳光直接发电的光电半导体薄片。它只要被光照到，瞬间就可输出电压及在有回路的情况下产生电流。在物理学上称为太阳能光伏（Photovoltaic，缩写为PV），简称光伏。太阳能电池主要是以半导体材料为基础，其工作原理是利用光电材料吸收光能后发生光电转换反应，根据所用材料的不同，太阳能电池可分为：①硅太阳能电池；②以无机盐如砷化镓III-V化合物、硫化镉、铜铟硒等多元化合物为材料的电池；③功能高分子材料制备的太阳能电池；④纳米晶太阳能电池等。

许多国家正在制订中长期太阳能开发计划，准备在21世纪大规模开发太阳能，美国能源部推出的是国家光伏计划，日本推出的是阳光计划。NREL光伏计划是美国国家光伏计划的一项重要的内容，该计划在单晶硅和高级器件、薄膜光伏技术、PVMaT、光伏组件以及系统性能和工程、光伏应用和市场开发等5个领域开展研究工作。

新闻热词

photovoltaic [fəʊtəʊvɒl'teɪɪk] adj. 光电池的

cadmium ['kædmiəm] n. 镉

inorganic [ˌɪnɔː'gænɪk] adj. 无机的

efficiency [ɪ'fɪʃnsi] n. 效率，效能
synthesize ['sɪnθəsaɪz] v. 合成，综合
nanocrystal ['nænəʊkrɪstl] n. 纳米晶体
solvent ['sɒlvənt] n. 溶剂
substance ['sʌbstəns] n. 物质，材料
parallel ['pærəlel] n. 平行，平行线 adj. 平行的，并列的
research [rɪ'sɜːtʃ] n. 研究，探究

新闻播报

Rapidly expanding solar cell technology currently relies on expensive **photovoltaic** materials such as silicon or **cadmium** telluride, which is why their production, installation and maintenance costs are still high.

Troy Townsend, an assistant professor of chemistry at St. Mary's College in St. Mary's City, Maryland, says less efficient but much cheaper **inorganic** materials could be used to create paintable solar cells.

参考译文

迅速发展的太阳能电池技术现在依靠如硅或者碲化镉等昂贵的光伏材料，这就是它们的相关产品，安装及保养维护费用持续高居不下的原因。

圣玛丽大学的助理教授特里·特温斯德表示低效但价格却非常低廉的无机材料可以用来制造可上漆的太阳能电池。

To make up for the low **efficiency**, this less expensive material may be used to cover large surfaces, such as the roofs of entire communities.

"Typically, silicon solar cells are between 16 and 18 percent efficient," Townsend said. "There have been some commercially available cadmium telluride solar cells, from First Solar, that have gotten up to 20 percent. Our devices right now are between 5 and 12 percent."

参考译文

为了弥补效能方面的不足，这种材料可用于覆盖比如整个社区屋顶等的大型表面。

“一般而言，硅太阳能电池的效能在16%至18%之间。”特温斯德说，“现在还可以找到First Solar公司的碲化镉太阳能电池，能够将效能提高到20%。我们现在的设备的效能是在5%至12%之间。”

The photovoltaic material can be **synthesized** by mixing **nanocrystals** with organic **solvents**. "All these layers we all have been able to produce as an ink. They can be printed, sprayed or spin-coated to make an entire device fully solution-processed."

参考译文

光伏材料是通过混合纳米晶体和有机溶剂而合成。“所有这些涂层可以做成油墨，它们可以印刷、喷涂或进行旋涂使整个设备完全经过溶液化处理。”

Once deposited on a suitable surface, such as glass, the photosensitive layers have to be heated, together with an agent. Instead of commonly used highly toxic **substances**, Townsend discovered that it can be done with nontoxic salts.Individual cells can be connected in series or **parallel** to build up either voltage or current.Townsend hopes that someday, solar arrays may become much more affordable for individual users.

参考译文

一旦被附着在如玻璃等的适当表面上，光伏涂层会连同一种媒介一起被加热。而且特温斯德发现可以使用无毒的盐来替代通常使用的剧毒性物质。单个电池可以通过串联或并联的方式形成电压或电流。特温斯德希望未来个人用户能够负担得起太阳能电池阵。

"The goal of this is to be able to put this in the hands of an average, everyday person," he said. "They have all the tools they need to build these devices in their home kitchen." He is also confident that further **research** will lead to the increased efficiency of paintable solar cells.

参考译文

"太阳能电池阵的目标就是每个普通人都能使用。"他说，"他们的家庭厨房中便有能建造这些设备的所有工具。"他同样相信更为深入的研究将会带来更高效率的可喷涂太阳能电池。

精彩解析

1. To make up for the low efficiency, this less expensive material may be used to cover large surfaces, such as the roofs of entire communities.
   为了弥补效能方面的不足，这种材料可用于覆盖比如整个社区屋顶等的大型表面。

   make up for 补偿，弥补

   例句 We'd better make up for the lost time.

   我们最好是弥补一下失去的时间。

2. Instead of commonly used highly toxic **substances**, Townsend discovered that it can be done with nontoxic salts.
   而且特温斯德发现可以使用无毒的盐来替代通常使用的剧毒性物质。

instead of 用……代替，用……而不用……

例句 Shall we have vegetables instead of meat today?

今天我们不吃肉吃蔬菜好吗？

读书笔记

5 第一辆自动驾驶卡车现身欧洲高速公路

First Self-Driving Truck Debuts on European Highways (VOA News)

新闻导读

自动驾驶汽车（Autonomous vehicles）又称无人驾驶汽车、电脑驾驶汽车或轮式移动机器人，是一种通过电脑系统实现无人驾驶的智能汽车。自动驾驶汽车技术的研发，在20世纪也已经有数十年的历史，于21世纪初呈现出接近实用化的趋势，比如，谷歌自动驾驶汽车于2012年5月获得了美国首个自动驾驶车辆许可证，预计于2015年至2017年进入市场销售。

自动驾驶汽车依靠人工智能、视觉计算、雷达、监控装置和全球定位系统协同合作，让电脑可以在没有任何人类主动的操作下，自动安全地操作机动车辆。德国老牌汽车厂商梅赛德斯-奔驰2014年10月曾在德国汉诺威举办的“IAA商用车博览会”（IAA Commercial Vehicles expo）中展示了一款重型自动驾驶概念卡车“Future Truck 2025”。该公司相信，这一概念设计将最终有可能帮助减少每年高速公路意外事故的发生。

新闻热词

division [dɪ'vɪʒn] n. 部门

passenger ['pæsɪndʒə(r)] n. 乘客，旅客

autonomous [ɔː'tɒnəməs] adj. 自治的

steering ['stɪərɪŋ] n. 转向装置

premiere ['premieə(r)] n. 首次露面

monitor ['mɒnɪtə(r)] v. 监控，监视

radar ['reɪdɑː(r)] n. 雷达

sensor ['sensə(r)] n. 传感器，感应器

automatically [ˌɔːtə'mætɪklɪ] adv. 自动地；自觉地

initial [ɪ'nɪʃl] adj. 最初的；开始的

新闻播报

The new 430-horsepower truck, loaded with 40 tons of cargo, slowly pulled out of the parking lot in Stuttgart, driven by the head of Daimler's trucks and buses **division**, Wolfgang Bernhard.

Chatting with him in the **passenger** seat was Winfred Kretschmann, the prime minister of Baden-Wuerttemberg, the first German state to issue a license for **autonomous** trailer-trucks.

参考译文

这辆载着40吨货物马力达到430的卡车缓缓驶出斯图加特的停车场。手握方向盘的则是戴姆勒公司卡车及巴士部门的负责人沃尔夫冈·伯恩哈德。

坐在副驾驶席和他谈话的则是巴登-符腾堡州总理温弗雷德·克利茨曼。这里是德国颁发自动驾驶拖挂卡车执照的第一个州。

Once on the highway, the driver lets the truck take over the **steering**, said Wolfgang Bernhard of the Daimler Trucks and Buses Division.

"If I press this button now, we are on the road and we have actually begun the world **premiere**," he said. "Shall we do it, prime minister?" "Let's do it."

参考译文

一旦上了高速公路，驾驶员就交由卡车自行驾驶，戴姆勒公司卡车及巴士部门的负责人沃尔夫冈·伯恩哈德说。

“我按下这个按钮，这辆卡车的世界首秀就开始了。总理，我们开始吗？” “开始吧。”

Soon, the truck was self-driving down the busy A8 highway, near Stuttgart, at 80 kilometers per hour, followed by a car with cameras and, just in case, a police car.

That doesn't mean the driver can zone out, there are strict rules for the person behind the wheel, said Bernhard.

"I'm not allowed to turn around," he added. "I'm not allowed to turn to the side because I have to continue to **monitor** the traffic situation. But I can take my hands off the wheel and, as you can see, the steering is smooth and the vehicle remains on track."

参考译文

不久这辆卡车就以每小时80公里的速度驶入了斯图加特附近繁忙的A8号高速公路，后面还跟有一辆摄像用车，以防万一还有一辆警车。

这并不意味着驾驶员可以走神，对于驾驶者而言有一套严格的规定。

“我不能回头。也不可以走神，必须时刻关注路况。但我的手可以离开方向盘，就像你看到的这样，这辆车仍然走得很稳。”

A **radar** and a number of video cameras and **sensors** constantly monitor the road conditions. In adverse situations the truck will ask the driver to take over and, if he does not, it will **automatically** slow to a stop.

Daimler says its advanced trucks will relieve the drivers from the strain of driving on monotonous stretches of the road and in stop-and-go traffic jams.

The company hopes necessary laws permitting such operations elsewhere could be passed before the **initial** goal of 2020.

参考译文

雷达以及一系列摄像头和感应器都在密切监测路况。如果出现状况，方向盘会交由驾驶员进行控制，要是他没有接手，车辆就会自动慢慢停下来。

戴姆勒公司称这款拥有先进技术的卡车能够解放司机，让他们摆脱长时间单调开车及交通拥堵时一走一停的烦恼。

这家公司希望在2020年初步目标达成之前，其它州也能通过必要法律允许这种卡车上路。

精彩解析

1. The new 430-horsepower truck, loaded with 40 tons of cargo, slowly pulled out of the parking lot in Stuttgart.
   这辆载着40吨货物马力达到430的卡车缓缓驶出斯图加特的停车场。

   load with 使装满

   例句 They loaded the ship with coal.

   他们把煤装上船。

2. Once on the highway, the driver lets the truck take over the steering.
   一旦上了高速公路，驾驶员就交由卡车自行驾驶

   take over 接手，接管

   例句 When he retired, his eldest son took over the farm.

   他退休时，他的长子接管了农场。

3. That doesn't mean the driver can zone out, there are strict rules for the person behind the wheel.

这并不意味着驾驶员可以走神，对于驾驶者而言有一套严格的规定。

zone out 走神，失去意识

例句 After 5 hours' work, I zoned out in front of my computer screen.

连续工作五小时以后，我坐在电脑前走神了。

读书笔记

用数学方法制作完美咖啡

Use Mathematical Methods to Make Perfect Coffee (BBC News)

新闻导读

咖啡是用经过烘焙的咖啡豆制作出来的饮料，与可可、茶同为流行于世界的主要饮品。日常饮用的咖啡是用咖啡豆配合各种不同的烹煮器具制作出来的，咖啡的制作方法也很多，例如：滴滤咖啡，是德国人发明的冲煮方法。简单的说就是把咖啡磨粉后，放在一个漏斗里或者再加层滤纸，上面浇上热水（理想水温90℃到95℃之间），由于地球引力作用，咖啡就从底下流出来。咖啡的量通常是7~10克粉可以做大约120ml的一杯。虹吸壶（Syphon），是坊间咖啡馆最普及的咖啡煮法之一。原理：在酒精灯的燃烧下，下层容器中的水温达到92℃时，水流被吸到有咖啡粉末的上层容器中，通过浸泡、搅拌后，制成的咖啡再原路返回。研磨度：比粉状略粗，接近特粒细砂糖。虹吸式煮法带有一种化学实验室的感觉。有人说因为它能萃取出咖啡中最完美的部分。

新闻热词

correspondent [ˌkɒrəˈspɒndənt] n. 记者，通讯员

mathematical [ˌmæθəˈmætɪkl] adj. 数学的；数学方面的

filter [ˈfɪltə(r)] n. 过滤器

equation [ɪˈkweɪʒn] n. 等式；方程式

variable [ˈveəriəbl] n. 可变因素

tailor ['teɪlə(r)] v. 按需定制；量身打造

increasingly [ɪn'kriːsɪŋli] adv. 渐增地；越来越多地

parameter [pə'ræmɪtə(r)] n. 参数；界限；范围

precision [prɪ'sɪʒn] n. 精确；精密

watery ['wɔːtəri] adj. 含水的，水分多的

involve [ɪn'vɒlv] v. 需要；包含

improvement [ɪm'pruːvmənt] n. 改进，改善，改良

新闻播报

Some students may feel they need coffee to help get them through their maths homework, but can maths help with making coffee? Scientists think it can as I heard from our **correspondent**.

Well, scientists wanted to make a **mathematical** model of the perfect cup of coffee using a drip **filter** machine. So they used **equations** to perfectly simulate or as much as they could the conditions inside the drip filter. So they really wanted to use this to design better machines.

参考译文

有些学生可能会借助咖啡来完成数学作业，那数学可以帮助制作咖啡吗？科学家们认为可以，本台记者报道。

嗯，科学家们希望用滴滤机制作完美咖啡的数学模型。因此他们用方程完美模拟或尽可能模拟滴滤机里面的条件。所以他们非常希望借此设计更好的机器。

Yeah, you wouldn't have thought there were that many **variables** when it comes to making a cup of coffee. How much difference does it make?

Well grain size is a key thing. I mean when you've got larger grains and water flows through them more quickly, it tends towards a more watery cup of coffee. You got smaller grains and water flows through them more slowly, and that tends towards a bitter tasting coffee. People want to **tailor** it because there's a big market in this. And you know the drip filter machines are **increasingly** coming within the home. So people want to kind of do it from that angle, getting the coffee out of the beans and working backwards to find out what **parameters** you need to achieve it.

参考译文

对，谁能想到做杯咖啡会考虑那么多的变量。这能起到多大的作用呢?

嗯，颗粒大小是个重要因素。也就是说，如果是稍大一些的颗粒，水流过它们的速度更快一些，那么这杯咖啡就会更稀一点。如果是稍小一些的颗粒，水流过它们的速度慢些，那这杯咖啡就有可能更苦一点。因为这方面市场很大，所以人们想定制。而且滴滤机越来越多地走入家庭，所以大家希望从这个角度来做，用咖啡豆磨咖啡，然后回过头来找出达到目的所需要的参数。

But presumably because each person has a different taste, it's gonna be difficult to come up with just one formula.

Yeah, that's right. There's no specific formula but what they might be able to do is by this mathematical understanding, make machines more **precision**, use a more scientific approach so that you can vary the grain size, vary the water flow through it. And that will maybe you know just allow you to kind of get closer to that ideal of your perfect cup of coffee, not too bitter, or maybe a little bit bitter or more **watery**, however you like it really.

参考译文

但可能每个人都有自己喜欢的口味，所以很难研制出唯一的配方。

是的，没错。没有特定的配方，但可以做到的是通过数学理解，让机器更精确，用更科学的方法实现改变颗粒大小，改变通过的水流等。这可能会让你更接近你理想中的咖啡，不太苦或可能有一点苦，或稀一点，反正就是按照你喜欢的方式来。

So is there an actual equation?

There's lots of equations that they used. What they described it as was the way that they use fluid mechanics to understand Formula One, so there's lots of maths **involved** in designing Formula One cars now. And that's they want to do for the drip filter machine. You know, the coffee market is huge. It's 100 billion a year. And there's about 16 million coffee machines sold each year in Europe. There're lots of other things they don't understand like the way that the coffee moves around when it's going through the filter. And they also want to know how you put the water in. That's a key thing that affects the tastes. And there're lots of big companies putting resources into you know really refining the technology behind some of these machines. So I think it's fully going on at the moment. You might see **improvements** in next five years and next ten years.

参考译文

有一个实际的方程式吗？

有很多可用的方程式，他们描述，这和用流体力学理解一级方程式赛车是一样的道理。设计一级方程式赛车用到很多数学方法。他们想把上述做法应用于滴滤机。咖啡市场很大的，一年市场价值为一千亿。而欧洲每年能卖出大概1 600万台咖啡机。还有很多方面科学家们并不理解，比方说咖啡穿过滤网时的流动形态。他们还想知道怎么加水，这是影响咖啡口味的关键。另外，很多大公司投入资源认真改善一些机器背后的技术。因此，我认为目前这个概念在完全实现，可能未来5-10年会有更多进展。

精彩解析

1. But presumably because each person has a different taste, it's gonna be difficult to come up with just one formula.

   但可能每个人都有自己喜欢的口味，所以很难研制出唯一的配方。

   come up with 想出，提出

   例句 Several of the members have come up with suggestions of their own.

   有几位成员提出了自己的建议。

2. …so there's lots of maths involved in designing Formula One cars now.

   ……设计一级方程式赛车用到很多数学方法。

   involve in 包括，被卷入中；涉及

   例句 We mainly involve in intellectual property right protection and commercial consultation business.

   我们主要业务范围涉及知识产权保护和商业咨询服务。

7 计算机更擅长推测我们的性格

Computers Can Be Better at Predicting Our Personality (BBC News)

新闻导读

Facebook是美国的一个社交网络服务网站，于2004年2月4日上线，主要创始人为美国人马克·扎克伯格（Mark Zuckerberg）。Facebook是世界排名领先的照片分享站点，截至2013年11月每天上传约3.5亿张照片。2015年8月28日，Facebook CEO马克·扎克伯格本周在个人Facebook帐号上发布消息称，Facebook本周一的单日用户数突破10亿。

2012年2月1日，Facebook正式向美国证券交易委员会（SEC）提出首次公开发行（IPO）申请，目标融资规模达50亿美元，并任命摩根士丹利、高盛和摩根大通为主要承销商；5月18日，Facebook正式在美国纳斯达克证券交易所上市。2014年2月19日，Facebook 宣布以190亿美元收购WhatsApp；2015年6月4日，Facebook推出安卓移动应用的简化版；美国时间2015年9月15日，Facebook首席执行官马克·扎克伯格表示会推出“不喜欢”按钮。2015年9月，Facebook与电商平台Shopify合作推出购物功能。

新闻热词

personality [ˌpɜːsəˈnæləti] n. 个性，性格

conclusion [kənˈkluːʒn] n. 结论，推论

detail [ˈdiːteɪl] n. 详情，信息

broad [brɔːd] adj. 宽阔的，广泛的

success [sək'ses] n. 成功，成就

accurate ['ækjərət] adj. 精确的，准确的

spouse [spaʊs] n. 配偶

charity ['tʃærəti] n. 慈善，慈善事业

emotional [ɪ'məʊʃənl] adj. 情感上的，情绪上的

concede [kən'siːd] v. 承认

creepy ['kriːpi] adj. 令人毛骨悚然的，令人紧张不安的

upfront [ˌʌp'frʌnt] adj. 正直的，坦率的

recruitment [rɪ'kruːtmənt] n. 招聘，招募

新闻播报

Computers can be better at predicting our **personality** than our friends and family. That's the **conclusion** scientists in Cambridge have drawn from an experiment with tens of thousands of volunteers. Julie Peacock has more **details**.

参考译文

相比亲朋好友，计算机更擅长推测我们的性格。这是剑桥大学科学家在成千上万的志愿者身上做实验后得出的结论。朱莉·皮考克详细报道。

Facebook was a social media researchers use to see how well computers could judge people's personalities. It studied the likes of more than 80,000 people to discover their **broad** personality traits. And it did so with great **success**. After analyzing just ten likes, the computer was more **accurate** at judging someone's personality than their work colleagues. After 150 likes, it knew people better than their own mothers. And it only took 300 likes to be more accurate than a person's **spouse**. One of the researchers David Sitwell says information could be used to target advertizing to suit personality types.

参考译文

研究人员用社交媒体"脸书"探究计算机在判断人的个性方面的能力，该实验研究了8万多人的爱好，广泛挖掘他们的个性，并且大获成功。计算机在分析10个爱好之后就能比当事人的同事更精准地判断他的个性；分析150个爱好后，这种能力就高于他的母亲；分析300个爱好，就能比配偶的判断更精准。研究员大卫·希特维尔称，可以利用这些信息制作定向广告，以迎合不同的性格类型。

Let's say, I'm viewing a **charity** website. And I want to find out about the charity. If I'm more of an **emotional** person, then the charity could give me more pictures and more messages sort of from the people that I'm trying to help.

参考译文

比方说，我正在浏览一个慈善网站，想寻找一些慈善信息。如果我这个人比较情绪化，那么慈善宣传可以向我展示更多我想帮助的人的照片和信息。

He **concedes** that some people may find the idea **creepy** and believes that social media websites would have to be **upfront** with users if they adopt the technology. Other possible applications would be on dating websites or in **recruitment**. But researchers see there is a lot that computer can't judge, such as whether or not someone is interesting. That's reported by Julie Peacock.

参考译文

他也坦言一些人会觉得这个想法令人紧张，他认为社交媒体网站如果采用了这种技术，就必须对用户坦诚。该技术还可应用于交友网站或用于招聘。但研究人员也清楚，许多事情是计算机判断不了的，比如某人是否有趣。朱莉·皮考克报道。

精彩解析

1. I'm viewing a charity website. And I want to find out about the charity.

   我正在浏览一个慈善网站，想寻找一些慈善信息。

   find out 找出，查明

   例句 You can find out many advantages in urban life.

   你会发现都市生活中有许多便利之处。

2. But researchers see there is a lot that computer can't judge, such as whether or not someone is interesting.

   但研究人员也清楚，许多事情是计算机判断不了的，比如某人是否有趣。

   whether or not 无论，是否

   例句 They'll find out the truth, whether or not you tell it to them.

   不管你是否告诉他们，他们都会查明真相的。

读书笔记

8 火星上发现液态水

Liquid Water Has Been Found on Mars (CNN News)

新闻导读

火星是太阳系由内往外数第四颗行星，属于类地行星，直径约为地球直径的一半，自转轴倾角、自转周期均与地球相近，公转一周约为地球公转时间的两倍。在西方称为战神玛尔斯星，中国则称为荧惑星，因为它荧荧如火，位置、亮度时常变动。火星基本上是沙漠行星，地表沙丘、砾石遍布。以二氧化碳为主的大气既稀薄又寒冷，沙尘悬浮其中，每年常有尘暴发生。与地球相比，地质活动不活跃，地表地貌大部份于远古较活跃的时期形成。有密布的陨石坑、火山与峡谷，包括太阳系最高的山：奥林帕斯山和最大的峡谷：水手号峡谷。另一个独特的地形特征是南北半球的明显差别：南方是古老、充满陨石坑的高地，北方则是较年轻的平原。火星两极皆有主要以水和冰组成的极冠，而且上面覆盖的干冰会随季节消长。

新闻热词

circumstance ['sɜːkəmstəns] n. 情况，情形

announcement [ə'naʊnsmənt] n. 宣告，公布

briny ['braɪni] adj. 盐水的，咸的

moist [mɔɪst] adj. 湿润的，潮湿的

lineae ['lɪnɪə] n. 线

hydrological [ˌhaɪdrə'lɒdʒɪkəl] adj. 水文学的

announce [ə'naʊns] v. 宣布，宣告

potential [pə'tenʃl] adj. 潜在的，有可能的

planet ['plænɪt] n. 行星

新闻播报

Under certain **circumstances**, liquid water has been found on Mars. This was the out of this world **announcement** from NASA following years of exploration on the Red Planet.

Scientists revealed **briny** water may flow on the planet's surface during its summer months. Different soils sampled were found to be **moist** and full of water. Dark streaks, known as Recurring Slope **Lineae**, or RSL, are now known to have been caused by flowing water.

参考译文

在某些情况下火星上发现了液态水，美国航空航天局经过数年的探索向世界公布这个消息。

科学家发现在夏季火星表面可能有咸水流过。采集的土壤是潮湿的，并且富含水。深色的条纹被称作季节性斜坡条带，现在发现是由流动的水造成的。

"These discoveries are very important, but they were only part of the **hydrological** cycle on Mars, that we are just now beginning to understand. What we are going to **announce** today is that Mars is not that dry, arid **planet** we thought of in the past."

参考译文

"这些发现很重要，但它们只是火星水文循环的一部分，我们现在才开始明白。我们今天要宣布的是，火星并不干燥，不像我们以前想象的那么干燥。"

So what does this tell us about **potential** life on Mars? Exploration by the Curiosity Rover proves that billions of years ago it was once a **planet** similar to Earth. But could the planet support life today? Scientists say, technologically, we will now be able to answer those questions.

参考译文

那么，这能告诉我们火星上存在生命吗？好奇号漫游者探索证明，数十亿年前，它曾经是一颗类似地球的行星。但是，今天火星上是否支持生命存在？科学家们表示，从技术上我们将能回答这些问题。

精彩解析

1. Different soils sampled were found to be moist and full of water.
采集的土壤是潮湿的，并且富含水。

be full of 充满，富含

例句 This task is full of challenges.

该项任务充满了挑战。

2. Mars is not that dry, arid planet we thought of in the past.
火星并不干燥，不像我们以前想象的那么干燥。

think of 有……想法，认为

例句 They all thought of her as a nice girl.

他们都认为她是一个好女孩。

新闻听力加油站

提高英语听力的6个方法

1. 跟读：这是遵循模仿的原则来使用的方法，也是语言学习过程中最有效的方法之一。跟读的方法有两种，一句一句地跟读，直到整篇文章读完；另一种是跟着原声将整段或者整篇文章跟读下

来。后一种方式，对整体文章的把握具有很好的效果，建议采用。

2. 大声朗读：这是跟读方法的延续。朗读当然就要出声，出声就会对耳朵和大脑有刺激，有刺激就会引起生理的变化，朗读到一定时候，你会发现你的舌头不再僵硬了。这对日后的口语表达奠定了良好的发声基础。

3. 听写：这个方法是从小孩学语文的过程中学来的。小学生经常要回家让家长给他听写生词甚至句子。这种通过手（写）、耳（听）的方法，对巩固所学的内容，非常见效。

4. 使用英英词典：在听的过程中碰到生词时，最好使用英英词典进行查询。使用英英词典越早越好。这不仅因为英英词典给你的词条解释是最清晰的（翻译过的词条解释往往会引起词义上的误解），还因为通过查询英英词典，能够使你对英语的把握和感觉更加直接，不需要更多的中英转换。

5. 主题集中学习：这个方法在听力的过程中非常有效。由于听力的素材非常宽泛，语音质量和词汇量的差别也很大，导致学习的选材比较困难。在分级原则的指导下，我们可以采用主题集中学习的方法，将一批自己感兴趣的、主题相关的有声资料作为听的对象，进步效果非常明显。

6. 阅读促进听力：阅读和听力材料相关的内容，也可以将阅读作为听力练习的辅助方法，大量地阅读小说、杂志、网络文章、新闻报道等自己感兴趣的内容。阅读是积累词汇的最有效的方法之一。通过阅读来进一步提高自己，尤其是增加对国外背景知识的了解，将反过来促进听力的进一步提高。要知道，你对某些知识了解得越多，你的英文听力就越容易，所以善于积累各种知识，对语言学习也是相当有裨益的。

9 新式轮胎或能使电动汽车获更远里程

New Tires May Help Electric Vehicles Get Greater Ranges (CNN News)

新闻导读

轮胎是在各种车辆或机械上装配的接地滚动的圆环形弹性橡胶制品。通常安装在金属轮辋上，能支撑车身，缓冲外界冲击，实现与路面的接触并保证车辆的行驶性能。轮胎常在复杂和苛刻的条件下使用，它在行驶时承受着各种变形、负荷、力以及高低温作用，因此必须具有较高的承载性能、牵引性能、缓冲性能。同时，还要求具备高耐磨性和耐屈挠性，以及低的滚动阻力与生热性。

最早的轮胎是由木头或铁制造的，这从中国古代的战车上和国外的绅士马车上都能看出。后来，当探险家哥伦布，在1493-1496年第二次探索新大陆到达西印度群岛中的海地岛时，发现了当地小孩所玩的橡胶硬块，这使他大吃一惊。后来他把这个奇妙的东西带回了祖国，若干年以后，橡胶得到了广泛的应用，车轮也逐渐由木制变成了硬橡胶制造。但这时的橡胶轮胎却还是实心的，走起来还很不舒服，而且噪声也很大。直到1845年，出生于苏格兰的土木技师R.W.汤姆生发明了充气轮胎，并以《马车和其他车辆的车轮改良》为题，获得了英国政府的专利。同年12月10日第一个充气轮胎诞生。1847年《科学·美国》杂志介绍了汤姆生的充气轮胎，称其为划时代的改良。

新闻热词

gasoline ['gæsəliːn] *n.* 汽油

range [reɪndʒ] n. 范围，里程

emission [i'mɪʃn] n. 排放，排放物

anxiety [æŋ'zaɪəti] n. 焦虑，忧虑

model ['mɒdl] n. 模型，模式

mileage ['maɪlɪdʒ] n. 英里数，英里里程

solution [sə'luːʃn] n. 解决，解决方案

recharge [ˌriː'tʃɑːdʒ] n./v. 再充电

generate ['dʒenəreɪt] v. 产生（能量），发（电）

rubber ['rʌbə(r)] n. 橡胶，橡皮

pavement ['peɪvmənt] n. 路面

battery ['bætri] n. 电池

新闻播报

Time for the "Shoutout." Which of these is not true about electric vehicles as compared with **gasoline** powered vehicles. You know what to do. Is it lower fuel costs, greater **range**, lower **emissions** or higher sticker price? You've got three seconds. Go. All of these statements are generally true about electric vehicles except option B. Their range is shorter than that of gas-powered cars. That's your answer and that's your Shoutout.

参考译文

又到了《大喊答题》节目环节。相比汽油动力车，下面电动汽车的哪一句描述是错误的？你知道该做什么。是较低的燃料成本，更远的里程，更低的排放还是更高的标价？你有3秒钟，开始。除了B选项外其他都是对电动汽车的正确描述。电动汽车的行驶距离比汽油动力车短。

你回答对了吗？这就是本期的《大喊答题》节目环节。

There's actually a term for when people fear running out of power in an electric car. It's called range **anxiety**. Most electric cars can travel between 70 and 100 miles before needing to be charged. There are some **models** that get considerably more **mileage**, but they cost considerably more money. Charging electric cars is cheaper than filling up a gas tank, but because it takes a lot longer, some scientists are seeking **solutions**.

参考译文

实际上，有一个术语，针对的正是人们所担心的电动汽车动力问题。它被称为里程焦虑。在需要充电前大多数电动汽车可以行驶70至100英里。有一些型号能够行驶更多里程，但造价则更为高昂。相比加满油箱，充电电动汽车价格更为低廉，但却需要很长时间，一些科学家正在寻求解决方案。

Typically, an all-electric car can travel about 90 miles before needing a **recharge**. But a newly unveiled tire concept from Goodyear aims to **generate** extra energy from where the **rubber** meets the road.

参考译文

通常，一款全电动汽车充电前可以行驶90英里。但新公布的固特异轮胎的概念旨在从橡胶接触地面时产生额外的能量。

You might call them energy tires. Goodyear isn't offering a lot of details about how it works, but here's the idea. Sunlight and **pavement** friction would generate heat inside the tire, which would be converted into electricity, which would help charge an electric car's **battery**.

It's still just a concept, but if it's successful and carmakers show interest, the idea could help win over drivers who reject electric vehicles because of so-called range anxiety.

参考译文

你可以称它为能量轮胎。固特异并没有透露关于它是如何工作的详细信息，但这里有个理念。阳光和路面摩擦会在轮胎内部产生热量将被转换成电能，能够帮助给电动车的电池充电。

这还只是个概念，但是如果能够成功而且汽车制造商们表现出兴趣，这个想法能帮助因为里程焦虑而不考虑电动汽车的司机们。

精彩解析

1. Charging electric cars is cheaper than filling up a gas tank.

相比加满油箱，充电电动汽车价格更为低廉。

fill up 使充满，填满

例句 They filled up with diesel at the petrol station on their way home.

他们在回家的路上去加油站加满了柴油。

2. Sunlight and pavement friction would generate heat inside the tire, which would be converted into electricity.

阳光和路面摩擦会在轮胎内部产生热量将被转换成电能。

convert into 使转而变为……

例句 All the bank money was converted into cash.

所有的银行票据都兑换成了现金。

读书笔记